LETTE

OF

BENJAMIN JOWETT, M.A.

MASTER OF BALLIOL COLLEGE, OXFORD

ARRANGED AND EDITED BY

EVELYN ABBOTT, M.A., LL.D.

AND

LEWIS CAMPBELL, M.A., LL.D.

WITH PORTRAIT

1899

PREFACE

THE present volume is merely a supplement to the
Life and Letters of Jowett, published two years ago.
It contains a number of letters, partly on special subjects,
and partly of more general interest, which could not be
included in the previous volumes, and yet seemed to be
worth preserving; and also some documents of a more
public nature, which throw light on important features
of Jowett's career. The letters have been divided
into sections, according to the subjects treated in them,
an arrangement which has the advantage of bringing
together what Jowett thought or suggested about
Church Reform, Education, &c., but the disadvantage
of separating the letters addressed to one person.
This separation is to be regretted, for nothing was
more characteristic of Jowett than his devotion to his
friends. If all the letters to Morier, for instance,
were collected together, they would form the record
of a watchful, unwearying friendship, outspoken yet
sympathetic, to which it would be difficult to find
a parallel. Such an arrangement was, however, incom-
patible with the plan of the work, and could not be
introduced into this volume.

The concluding section contains a few passages
gleaned from Jowett's note-books, and some sayings
which live in the memory of his friends.

EVELYN ABBOTT.

CONTENTS

LETTERS OF BENJAMIN JOWETT

I. CHURCH REFORM AND THE ABOLITION OF RELIGIOUS TESTS

As Convocation was still in abeyance, synodical action on the part of the Bishops of the Church of England was at this time only occasional. The Episcopal Conference referred to in the following letter may have been a consequence of the alarm to which the secession of J. H. Newman and other recent events had given rise.

To A. P. STANLEY[1].

[? *November*], 1846.

What fun it would be to be up the chimney at that Synod of Bishops ! . . . The conference lasts three hours : at the end

[1] In a letter quoted in the *Life of Bishop Wilberforce*, vol. i. p. 380, the Bishop says : ' I hope to go down to Fulham to-day, to meet the Bishops of Winchester and Sarum on Lay Reading,' &c., &c., &c. The following letter may refer to this or to some similar conference of which Stanley knew. ' It was during the Parliamentary recess of the autumn of 1846 that the first stirring of controversies respecting the details of the mutual action of Church and State, in the matter of elemen- tary education, began to make themselves felt. . . . National education was part of the programme of Lord John Russell's Government. It was well known that the Government were considering some comprehensive plan, and the air was full of projects. The attention, too, of Churchmen had been peculiarly excited by a pamphlet by Dr. Hook, the Vicar of Leeds. . . . Meantime the Bishops were being consulted by the Government.' *Ibid.*, p. 379.

B

of it, they all by the most different routes arrive at one conclusion, that the great thing they want is Money.

Excuse all this nonsense. Is not the conclusion the only
one a wise man can come to? Can there be any real
Church Reform, such as giving up Subscription, or Arnold's
Pamphlet, without a second Reformation? Has there ever
been any organic change made in it, like an old Shop 'established ever since 1572'? What I want to see is the Universities
made somewhat more dependent on the State, so as to become
a real link between Church and State, instead of representing
the worst half of the Clergy. Catch them young: you may
undermine their fierce Tory and High Church principles at
College. National Education will grow up without the Church:
in the next generation men will find the limit imaginary and
jump over it, and the Church become a truly National Establishment—*ne sis mihi patruus*—wanting no money nor anything else.

To B. C. Brodie.

Under the existing regulations no one could proceed
to the degree of M.A. without signing anew the Thirty-
nine Articles of Religion. Brodie's scientific studies
had suggested doubts which made it impossible for him
to do so conscientiously. But with a view to an
Examinership in Physical Science, under the new
Examination Statute, or to such a Professorship as he
afterwards held, the degree was indispensable; and it
occurred to him that by having recourse to the obsolete
method of 'graduating by incorporation' he might avoid
the odious requirement. But for this purpose certain
consents were necessary, and he had written to his
friend Jowett for assistance and advice.

Balliol, *Feb.* 16, [1851].

The Master is absent and will be away for the next fortnight:
when he returns, if you still wish it, I will bring your case
before him. I ought to say that, after looking into the matter,
I doubt not exactly the legality, but the expediency of pressing

your claim [1]. I should be indeed glad if you could ever be induced to come to Oxford as a Physical Professor, and glad too that you and others should be relieved from signing the 39 Articles. But, in the first place, it is impossible to try your right without the reason of it becoming apparent. The Master will of course ask why you take this circuitous mode of obtaining an M.A. degree instead of the common one. And I think you will rouse the *odium theologicum* without any grounds to justify you in the eyes of the public. Secondly, I cannot see any reason to suppose that this process of incorporation was intended, in the case of members of the University, to relieve men from any of the forms gone through at the time of taking the degree, but only from the residence and exercises at that time required for a superior degree. The reason why the statute has become a dead letter may probably be that there is no object in any one's availing himself of such a privilege. Thirdly, the statute can only be applied with the consent of the V.-C. and Proctors, which, considering its obsolete character and the object sought to be obtained, they would certainly withhold, and rightly—in the opinion of the public. Fourthly, it seems to me that you would be placed in an awkward position from having signed the Articles once and now declining to sign them and yet seeking an Academical position which in part results from that first signature. In throwing the onus on them I fear you would only injure yourself : much as I wish that you should come here and dislike subscriptions of this sort, I could not think the V.-C. wrong for interposing his veto.

This is the chief reason I have for not wishing you to proceed further in the matter. Even if the right is clearer than I see it to be I think you will put yourself in a false position by claiming it, after having once signed. I consider it chiefly in reference to the probability of your some day coming here. I do not understand this to be your object in pressing the claim ; but, supposing it to be so, I think it will make a material difference in your comfort in coming here, whether or no the Master, the Hebdomadal Board, &c., already

---

[1] For obtaining the M.A. degree without subscribing the Articles.   See *Life*, vol. i. p. 231, where part of this letter is quoted.

regarded you with suspicion. I think it is quite possible they might be induced in consequence to exert themselves to prevent your appointment, and, on the other hand, it is not impossible that in the course of the next few years some relaxation of the Tests may take place for non-Theological Professors. However this may be, I fear your attempt might not succeed and only do harm to yourself without establishing any principle.

Excuse my writing (in haste) in this abrupt manner. I will gladly take trouble about this or any other matter for you.

To B. C. Brodie.

BALLIOL, *March* 12, [? 1851].

I should have answered your letter sooner, but for a great press of work which I have had during the last fortnight.

Stanley is of opinion, and I agree in thinking, that it would be better for you to try your right when the Examinership is offered and not now. Suppose you try the right at present it is not possible to conceal the reason, viz. that you decline to sign the Articles. The V.-C. then says, 'This is an evasion of subscription which it is my duty to prevent.'

But supposing he, in the dearth of men of science in Oxford, goes out of his way to offer you the Examinership. You then state openly the difficulty, and propose your remedy. I think it is possible that he would think twice (in the present day) before he prevented you from coming in at the Back Door, as otherwise he would display the University in the ludicrous position of looking in vain for an 'Orthodox' chemist, and finally giving up the Chemistry for the Orthodoxy.

This is the way in which the matter strikes me. With the example of Everett, and the fear of Convocation before the V.-C.'s eyes, it is quite uncertain what he will do: but in this way I think you right yourself best and really throw the onus on them.

To a Friend, who was hesitating about accepting a Living.

BALLIOL, *July* 6, [1851].

I was very glad to hear that you were likely to obtain a living. You must not think me lax, if I say that I should think it extremely wrong in you to refuse it from any scruples respecting Subscription.

I do not mean that a person is justified in subscribing in all cases. If he feels himself a Papist or a Unitarian at heart, or were actually engaged in plans for upsetting the existing constitution of things in the Church, or if he were prone to speculative doubts about the first principles of religion, I would not have him subscribe. But if he feels that he is really a member of the Church of England and willing to submit to its authority, and also feels that this is the field where he has been placed and in which he can best work, and that he would be in a false position by transferring himself to any other communion, then it seems to me it would be absolutely irrational in him to throw away his life by refusing to take a living.

Do you think religious scruples are a thing to be encouraged? I have known persons give way to them on particular subjects. They have ended (sometimes almost unavoidably from the position in which they placed themselves) by doing things really wrong, or they have cut themselves off from all opportunities of usefulness and of moral or religious improvement.

I do not like subscriptions, whether to the Articles or the Creeds or anything. I think they are the worst bond of a Church, because to a great number of persons they will always imply that to each of those five hundred (say) propositions you strictly bind yourself, and tyrannical Bishops will be seeking from time to time to enforce the letter and declaring, as the Bishop of London does, that everybody takes them in the same sense, which we all know to be untrue. But I cannot doubt that any one may fairly sign our Articles—

1. Who is a sincere member of the Church of England, i. e. not a traitor to it, seeking to undermine its faith or uniting with Rome, &c.

2. Whose opinions are such as agree with any of the recognized parties in the Church whom Bishops have been in the habit of ordaining from time immemorial.

3. (This is more a question for himself to consider than for the Church to demand of him) Who feels that there is nothing in the services of the Church of England which is such a

stumbling-block to him as to prevent his working heartily in general as a labourer in the cause.

I have rather stated what I feel myself than endeavoured to give a definite answer to the question you asked. If it is said, 'All this does not meet the difficulty of doing evil that good may come, of signing some proposition which I do not think true for the sake of some practical result,' I fear I am unable to answer this except by saying that it may be, and I think in this case is, pushed to an absurdity. The same principle which in ordinary cases leads men to refuse to sign the Articles would, if carried out, destroy all common action or communion with one another, and would make a Church Establishment or any Church or even public worship impossible.

We must all stand isolated and independent of each other, because we are all individuals, and must have our common belief modified in some degree by our individual peculiarities, which no single form of words, whether used in Articles or as a Liturgy, can equally express for us all. All arguments that can be urged in favour of subscription to any form of words apply, I think, with increased force to the Articles and Liturgy, because they are not in the strictest sense consistent with themselves, and were written at a time when men were forced to make compromises and were in a state of compromise themselves between the remains of Romanism and the religion of the Reformers. I mean that this is a strong reason why their words should be interpreted in a large and liberal spirit for us their posterity who do not live in the same circle of ideas exactly and are not subject to the same influences. If a person goes on further to say, ' But there is great danger of my applying these casuistical arguments to my own temporal advantage,' I would ask him to consider whether he is to be deterred from doing what in a doubtful case seems on the whole right because it is to his interest. Temporal good in this life, and in the present state of society, seems to me the vantage-ground from which a religious man starts, to pour forth by the assistance of worldly prudence unnumbered blessings on those around him. No man can say that it makes no difference to him, considering the subject merely in a religious point of view, whether he can have his mind free from care, and time for prayer and meditation, whether he has an employment suited to him and opportunity of doing good among the poor, whether he has the means of giving his children a first-rate education. And, in reference to this particular case, may it not be said that the scruple is settled for you by the custom of the Bishops who ordain, and of many good men who were far better than ourselves and felt no difficulty on this subject, whose opinion, although we cannot altogether throw off the responsibility on them, must be allowed to have some weight?

If all good men refused to sign the Articles, the Church of England would probably go on with bad ones—so great is the difficulty in getting these things changed. And yet this seems almost a practical 'reductio ad absurdum' of the question at issue.

I have put down these things as they occurred to me. I hope you will excuse the want of arrangement. Two other things come into my head to say—first, that if there is any party who has a right to the Protestant Church of England, as the descendants of the Reformers, it is the Evangelical party—not the less so if verging towards Calvinism; secondly, that from knowing you many years, since the days when we associated with Goulburn and Waldegrave, I feel persuaded that you would not take a living from motives of interest, and that if you ever thought you were doing so you would be deceiving yourself. Only make up your mind to quit these scruples for ever, if you now see that you can do so, and do not let the ghost of them rise up hereafter and enfeeble and embitter your life. If you feared that from state of constitution or nerves they might do so, and that hereafter you would have no rest, I could not urge you to take a living.

It is a good thing in the best sense to have a parish in which to work and labour until the evening, and, if life is spared so long, to see a new generation creep up trained by our hands. I trust that you will have this happiness. I have not had much experience of parochial work, but it seems to me that as a fact with older persons it consists chiefly in giving them comfort and consolation under affliction, while the real moral and religious change is made in the school and among the children.

Forgive the length of this letter, and also any faults in the manner in which it is written.

[PS.] I believe that numbers would acknowledge that they take the Articles, &c., with the latitude you allow, and that the great majority really do so.

To A. P. STANLEY.

This letter seems to have been prompted by Stanley's report of the audit at Canterbury in July, when, as Stanley's biographer tells us, 'he had accomplished the Eastern tour which had been the cherished wish of years,' and 'nothing now stood between him and Canterbury. Into the duties of his Canonry and the interests of his Cathedral he threw all the energies of his nature' (*Life of Dean Stanley*, vol. i. p. 466). It will be remembered that before Stanley's visit to Palestine Jowett pressed upon him a scheme for a Hall of residence attached to Balliol College, with Stanley as Principal. Stanley did not see his way to this, and Jowett now returns to the charge, with practical suggestions of a different nature. Jowett afterwards repented of this insistence, which appears to have somewhat annoyed his friend. See *Life*, vol. i. pp. 212, 280.

ST. GERMAIN, *Aug.* 30, [1853] [1].

'How may Cathedral Institutions be made to teem with life at every pore?' It is a kind of an impertinence for me to write to you on this subject—'that confounded πολυπραγμοσύνη of his which makes him desire to have a finger in every pie.' Yet suffer me to disgorge myself. I am not desirous to do anything myself, as it is out of my way. But I really think that in your position it would be a mistake not to stir a little, and [I] offer a few recommendations. The 'finances' are a bugbear. Do talk to that wisest among ladies (for whom allow me on all occasions to express my regard and veneration),

[1] *Life*, vol. i. p. 214.

Mrs. Stanley, and to the judicious Vaughan, best of counsellors, on the subject.

'Well, what is his nostrum?' Nothing new, but chiefly a few plain principles of that kind which younger men see more clearly than old ones, and laymen more distinctly than clergymen.

The first is, 'He that will not work neither shall he eat.' No Dean, Canon, Minor Canon, Organist, or Verger should receive too much or do too little. The strictest economy should be practised among all servants and inferior people —the Scoutocracy of the Cathedral,—indeed, in all but two points where liberality would be well bestowed, (1) the fabric, (2) the services.

The second principle would be to reconstruct rather than to destroy. To raise all poor livings £20 out of the spoils of the Cathedral would put a stop to the abuses and the outcry, but it would not be doing the best thing possible : it would be losing an opportunity of doing something different in kind, and which could not be done so well elsewhere ; it would be throwing away the rank and position of the Cathedral clergy, and leaving the building a useless monument of the past.

At the same time, until every sixpence of the Cathedral property is applied in the most useful manner, there will be no cessation of Mr. Horsman's and Sir B. Hall's [objections?] to the Chapter. The public like Architecture—they will be very tolerant of large sums spent in preserving the building: they love music—they will not object to £1,000 a year appropriated to the Choir, if well managed. But sinecurism or half-sinecurism, the ghosts of imaginary duties and offices, they will not tolerate. Any concealment of incomes, accounts, &c., they will not tolerate. But they will soon be patient and lovers of Cathedrals if they see new Institutions, the want of which is really felt, growing up under the shadow of Canterbury Cathedral.

I have not read the many pamphlets on this subject, but just add a few suggestions as to the possible ways of carrying out these principles which may suggest better ones to you.

Suggestions respecting the fabric—

1. To appoint a Conservator or Inspector of Cathedrals, such

as Willis or Ruskin, under whose care all repairs of the buildings should be carried on.

2. To devote a large annual sum for repairs: in most Cathedrals at least £1,000 a year, in some much more would be required.

3. In addition to this each Cathedral should contribute at least £200 a year to a general fund (making in all £5,000 a year and upwards) to be reserved for larger restorations, such as York and Hereford, out of which grants should be made to meet private subscriptions.

Choir.

The only remark I would make respecting the services is that the singers should have, if possible, some other employment, and that the boys of the Choir should be boarded and carefully educated. It is a duty we owe them for demoralizing them by familiarity with the service.

Estates.

1. Management to be vested in the Archdeacons (whose office requires a knowledge of business as a condition of their appointment) subject to the approval of a Government Surveyor.

2. It seems undesirable, for political reasons, that the Chapters should be reduced to the condition of pensionaries, and also that the stimulus should be lost which would be given by private interest to the improvement of their estates. On the other hand, it is still more undesirable that the income of members of the Chapter should increase with the increasing value of land, houses, mines, &c. To obviate the evil of either alternative it is proposed that the Dean and Chapter should receive or retain such a portion of their estates as would at its present valuation suffice to pay their expenses and incomes. That in case of an increase they should be allowed to divide such a sum as would give each Canon an annual income of £800 a year, the remaining surplus to be added to the Domus fund and spent for public objects connected with the Cathedral, under the control of a Government officer, to whose inspection the accounts should be annually submitted and published.

Applications and Uses

must in some measure vary with the circumstances of each Cathedral.

Deans

to be Suffragan Bishops of large towns (not quite half the Cathedral towns are large towns ; with the smaller ones it would be easy to unite others, e. g. Wells and Bath, Salisbury and Southampton, Durham and Newcastle, Rochester and Gravesend).

Their duties would be—

1. To confirm, but not to ordain, independently of the Bishop of the Diocese.

2. To exercise Episcopal Authority over the Clergy of the town, who should have an appeal to the Bishop of the Diocese, and in case of disagreement between the Bishop and his Suffragan to the Archbishop.

The incomes of the Suffragans to be £1,500 a year.

Canonries.

1. Two, as at present, to be attached to the Archdeaconries.

The two remaining Canonries and the minor Canonries to be appropriated to a

Theological College,
Training School or
Grammar School.

The two Canonries might be appropriated to Professorships at the Theological College which should be placed under the newly constituted Chapter—the Minor Canons also assisting in tuition.

Or, one Canonry might be appropriated to a Professorship of Theology at the Theological College, another to the Training School or Grammar School—the choristers receiving their education at one of the two.

For the efficiency of the Training or Grammar School it would be necessary to have (1) exhibitions to support the pupils at school or College given by examination, (2) cheap means of boarding.

Before the Canonries became vacant a portion of the funds in the hands of the Ecclesiastical Commissioners might be advanced for buildings and salaries.

The Canons are thus absorbed into Professors and masters of schools, and the Minor Canons into teachers and under-masters.

Library.

Every Cathedral town to have a library endowed with not less than two hundred a year, either as a Clerical library for the Diocese or as a general library for the use of town.

CANTERBURY.

(Shall I venture into the precincts?)

With four Canonries besides the Archdeaconries at disposal it would be quite possible in the course of time to raise up and foster three institutions.

1. St. Augustine's College.

It is already built, which is a great advantage : it does not answer as it is : it is vicious in principle, because it pledges mere boys to a missionary life.   There are some noble exceptions, but I should imagine that in general you get a few under-educated youths who cannot afford the expense of going to the University.

Without interfering with its missionary character it might be made with great advantage a general Theological College, and endowed with two Canonries, one for Divinity (say), another for Hebrew.   It would be a positive advantage to the missionary students to have (1) other associates, (2) better paid and therefore better teachers.   They might always have the priority of admission into the College and be encouraged by exhibitions : the other students, as at Wells, might lodge in the town.

2. Grammar School.

Might be assisted by appropriating a Canonry to the head mastership and two Minor Canonries to the under-masterships, the funds at present appropriated to those objects being partly reserved for exhibitions at school and College.

The choristers to be educated at the Grammar School.

A department for general and commercial education and modern languages to be added.

3. A Canonry and two Minor Canonries to be appropriated to the training school.

All this would come into existence gradually during the next forty years ; only St. Augustine's Theological and Missionary College immediately. Where there is an existing master of a Grammar School not very efficient, yet not to be got rid of, that part of the scheme might commence last.

'Thus have I finished a little globe of the Ecclesiastical world.' I hope you will do something at least about St. Augustine's, and speak to the Archbishop and, if expedient, to Hope.

Upon reading this over it appears to me hardly worth sending. The opportunity for good is a great one, however.

LETTERS TO MR. FREDERIC HARRISON.

In urging Stanley to take part in *Essays and Reviews*, Jowett wrote (Aug. 15, 1858): 'I entirely agree with you that no greater good can be accomplished for religion and morality than the abolition of all subscriptions, but how will this ever be promoted in the least degree, or how will it be possible for any one in high station ever to propose it, if we only talk it over in private ? We shall talk A. D. 1868 [1].'

Stanley declined the enterprise, and disapproved of it as impolitic, but when the book was rudely assailed, he threw himself with chivalrous ardour into the defence. His article in the *Edinburgh Review* for April, 1861, went far to save a critical situation ; but it contained a paragraph severely censuring the writer of 'Neo-Christianity' in the *Westminster Review* for Oct. 1860, whose article, originally suggested to him by a friend and colleague of Jowett, produced a somewhat unexpected sensation [2].

· Stanley's strictures were in accordance with the feeling of many ' Oxford Liberals' at the time, but were distasteful to Jowett, who desired to conciliate all earnest lovers of

---

[1] *Life,* &c., vol. i. p. 275.   [2] *Ibid.,* pp. 291-2.

free inquiry. The passage referred to in the following letter will be found in vol. 113 of the *Edinburgh Review*, at page 464.

To FREDERIC HARRISON.

FRESHWATER, I. OF W.,
April 23. [1861].

In an article in the recent number of the *Edinburgh*, I observe a severe and I think undeserved criticism on an able article in the *Westminster*, which is generally attributed to you. Knowing as I do that the article in the *Westminster* was not dictated by the least degree of unkindness or ill feeling, I am very sorry that words have been used which have, perhaps, given you pain. I believe the writer of the article (of which I need hardly say I never saw a line until it was published) regrets it too, being aware that he wrote under some misconception of the object of the *Westminster*.

Any one has the most perfect right to attack me for mistiness or want of logical consistency (in not pushing premises [*sic*] to their conclusions) or dishonesty. But, perhaps, you will excuse my saying that I think it a mistake for one who is placed in very nearly the same circumstances as I am, in reference to subscription, to provoke (not with my good will certainly) this sort of retaliation.

If you and I and the gentleman in the *Saturday Review* who attacks us both, as well as other Liberals, keep bringing before the world the various shades of difference by which we are divided, instead of joining in the attempt to obtain the abolition of subscription, about which we are all agreed, it is clear that another generation may pass away and Oxford remain as it is. There is nothing our opponents desire more than to see us at variance with one another, each trying to prove the ground of the other to be untenable.

My chief reason for writing to you is to urge you (if I may take the liberty of doing so as a stranger) not to join in a barren protest about the Articles (which will at once set the public against you and put you into the power of the Visitor of your College), but to co-operate heartily in attempts for the removal of subscription. No doubt some terms must and ought to be kept with existing institutions when you have the advantage of being within them. But I believe that it is right (and possible within this limitation) to do and say all that it is really desirable to do and say.

As to the imputation of dishonesty, that of course will be urged, like any other weapon which is likely to tell with the public. It is impossible to avoid it, and not, I think, desirable to answer it. The considerations which justify the position of a liberal clergyman or Fellow of a College are not of a kind to tell with the public, and lead away from the main purposes of life into a sea of polemics and recriminations. The position may be tenable, but the sooner it is altered the better. Time and your own course of life set you right at last, and the public, so far as its opinion is of any importance, ought not to be challenged to express an opinion. I am strongly against the writer of the article in the *Westminster* doing anything to vindicate his position, except making energetic and persevering efforts to alter it.

Mr. Harrison's reply probably perished in the holocaust of Jowett's letters [1]. It led to the following rejoinder :—

FRESHWATER, *April* 30, [1861].

Many thanks for your letter, which I fear I have not time to answer as it deserves. . . .

I have no reason to suppose that the Liberals in Oxford regard me as their head, and have no wish to be thought so. I want to work with others, not to lead them. I would gladly follow in the wake of the Dean of Christ Church or Arthur Stanley, or even our friend 'the gentleman in the *Saturday Review*,' if they would help to carry the abolition of subscription.

I agree with you in thinking that great religious changes are needed, and that religion must be much more based on fact. Only fact and demonstration must not exclude right and conscience, or the hope of a future life, or communion with God, or the sanctifying and elevating influences of the New Testament, or the 'fact' of the religious and moral nature

---

[1] See Preface to *Life*, vol. i. p. vi.

of man will rise up and condemn them. Above all, any religious movement must take into account the poor and un-educated.

I was glad to hear that you were not a Positivist. Not that I do not respect Comte (whom I read and analyzed about ten years ago). But he seems to me to have got a false and absorbing hold on some minds. They do not seem to me to recognize sufficiently the enormous difference between saying that things must be based on facts and showing how they are based on facts. And his enormous generalizations, while they are no doubt a stimulus and help to thought, yet lead people to warp or overlook facts. Comte appears to me to be much more of a metaphysical and speculative thinker, under the name of Positivism, than is commonly supposed. And the enthusiasm which he excites in some minds seems to me a characteristic of the metaphysical disorder.

I think you might do great good by turning your mind to religious subjects; endeavouring to supply as far as possible the constructive side, which (as you rightly say) is too much left out of sight in *Essays and Reviews*. I hope some of us may do something more ourselves in that way hereafter. It should be addressed, not to a small circle of Liberals, but to the mass of the world, and especially of the semi-religious world. Every one who takes part in any political and religious move-ment must count to be misrepresented, and sometimes the best way out is by silence, or at least by speaking altogether irrespectively of the attack. I know the annoyance, having been compelled to sign the Articles by the Vice-Chancellor at a time when no friend supported me. I think at the present moment you can't be too cautious: weak people set on by deeper ones may do you harm.

[PS.] The author of the article in the *Edinburgh* is perfectly honest and kindly to you as to every one else. But he has written under a mistake. No one would be more grieved at driving you out of your Fellowship. He thought that you wanted to drive us out, and hence his strong language.

The movement for abolishing or relaxing religious tests reached an important stage in 1864. Two Bills were then introduced into the House of Commons, by Mr. Dodson for the Abolition of Tests, and by Mr. Bouverie for the relaxation of the Act of Uniformity. Resolutions in support of these measures were passed at a meeting held at Liverpool on June 10, 1864. They were proposed and seconded by Mr. Goldwin Smith, Mr. Neate, Sir Benjamin Brodie, Mr. (afterwards Lord) Bowen, Mr. Henry Fawcett, and Prof. H. J. S. Smith; and were subscribed to by 123 distinguished men.

Amongst the speakers to the first resolution were Jowett and John Bright. According to Mr. Charles S. Roundell, who was present, 'each made a notable contribution.' 'It was on this occasion (I am as good as sure) that Jowett remarked *à propos* to a suggestion which had been made about our accepting tests in a mitigated form, that "old fetters are easier to wear than new ones." Bright made the remark that hitherto he had been accustomed to regard the Universities as "places devoted to the dead languages, and to undying prejudices." '

In 1865 a Bill was brought in by Lord Granville, and passed into law, enacting that in lieu of the old form, whereby the declarer pledged his assent and consent to all and everything contained in the Book of Common Prayer, &c., the declaration to be made by every clergyman before his ordination should be as follows :—' I assent to the Thirty-nine Articles of Religion, and to the Book of Common Prayer, and the Form for the Ordering of Bishops, Priests, and Deacons; I believe the doctrine of the United Church of England and Ireland, as therein set forth, to be agreeable to the Word of God; and in public prayer and administration of the Sacraments I will use the book prescribed, and none other, except

c

so far as shall be ordered by lawful authority.' In the same session of Parliament, Mr. Goschen introduced a Bill to abolish tests in connexion with University degrees. This measure passed the second reading in the House of Commons by a majority of 206 to 190, but could not be carried further in the course of that session.

In 1867 two measures were before the House, Mr. (afterwards Lord) Coleridge's Bill for the Abolition of University Tests, and Mr. Fawcett's for the Abolition of Tests in Colleges. A conference in support of these, and also of Mr. Ewart's Bill for the Extension of the University, was held at the Ship Hotel, Charing Cross, July 1, 1867, on the invitation of persons chiefly connected with the University of Oxford.

At that conference several important resolutions were agreed to, and a working Committee, consisting of Mr. Goldwin Smith, Mr. Fowler, and Mr. Roundell, was appointed, with power to add to their number, for the purpose of keeping on foot the objects of the conference. After this came Lord Salisbury's Executive Commission, which did less in this direction than had been anticipated. But in 1870 Mr. Gladstone's Government introduced a measure for the Abolition of University Tests except for Degrees in Divinity, and a Committee of the Lords took evidence upon the question. This measure passed the House of Commons early in the session of 1871. Amendments by Mr. Stevenson, for freeing the Divinity Degrees, and by Mr. Fawcett for abolishing Clerical Fellowships were rejected, but had been supported by strong minorities of 160 and 140 respectively. · Lord Salisbury, in the debate on the second reading in the House of Lords, had thrown out a hint of requiring a new test in place of the old one. It was at this juncture that Jowett gave his evidence before the Committee of the

Lords, which was still sitting. It may be mentioned
in passing that an important meeting was again held in
Liverpool on March 27, 1871.

The following excerpts from Jowett's evidence before
the Committee of the House of Lords[1] have been taken,
with permission, from the authorized report. The Marquis
of Salisbury was the Chairman and the Earl of Morley
led the examination in chief.

EARL OF MORLEY. *Q.* Are you in favour of the entire
abolition of tests from the Universities[2]?
J. Yes, I am in favour of the entire abolition of tests. The
Bill does not go to that length; it excludes the Divinity Professors from its operation.
Q. What do you consider to have been the effects of tests as
they have been up to the present time enforced?
J. I think that they have not prevented very great diver-
gencies of opinion from springing up; I do not think that if
tests were abolished the differences of opinion would be greater
than they are at present.
Q. You will be against any test whatever, however comprehensive, if I understand you rightly?
J. Yes, I am, because, however comprehensive tests may be,
there are still persons who are excluded by them, and there is
an ambiguity about their meaning. Supposing we require as
a condition of becoming a teacher a declaration of the general
faith of a Christian, still an ambiguity arises. There is
a difference of opinion amongst persons as to who are to be
called Christians, and who are to be included. We are apt
to speak of everybody as an infidel who does not agree with
us, and we should have the old disputes revived. Is a Quaker,
or is a Unitarian a Christian? Then, again, the Jew or free
thinker would be excluded; the Ultramontane admitted. Let
me also put the case of particular scientific men who are not
at all opposed to Christianity, but yet who might have a great

[1] First Report from the Select   293-317.
Committee of the House of Lords   [2] *Ibid.*, p. 293 ff. Queries 3015-
on University Tests, 1871, pp.   3023.

objection to signing such a test, both on general grounds which would apply to signing any test whatever, and on particular grounds with reference to the sense in which the word 'Christian' was employed. It is a very invidious thing to compel a conscientious man to say, 'I am not a Christian, and I object to signing that test.' I think you would find difficulties about a comprehensive test. It goes upon the supposition that the Universities are divided into two great classes, one consisting of Christians and the other of infidels. That is not at all really the case. We shade off into one another, just as people do in society, by every degree of difference, and sometimes pass from one class to the other, and you would do harm if you introduced artificial distinctions which stereotyped us as Christians or non-Christians, just as you would if you introduced similar distinctions in society.

Q. You would attach no importance to the imposition of a kind of negative test [1] ?

J. I think that it would have no positive effect in attaining the end for which it was intended, and that it would have some very bad effects. One effect, I think, which would obviously arise from its introduction, would be a great silence on the subject of religions, and upon all questions of opinion connected with it. An honourable person would say, 'I have taken this test, and therefore the best thing I can do is to close my mouth. I will speak on history, I will speak on physical science, but about religion I will say nothing.' I would submit that there cannot be a more unfavourable position for religious opinion than that of absolute silence and indifference to it. Anybody who takes any interest in such subjects knows that although there are difficulties about opinion and belief, they are nothing as compared with the difficulties which arise from indifference.

Q. And you do not anticipate that if these tests are abolished it will have any practical effect upon the religious teaching of the Universities ?

J. No, I do not.

---

[1] First Report from the Select Committee of the House of Lords   on University Tests, 1871, Queries 3024, 3025.

Q. Would you propose to abolish the tests even for Divinity professors [1]?

J. That is not included in this Bill; but I should wish to abolish the tests even for Divinity professors. In the appointment of Divinity professors, I think the persons who appointed them would have a certain regard for public opinion, but the object in view is very ill-secured by tests. They appear to me to be useless and superfluous in the case of Divinity professors as well as other professors.

Q. You would leave them entirely free, would you?

J. I should not bind a person by the obligation of a test. I should like to put before the Committee this consideration. Supposing you had one class of professors bound by tests; for instance, supposing the Church of England Divinity professors were bound by tests and other Divinity professors were not bound by tests, which do you suppose would have the greater authority and weight—the persons who were free to speak what they thought, or the persons who were obliged to speak within a certain limit? Of the latter a great suspicion would arise that they said not what they thought, but what they were compelled by the test to say.

. . . .

Q. Do you anticipate that if tests are abolished you would get, especially in the smaller colleges, a society consisting of persons of so many different denominations that it would be impossible to keep up any kind of religious teaching or worship, their views being so conflicting that they could not agree upon any particular form?

J. No, I do not anticipate that; I think that difficulties of this sort would disappear in practice. I think that 'the case of a college is very much like that of persons meeting on a school board. Sensible people feel at once, under such circumstances, that what they have to do is not to enforce their own peculiar religious opinions, whatever they may be, but to do the best they can for the young persons who are brought under their care; and I do not imagine, as I think I implied in a previous answer, that the divergence would be

[1] *Ibid.*, Queries 3026-3039.

much greater if the Bill were passed than it is at present; but even if it were, I should not expect that persons in authority would be attempting to enforce their own individual opinions, irrespective of their duties to the younger persons who were placed under them.

.   .   .   .

Q. Is it true that there is a great deal of German philosophy now taught at Oxford, if not directly, yet filtering through the studies in preparation for the Final Schools[1]?

J. German philosophy is such a general name that I hardly know how to reply to the question. There are all kinds of things which may be called German philosophy, having the most various tendencies. I should be very sorry if there were not some knowledge of German philosophy at Oxford. There seems to be too little study of German, rather than too much, at Oxford. Very few persons read German books. I have no doubt that there has been an interest shown about German philosophy, and about Hegel in particular, just as there has been an interest about a great many other things; but it would be a great mistake to look upon the philosophy of Hegel as a mere infidel philosophy. He was, or believed himself to be, a Conservative both in religion and politics. There are all sorts of persons, from the most extreme of orthodoxy to the most extreme of the opposite view, who have professed themselves disciples of Hegel. And it does not at all follow that because persons read Hegel they share all his opinions, even supposing him to be of a different character from what I am describing. They read the book as a valuable work on Logic, in fact. So again with respect to Mr. Mill's Logic. Without expressing anything but the greatest respect for Mr. Mill, it would be ridiculous to suppose that the persons who read about the syllogism, and the proposition, and the experimental methods in Mr. Mill's Logic share all his opinions. The book has forced its way because it is the best and most available English treatise on Logic.

CHAIRMAN (The Marquess of Salisbury).—*Q.* I did not quite

[1] First Report from the Select Committee of the House of Lords on University Tests, 1871, Queries 3042–3049.

understand what view you took with respect to the Divinity professors ; are they to be of all religions, or only of one ?

J. I did not say that they were either to be of all religions or only of one, but what I said was that I thought it was not desirable to impose tests on the Divinity professors. In a Church of England University for Church of England students, no doubt the professor appointed would be a clergyman of the Church of England, but I do not think it is desirable to enforce that by any test to be imposed upon him.

Q. It is not the result, but the instrument, to which you object[1] ?

J. Yes, it is the instrument.

Q. I think you used the words, 'Church of England University'; do you recognize the University as being Church of England by right as well as by fact ?

J. No ; I think that while the Church of England was the Church of the whole nation, it was reasonable that the Universities should be Church of England, but now that the Church of England is only the Church of half the nation, I think it is very unreasonable that the rest of the nation should be excluded. Perhaps your Lordship will allow me to make a slight correction in the words I used just now. I meant to say the Divinity professors for Church of England students.

Q. If it is unreasonable that the Universities should be exclusively Church of England, it would be equally unreasonable to suppose that the Divinity professors should be exclusively Church of England, would it not ?

J. No. I do not think that the inference holds ; I think it is quite possible to have Divinity teachers for the Church of England students, and Divinity teachers for Dissenting students, and, perhaps, Divinity teachers for Roman Catholic students, in the University.

Q. Then it does rather come to that, you would have Divinity teachers of as many religious bodies as there were pupils to attend them ?

J. Yes.

. . . .

Q. And when the persons were once appointed, I suppose

[1] *Ibid.*, Queries 3050–3057.

you would not think it right that they should be liable to deprivation or supervision, if they taught differently from what was expected of them?

J. I should leave that to the different sects to arrange for themselves.

Q. You would have no objection to the sects, then, imposing a penal prohibition upon the Divinity professors[1]?

J. There is a good deal of difficulty about subjects of this kind. I am not prepared to solve it. I would rather say generally, that while there are Divinity students of different religions there must be Divinity professors of different religions; but I should leave to the different religious bodies both the mode of appointing them and the mode of removing them.

. . . .

This is a very difficult subject; I will tell you as nearly as I can what I think. I think it would be much better if Divinity were altogether free, and if there were no such divisions of opinion as exist at present, if facts and opinions in theology could be examined like other facts and opinions. But in the present state of this country—I might say of the Christian world—that appears to me to be impossible; and, therefore, though I do not think it the very best thing, I should be willing that the Divinity professors should be appointed by the several bodies of Christians.

Q. But your view, looking to a higher ideal, would be that a man should examine theology as he would any experimental science, and teach his pupils such theories and views as might occur to him in consequence of that examination?

J. I should object to the comparison with experimental science, because you must allow for a great difference in the nature of the subject-matter.

Q. But you would hold that there was no objection to a teacher of theology indulging any amount of individuality or eccentricity in the doctrines that he taught, any more than you would in the case of any other science, so that they were the result of a careful examination and a conscientious desire for truth?

[1] First Report from the Select Committee of the House of Lords on University Tests, 1871, Queries 3058-3067.

J. I should hold that there was the greatest objection to eccentricity in all cases.

Q. I will say departure from conventional and ordinary standards [1].

J. It would depend upon how far it was a nearer approach to the truth or not, I think.

Q. I understand you, without accepting any standard of external truth on their behalf, to wish to give them the utmost latitude and freedom?

J. I think that the true principle would be to give them latitude and freedom; at the same time a man is very responsible for the conclusion he comes to, and for what he teaches.

Q. But I understood that that opinion of yours adapted itself to another opinion which you stated in your examination in chief, which was, that the authority of a teacher over those whom he was teaching depended almost entirely upon their belief in his perfect freedom in the utterance of the opinions which he held?

J. No, I do not think I said that or anything quite like it. What I said was that I thought that anybody who was bound by a test would be at a very great disadvantage in point of authority; but I did not mean to say that mere freedom would give him weight or respect. Nobody values less than I do the mere power of saying what you please, whether you are fit to say it or not.

Q. Your view is that, other things being equal, a person free from any pledge would have much greater weight than a person who was not free?

J. That I did mean to say; but that is quite a different thing.

Q. Would you not think that that must go a great deal further than the Universities, and apply to the clergy also?

J. I hesitate to answer these questions, because, though I am very glad to give my opinion, they are very difficult questions to answer offhand, and I do not quite see, if I may be allowed to say so, how they bear upon the question about which I am examined. I do not mean any disrespect to the Committee; but the truth is that these questions are very difficult to answer

[1] *Ibid.*, Queries 3068-3072.

offhand without consideration. I would wish to say shortly, in answer to your Lordship's question, that I do think it would be desirable that tests should be abolished for the clergy as well as for the Universities.

Q. I have no wish to ask you any questions which may seem to you irrelevant; but you will see that you and others are urging very great changes upon the ground of broad general views; and, of course, before those broad general views can form a ground for legislative action, it is necessary that we should ascertain how far, and in what direction, they will carry us [1].

J. Very well; I will not object to your Lordship asking what you think proper.

Q. I wish to ask you again with reference to the clergy. I think one of the present institutions of Oxford to which you took the strongest objection was the clerical fellowships?

J. Yes.

Q. And one of the grounds on which you stated that objection was, that persons were induced to take orders for the sake of obtaining clerical fellowships who would not otherwise have taken orders?

J. Yes.

Q. Do you not think that that objection applies to any other system upon which the clergy are remunerated?

J. It does.

Q. There must be many persons who take orders for the sake of livings who otherwise would not take orders?

J. It is a matter of degree, I think. What your Lordship says is quite true. I have very little doubt that that has the same bad effect. Many a man has taken orders because he has had a living waiting for him; we must be all familiar with that fact; and I think that that is an equally bad thing.

Q. You would not on that account refuse to accept the principle that they who minister at the Altar shall live by the Altar?

J. Certainly not.

Q. Do you not think that one of the remunerations of the clergy may fairly be derived from fellowships attached to

[1] First Report from the Select   on University Tests, 1871, Queries
Committee of the House of Lords   3073–3079.

colleges, supposing that the money comes from persons who wish it to be so disposed of ?

J. The restriction of fellowships to clergymen presents a very direct temptation, to which I admit that livings may sometimes offer a parallel, but it has other evils besides. You appoint a man of inferior merit instead of a man of superior merit because he is willing to go into orders, and that is an evil which does not apply to livings equally.

Q. Do you look upon clerical fellowships as an evil absolutely or comparatively ; I mean, would you rather that a man having money to leave should not leave it to a college at all, or that he should leave it in the shape of a clerical fellowship[1] ?

J. I would rather that he would not leave it to a college at all than leave it hampered by any kind of restriction, clerical or otherwise, distinct from the main purpose of the college.

Q. You do not think that the promoting of religious belief in any form is an end to which the machinery of colleges ought to be applied ?

J. Not the promoting of particular religious belief. Religion is a very important element of education, and I do not wish to see it diminished in the colleges, but I do not think you are at all likely to be successful in promoting it by confining endowments to one particular form of religious opinion, or to the teaching of religion generally.

Q. Would you forbid by legislation the application of any funds to the teaching of religion generally in the Universities ?

J. No, I should not, any more than I should wish to prevent by law property being left for other purposes to which it would be very undesirable that it should be left.

Q. Still you regard it as highly inexpedient that property should be left for the purpose of teaching religion in the University ?

J. Yes, I do ; but there are a great many other things which are inexpedient, which I should not wish to prohibit by law.

Q. Therefore you would not wish to prohibit in any way denominational colleges ?

J. I do not think them desirable, but I should not wish to prohibit them.

- - - - - - - -

[1] *Ibid.*, Queries 3080–3090.

Q. Then your objection generally to all this machinery for producing religious teaching may be summarized thus, may it not, that you do not wish for religious teaching in the University?

J. No; I wish that religious teaching should exist in the University, and that religious influences should exist there, but I think that you are not likely to obtain them in the best manner, or in the greatest degree, by tests, or by confining endowments to the encouragement of them.

Q. Did not I understand you to say that you objected to any money being applied to the teaching of religion in the University [1]?

J. That is what I mean in the answer which I have just given.

Q. If I understand your doctrine rightly, it is that you wish that religion should be taught in the University, but that you do not wish that any provision for that purpose should be made?

J. Yes, that is what I meant to say, but I would put it in rather a different way. I wish that religious teaching should exist in the University; but I do not wish religious endowments to be appropriated to it simply. My reason for not wishing religious endowments to be appropriated to it is because I think that is the least likely way to encourage it, and the worst way of promoting it.

Q. You would prefer that it should be taught without paying any person to teach it?

J. Not without any person being paid to teach it. That is not what I said. I said without any endowment being specially confined to it.

Q. Any payments which are made for the teaching of religion in the University must come from living persons?

J. I presume your Lordship is speaking of the Divinity professors?

Q. I speak of any teaching of religion in the University.

J. In order to prevent misunderstanding, I should wish to explain the state of matters which exists at present. There are the Divinity professors, on whose lectures candidates for

---

[1] First Report from the Select Committee of the House of Lords on University Tests, 1871, Queries 3091–3095.

orders are compelled to attend, and besides that there are the tutors of the colleges in the University who teach Divinity. The first are already furnished with endowments, and I have said that I do not propose to touch those. With respect to the second, I think it is better that they should be paid out of the general tutorial fund of the college, as they are at present, than that any special endowment should be set apart for them.

Q. The result of that, of course, would be that they would be paid without reference to the kind of religious teaching which they might give[1]?

J. They would be paid with reference to what the governing body, chiefly consisting of members of the Church of England, thought to be their duty with reference to the undergraduates.

Q. How do you know that they would be chiefly members of the Church of England?

J. I think there is very little reason to suppose, in the present state of education, that Dissenters or persons of other opinions would form a majority either of the University or of any of the colleges. What we have to consider is, what will probably be the general state of the University.

Q. But still I understand you, that desiring, as most of the parents in England do desire, that there should be religious influences in the University, you do not wish that any special arrangements involving pecuniary payments should be made for the teaching of any religious belief?

J. Not exactly so. I have said, I think, that it is desirable that special arrangements should be made; but that they should be made by the colleges themselves, or by the University itself, and not maintained by the appropriation of any new endowments to them, and not enforced by Act of Parliament.

. . . .

EARL OF HARROWBY.—*Q.* You conceive that the election to the government of a college should depend entirely upon success at the age of twenty-two or twenty-three in the literary career which was pointed out for the education at a college?

J. Yes; I think that that is the system which is least liable to abuse, and most likely to succeed in the long run. You will

[1] *Ibid.*, Queries 3096–3115.

get some persons who are not fit, or at all events who are not
the best persons you could have; not so good as you could
have if you supposed some wise man who had a great knowledge of the world and of mankind selecting them, perhaps;
but, upon the whole, you will get a much better governing
body in that way than in any other; and I may mention that
I can see the effects of that already at Oxford in the great
improvement which has taken place in education, and the
greater care and attention to the undergraduates, and the better
teaching in the colleges, since the colleges have been thrown
open.

Q. For instance, supposing there are two persons, one
professing anti-Christian views, and the other not, you see no
objection in an elector saying, I prefer the one for the education
of the youth who are put into my charge who has Christian
views to the one who has the reverse, although the one who
has the reverse may have proved that he was a deeper Greek
scholar than the other. Should you see any objection to that
element entering into an elector's consideration in the choice
of a tutor for a college [1]?

J. I should see great objection to that element entering into
the elections to fellowships; because, though I should wish
the fellows of a college to be a Christian body, that opens the
door to abuse. Let me observe two or three things about it.
In the first place, young men are not so divided at the age of
twenty-two or twenty-three that you can tell who is Christian
and who is un-Christian amongst them. If you admit the consideration of requiring a person to be a Christian, it carries you
much further than you intend. It brings into operation much
stronger motives than the interest of Christianity, namely,
party feeling as between High Church, Low Church, and Broad
Church. You are constantly liable to have a man elected
because he is a High Churchman if the majority of the electors
are High Churchmen, and because he is a Low Churchman if
the majority are Low Churchmen. Merely social considerations, as well as party ones, may sometimes enter in. In that
way you take away all confidence in the election. I do not

[1] First Report from the Select   on University Tests, 1871, Query
Committee of the House of Lords   3116.

deny that, upon the present system, you may occasionally get a man who is out of harmony with the place, but I think the evil of that is much less than the evil of the system which your Lordship suggests.

Q. How do you think a parent would look at it himself in the choice of a tutor for his own son? Would he, of necessity, choose the best Greek scholar; or would he choose a man who was a good Greek scholar, and at the same time of good moral and religious character [1]?

J. I think the tutors of colleges will generally be men in whose moral and religious character parents may have confidence.

Q. Is that secured merely by their literary qualities?

J. It is secured by their literary qualities, and the influences of the place, and many things. I think that a parent generally will not, as far as my experience goes, enter nicely into the religious opinions of the tutor of a college, but he will choose the man who he thinks will be most careful and attentive about his son, and take the most pains with him.

. . . .

Q. I think the tendency of your mind would be against all religious endowments; you would think that the religious teachers should depend upon the support of the professors from time to time of the different religious creeds : that would be the tendency of your line of thought, would it not?

J. I think that the best way of supporting both religious teachers and all other teachers is to make them partly dependent on their pupils or congregations, and partly independent of them.

. . . .

Q. Supposing you had a number of teachers of Divinity, or theology, or religion, or whatever it may be called, not supported by endowments, but simply supported from time to time by those persons who professed the different professions of faith, would there not be a temptation among the subscribers to choose a man not simply from his literary qualifications, but from his accordance with them in religious opinion, and from his general religious character?

---

[1] *Ibid.*, Queries 3117–3123.

J. Your Lordship means that, owing to those causes, a person would be appointed who would not be a suitable teacher in point of literary qualifications? I think there is that temptation.

Q. A person who would not have the highest qualities of a literary teacher, but would have those which would be, perhaps, more important in the minds of the subscribers, namely, an agreement in religious opinion with themselves, or eminence of religious character [1]?

J. Two things occur to me with reference to that. In the first place, I do not think it would be desirable for a professor of Divinity to be dependent entirely upon the subscriptions of some religious body ; and, secondly, that the religious bodies would find it very important to choose able men ; and that they would not think it a sufficient qualification for a Divinity professor that he was a religious man simply, because they would find that he had no influence, and did nothing with his pupils.

Q. Have there not been instances, in not very remote times certainly, where a man was removed from his fellowship, though he was of the highest qualifications, because his opinions were not considered orthodox by those who managed the college—I refer particularly to Dr. Davidson?

J. Yes ; and I should think that the managers of the college acted very unwisely in removing Dr. Davidson.

Q. You think it was very unwise to remove a man whose religious opinions they did not think were safe and sound?

J. Yes, in that instance.

Q. You think it would have been better for them to have gone on encouraging and supporting a man who was what they considered unsound in religion?

J. I think it would be better for any religious body to tolerate within their body a good deal of difference from their own views ; and, so far as I could have any opinion about them from a slight knowledge, I think the Dissenting bodies would gain very much by allowing the same toleration which appears to exist in the Church of England.

. . . .

[1] First Report from the Select Committee of the House of Lords on University Tests, 1871, Queries 3124-3127.

EARL STANHOPE.—*Q.* Does it not follow that there might be some strong reasons for retaining the tests in the case of the Divinity professors, even if tests were abolished in other cases ; for might it not happen that a layman appointed to that professorship without a test might be found to lecture to these young men who were intended for Holy Orders in terms not conformable to the tenets of the Church of England [1] ?

J. I am afraid I can only repeat what I have said before : first, that I do not think denominational teaching the best mode of teaching religion ; but I regard it as a necessity, and looking at it as a necessity, I think you can obtain it quite sufficiently by the mode of appointment without further requiring tests. I do not propose that a layman should be appointed ; but even if a layman should be admitted to a Divinity Chair (and it is very desirable that laymen should be students of Divinity), the same thing would apply. I think you may obtain all the safeguards which you require by the mode of appointment.

Q. How would you supersede the necessity of tests in the case of the Divinity professorships in this event, that a person who had been appointed, we will suppose, when he held tenets in strict conformity with the tenets of the Church of England, afterwards deviated in his teaching from those tenets ? You can now, as I understand, ask those professors to take the test a second time. Supposing there was no test, what measures would you adopt in the case supposed ?

J. A Divinity professor is liable to the Church Discipline Act just as any other Church clergyman is.

Q. But supposing a layman were appointed as a Divinity professor—and many laymen have been highly qualified to teach Divinity—what step would you take ?

J. If you insist upon his being strictly a denominational teacher you must make some provision to meet the case.

. . . .

LORD HOUGHTON.—*Q.* During your residence at Oxford, have there not occurred several violent controversies within the circle of the Church of England ?

J. Yes ; I am afraid that is very notorious ; we have always

---

[1] *Ibid.*, Queries 3129–3157.

D

been in a state of unrest since I have been in Oxford, and
I believe antiquarians tell us that we were so in the Middle
Ages too. We have certainly had many controversies, which
have a good deal affected the minds of the young men. There
has been a good deal of action and reaction; for you cannot
have a movement in one direction without creating another
movement in the opposite direction. Ever since what is
called the Tractarian Movement, which began in 1835, there
have been disturbing influences: the Hampden agitation, the
Reform of the University, the changes in the examination
statute, the growth of ritualism, and during the last six years
the movement for the abolition of tests; and allowances should
be made for these influences by those who would fairly judge
the opinions of young men.

Q. Has not what might be called a certain amount of
sceptical tendency in the University been almost a necessary
reaction from these controversies [1]?

J. Yes, I think so. The tendency of one party, perhaps of
all parties, is to exclude the other party as much as possible.
There has been an attempt to divide the University—more,
I think, than is the fact at all—into two parties; and the old
argument has been used, that if you are not High Church or
Catholic, or whatever it is called, you must be in the other
extreme.

Q. Have the tests which have hitherto existed in the University been of any effect in checking these differences of
opinion?

J. I should think they have been of no effect whatever.

Q. Have the tests, the object of which was to preserve conformity to the Church of England, had any effect in checking
the tendencies towards the Church of Rome?

J. As far as I can judge, they have had none whatever.

Q. Therefore the existing tests have been no more effective
in checking positive diversities of opinion from the Church
of England than in checking negative tendencies?

J. Certainly not. All that the tests could expect to do would

---

[1] First Report from the Select
Committee of the House of Lords   on University Tests, 1871, Queries
3158–3161.

be negative, to produce a silence upon particular subjects. All that those who impose them could possibly expect of them would be that kind of check, but that is as nothing when you come across the influence of an eminent man acting in another direction. What I mean to express is, that tests must always be purely negative, and that the greater influences which act upon the undergraduates are really positive, and that the tests do not touch them.

Q. Would not a test, the object of which was to secure conformity to the doctrines of the Church of England, act as an impediment to the introduction and sustenance of doctrines tending towards the Church of Rome [1] ?

J. We might suppose so beforehand, but I do not think, judging from experience, that this has been the case. During the last thirty years the doctrine of a great part of the Church of England has entirely changed, and the appearance of many of our churches has become like that of a Roman Catholic Church. Judging from these general facts, I should say that tests have had no appreciable influence in checking the movement towards the Church of Rome.

Q. And having had no appreciable influence in checking the tendencies towards the Church of Rome, have they had any tendency, on the other hand, to check the development of freer forms of opinion ?

J. No, I think not.

Q. You regard the tests, therefore, as comparatively ineffective on the positive as well as on the negative side ?

J. Yes, on both sides.

Q. Was there not in the Tractarian Movement a resistance to the predominant tests in the University, which led even some of the highest and best minds into a line of conduct which was hardly thought compatible with legitimate controversy ?

J. Your Lordship refers to the casuistical explanations of the tests. Yes, I certainly think so ; and that shows the great evil of tests. There are two ways of escaping from them. One is the casuistical way, which, as your Lordship was saying,

---

[1] *Ibid.*, Queries 3162–3165.

D 2

is justly to be reprobated ; and the other is the more general way of regarding them without reference to their sense ; not casuistically evading them, but taking them in the most general sense possible, or in no sense.   Both seem to me to be bad.

Q. Has there been of late years any tendency to take these tests casuistically upon the negative side [1] ?

J. There has been a tendency to take them casuistically in one sense, but not in the same manner as before ; that is to say, they have been taken in a general sense in so far as they are supposed to be enforced by law, but not explained away in detail as they have been in such writings as the famous tract, No. 90. I think that both ways of escaping from them are almost equally objectionable, and show the great evil of tests.

. . . .

EARL OF CARNARVON.—*Q.* The only guarantee you would look to would be the guarantee of public opinion and their own sense of responsibility?

J. I would impose no tests.

Q. When you say that you would impose no test, do you mean that you would take any other kind of guarantee short of a test?

J. I would take no test or declaration.

Q. Is there any guarantee for the teaching of any particular opinion which does not resolve itself into some form, either of declaration or of test?

J. Yes, I think there is.   I do not think the object a desirable one, but I think it is very easy to accomplish it without a test. For example, you may put any endowment in the hands of trustees. Take such an instance as the Simeon trustees ; there is no test there, but yet, from generation to generation, they seem to go on appointing clergymen of a certain class of opinion.

. . . .

Q. Having no objection to the use of the Church of England Service in the chapels, would your objections extend to a declaration of a negative character, such as that which was proposed by Sir Roundell Palmer in the House of Commons,

---

[1] First Report from the Select Committee of the House of Lords on University Tests, 1871, Queries 3166-3218.

that all persons in offices of trust as respects teaching should declare that they would teach nothing in opposition to the doctrines and discipline of the Church of England?

J. Yes, I should object to that. That is a new test, and, if enforced strictly, requires not only every tutor but every lecturer either to teach the doctrines of the Church of England or to teach nothing. Such a test is more stringent than the existing declaration of conformity, and would be imposed on some persons of whom the declaration of conformity is not required. Other sects of Christians must in fairness receive a similar protection. And however stringent tests are made, you cannot touch the private tutors, who have a great part of the teaching in their hands. No one proposes to impose a test upon bachelors ; nor can you prevent anybody from coming down and settling at Oxford. If a man comes and settles here who is a man of force of character, and has the power of teaching, he may exercise great influence, possibly more than any one else in the place. That is another point of view in which tests are ineffectual, and which, I think, should be considered.

Q. I conclude from your last answer that had Dr. Newman held any office of trust in the University at the time when he left the Church of England, you would not have been willing to see his removal from that office ; you would have preferred to leave it to the simple effect of public opinion, and to have allowed him to retain whatever power his own individual character and influence might have given him [1] ?

J. Yes, for good or for evil, whichever it might be.

Q. The influence of his character, it must always be borne in mind, would receive greater weight from the chair from which he pronounced his opinions?

J. That would depend upon the position he was in. We have already separated off the Divinity professors, and if he were a college tutor it would depend upon the college, and upon the Vice-Chancellor, whether they were willing to continue him or not.

Q. I think the general tendency of your evidence and the

----

[1] *Ibid.*, Queries 3219–3221.

drift of your own opinion, as expressed to us, go to leaving
him in the position which he occupied, no matter what it was?
J. Quite so. As far as it is an evil, I think it would be the
lesser of two evils.

. . . .

LORD COLCHESTER.—*Q.* I think you stated that it would be
unjust that the Church of England, which forms only about
one-half of the nation, should possess the whole of the
University; do you think that there would be any objection to
retaining less than half the colleges for the Church of England,
if there was a large portion, though not a majority, of the
nation that desired that some such colleges might exist[1]?

J. I do not think there would be any injustice in it; but I
think it would be very undesirable, and that it would be absolutely impossible to carry out such a proposal in practice. It
would be very undesirable, because one of the great advantages
of opening the University is the bringing different classes of
persons together. Churchmen will, I hope, learn something
from Dissenters, and Dissenters will learn something from
Churchmen, and so on. I may mention in illustration of this,
what an eminent minister of the Church of Scotland said to
me a day or two ago. He said that the relation in which the
Dissenting bodies in Scotland stand to the Established Church
is far better than that which exists in England, and this, as he
thought, arose from their all having been educated at the same
Universities. That is a benefit which I want to secure; but
according to the plan now proposed, instead of really opening
the University to Dissenters, I should have brought the
Dissenters to the place called Oxford, where they might have
a portion of the endowments, and be examined like other
persons, and that would be all; they would not enter into the
spirit or society of the colleges; they would still be educated
in Wesleyan, Independent, or Presbyterian seminaries. I would
point out further that the plan is impracticable, and could only
be carried out by violence. There may be some colleges, in
the first instance, which would be willing to be Church of

[1] First Report from the Select   on University Tests, 1871, Query
Committee of the House of Lords   3229.

England colleges, possibly, for a time ; but they would, perhaps, find that the open colleges gained upon them, and then they would want to give 'up being Church of England. But there would be absolutely no colleges willing to become Nonconformist, or of any other religion, and they would be all agreed in refusing to make over half their endowments to the State for the support of other denominational colleges[1].

In 1880 Mr. Charles Roundell proposed a resolution in the House of Commons to which he spoke at length on July 9. He had previously communicated with Jowett on the subject of his resolution, which ran as follows :—

'That this House, while fully recognizing the obligation to make provision for the due fulfilment of the requisitions of sections 5 and 6 of the "Universities Tests Act," 1871 (relating to religious instruction, and to morning and evening prayer in colleges), deems it inexpedient that, save in the case of the Deanery of Christ Church, any clerical restriction shall remain or be attached to any Headship or Fellowship in any College of the Universities of Oxford and Cambridge.'

The following is Jowett's letter to Mr. Roundell on the subject :—

BALL. COLL., *July* 6, 1880.

I quite agree with the principle of your resolution.

I think that after provision has been made for the Chapel

---

[1] The following anecdote is well authenticated. When Dean Stanley was dying, in July, 1881, Jowett called at the Deanery, but Stanley was too ill to see him. The Dean was, in fact, already unconscious. Jowett was much agitated, and urged Canon Hugh Pearson, who was there, to express to Stanley, should he recover consciousness, his (Jowett's) deep regret for having done so little, of late years, in support of his friend's continued efforts towards obtaining a greater latitude of opinion for the clergy (*Life*, &c., vol. ii. p. 183).

Services and the religious instruction of the Undergraduates, all clerical restrictions should be abolished.

It is an invidious thing, partaking of the nature of a bribe, to elect an inferior man because he is willing to take orders, to reject a superior man because he is unwilling.

It is a bad thing both for the colleges and the clerical profession that the management of colleges should pass into the hands of inferior men because they are clergymen. . . .

I am anxious that religious education should revive in Oxford, but such a revival will never be brought about by the maintenance of Clerical Restrictions.

The Commission are inclined to let the Colleges do as they like, and settle the matter by a chance majority. But a great national institution should not be left to this sort of caprice, and the principle adopted by the Commission has a tendency to divide the University into Clerical and anti-Clerical Colleges.

Where the Colleges are nearly divided, the Commission appear to throw their weight into the clerical scale.

I think it much better in general that Religious Instruction should be given by clergymen, because laymen are not sufficiently interested in it, and that the persons who give the instruction or are employed in the Chapel services should be Fellows. I would give every facility for such an arrangement, but I would rather not enforce it.

The attempt to maintain Clerical Restrictions is an anachronism in the present state of Oxford opinion.

I am afraid that I have nothing new to add on a subject which has been thrashed out so often. I send these few remarks because I promised them.

After a debate in which, amongst others, Mr. Gladstone, and also Sir Matthew White Ridley (one of the Oxford Commissioners) took part, Mr. C. Roundell said that 'having regard to the promise of the Prime Minister, that the Government would afford a full and fair field for the discussion of the Statutes of the Commission next year, &c.,' he begged leave to withdraw his motion.

NOTES ON CHURCH REFORM.

These notes on Church Reform were written in 1874, at Caterham, where Jowett was staying with R. Lowe (Lord Sherbrooke), with whom he discussed the question.

The great objects to be arrived at in a reform of the Church are :—

1. To reconcile the Church and the Dissenters.
2. To make the Clergy more truly representative of the Laity.
3. To give the services of the Church of England some power of self-adaptation to public opinion.

1. The relation of the Church to the Dissenters, and of the Dissenters to the Church, is the greatest and worst schism in the Christian world. They divide the nation: these divisions affect all our politics, e. g. education, Church reform, &c. This division affects society, upper and middle classes, gentlemen and tradesmen—'See how these Christians' look down upon one another or hate one another. The sense of injustice has passed into the blood and bone of one half of the people of England. They were driven out in 1661, and have never been restored.

2. The laity want morality, education for their children— no popery. The clergy want sacerdotalism, sacramentalism, power. The laity are not sceptics, neither are they conservatives. But they do not want to go in for a crusade against geology, science, &c. At present while the clergy are moving in one direction, the laity are moving in another, or standing indifferent and in amazement. The High Church clergy insist that they alone possess the Church of England ; and they must be admitted to find certain germs of their doctrine in the Baptismal Service, in the Service for Ordination, &c. If these were in parts made optional, they and the Low Church man would be placed on the same footing, and probably a section of them would drop off.

3. The services of any church must rather fall behind than be in advance of public opinion, except so far as they

express general truths, which belong equally to all branches of knowledge. But if they are framed with a proper elasticity, so that some portions of them can be dropped and others retained, by the voluntary action of the clergy and congregation, they adapt themselves to the altered requirements of the age. Nothing can be more absurd than to suppose that our religious belief was settled once for all 301 years ago by the compromises and accidents of the sixteenth century, or by the intolerance of the Restoration. As little ought its ritual and form to be determined by a passing movement among the clergy, altering the position of the Communion table in the seventeenth century, reviving the surplice and various positions in the nineteenth.

The means are:—

1. The alteration of the Liturgy so far as to allow the omission of certain passages:

(a) Athanasian Creed.

(b) Phrases about regeneration and new birth in the Baptismal Service.

(c) Form of Ordination.

(d) 'Sure and certain hope' in Burial Service.

2. No alteration to be made in the form of service without the consent of the congregation. Certain alterations to be allowed with their consent:

(a) The services may be abridged, provided that not less than two-thirds of them are retained.

(b) Hymns may be introduced.

(c) Verses and passages from Scripture, &c.

(d) In the Communion Service nothing essential to the service shall be altered. The prayer for the Church Militant and the Exhortation may be omitted.

3. Dissenters should be allowed to preach in the Church, and clergymen in dissenting Chapels.

II. EDUCATIONAL

In the two years preceding the Universities Commission
of 1850, Jowett and Stanley were engaged upon a joint
work on University Reform (vol. i. p. 177). The appointment of the Commission, however, with Stanley as
Secretary, prevented the publication.

To A. P. STANLEY.

Jan. 10, [1849].

One or two things have occurred to me respecting the book,
at which I am at work regularly. In your part—'A short
comparison of Cambridge and Oxford, answer[ing] the objection
that Cambridge with [the] open system has done so little more
than Oxford with the close system'—I believe the answer to
be, partly that the Cambridge system is closed to Colleges,
although not to Counties, partly that Cambridge is eaten up by
examinations : how to make Senior Wranglers seems to be
the great question. If I may judge from what Spottiswoode and
Price tell me, Mathematicians are as much dissatisfied with the
results as we are. One part of your letter rather dismayed me—
where you said you had been writing a history of the University
from the beginning. Unfortunately I have done the same as
introductory to the account of the Constitution. Mine is
very short, 'mehr objectiv als subjectiv,' says little about the
Reformation, and finally terminates with the Caroline Statutes.
I am quite willing to cancel it, but think it might stand, if you
would make yours not so much a constitutional history as an
account of opinions and other changes.

I suppose the chief reason why the Colleges have increased
in wealth since the Reformation is the increase in the value of
landed property. Suppose money to have fallen in value eight-

fold since that time, and land, as is often said, to have increased fourfold, this would make the money-income of the Colleges thirty-two times what it then was. In Balliol College this seems to be about the case.

When the scheme for a new mode of appointing persons to the Civil Service, both at home and in India, was under consideration, Jowett was consulted by Sir Charles Trevelyan, to whom he wrote the following letter[1].

BALLIOL COLLEGE,
January, 1854.

DEAR SIR,

I think two objections are likely to be made to the Report you are so good as to show me on the 'Organization of the Permanent Civil Service.' First, that it is impossible to be assured of the moral character of persons elected by examination into the public service. Secondly, that it is impossible to carry on an examination in so great a variety of subjects as would be required, and with such numberless candidates ; in other words, that the scheme, however excellent, is not practicable.

I am convinced that neither of these objections has any real foundation.

I. For the moral character of the candidates I should trust partly to the examination itself. University experience abundantly shows that in more than nineteen cases out of twenty, men of attainments are also men of character. The perseverance and self-discipline necessary for the acquirement of any considerable amount of knowledge are a great security that a young man has not led a dissolute life.

But in addition I would suggest that there should be a system of inquiries and testimonials, which might be made considerably more efficient than testimonials for Orders are at present. The analogy of insurance offices would afford the best model for carrying out such a system. I would propose :—

1. That the candidate should give notice (as in the case of

[1] Vol. i. p. 185. The letter is reprinted by permission.

Orders) of his intention to offer himself at least three months before the examination.

2. That he should, at the same time, send papers comprising a certificate of birth and baptism, with a precise statement of all the places of his education, whether at School or College, together with testimonials of his conduct for two years previously from the head of the School or College in which he was last a pupil, and also a statement of his present occupation and residence.

3. That he should give references :—

(a) To a medical man ;

(b) To a magistrate ; or, in case of inferior situations, to two respectable householders ;

(c) To a clergyman or dissenting minister ;

to all of whom carefully-drawn questions respecting the candidate, in the form of an insurance office paper, shouldbe submitted : the answers to be confidential. To prevent the possible forgery of a character, an independent letter might be sent to a clergyman or magistrate in the district, with the view of his certifying to the existence and respectability of the references.

The scrutiny of the character and testimonials of the candidates ought to be quite separate from the examination. The rejection should be absolute and without reasons ; whether it took place on medical or moral grounds would remain uncertain. In case of Parliamentary inquiry, however, a register of the reasons might be privately kept in the office.

With such or even a less amount of precaution the standard of character among public servants would surely be maintained as high as at present, or higher ; as high, certainly, as the standard of character which can be ensured in persons admitted to Holy Orders.

II. The second objection relates to the mode of examination.

A. To meet this let us begin by supposing a division between the superior and inferior appointments, and further, let us estimate the annual number of vacancies of the superior class at 250, and the number of candidates for the 250 vacancies at 2,000.

This last (which, however, is probably the outside number)

is somewhat alarming. The best way to disperse the crowd will be by holding examinations continually, say five in each year, three in London, one in Edinburgh, one in Dublin. Thus the number is reduced to 400 for each examination, a number which may be easily managed.

The examination should consist both of paper and viva voce work. Where, as here, the object is to select a number of young men for practical life, the latter is of great importance. The aim in either should be to test general intelligence and power of thought and language quite as much as knowledge of a particular subject.

The examination on paper of each candidate should last for about a week, to which would have to be added an hour of viva voce. The amount of labour thus entailed (equal to the perusal of 4,800 long papers and 400 hours of viva voce), no less than the variety of subjects, would make it necessary that the number of examiners should be not less than eight.

Considering the nature of the employment, and that everything depends on the fitness of the examiners, their salary should be liberal. They should be permanent officers, and, except for proved misconduct, irremovable. It is only by the office being made permanent that able men will, in the first instance, be induced to devote themselves to it, or will have the opportunity of acquiring the experience and facility necessary for doing their work well. Their irremovability, as in the case of the judges, is the best guarantee for their independence. To relieve them as much as possible from details of business, they would require several clerks and a secretary. It would be very desirable that at the head of this 'College of Examiners' some eminent person should be placed, of the rank of Privy Councillor.

I will next proceed to the subjects of examination, in reference to which I think three principles should be kept in view. We should consider what are :—

1. The indispensable requirements of public offices generally.

2. What are the best elements of higher education in England, without special reference to the wants of the public offices.

3. What are the special attainments needed in any particular department of the public service, as, for example, the Treasury and the Foreign Office.

1. The qualifications most universally required of officials are to write fast and neatly, a thorough knowledge of arithmetic and book-keeping, and English composition. I should propose to make these the subject of preliminary examinations, which might last for a single day. No candidate by whom this examination was not satisfactorily passed should be allowed to compete further. on this occasion. This would have the advantage of limiting the number of candidates. No able man who was fit for the public service would be excluded by the requirement of arithmetic, if it were known beforehand to be indispensable. It is necessary to require it, for otherwise you will not get it.

2. When this preliminary examination has been disposed of, we come to the principal one, in arranging the subjects of which we have to consider what is the main staple of English education at the present day. It will not do to frame our examination on any mere theory of education. We must test a young man's ability by what he knows, not by what we wish him to know. The system of our public schools, of our two English, as well as of the Scotch and Irish Universities, as well as the case of those who have not been at a University or public school, should be fairly considered in the arrangement of the plan. The knowledge of Latin and Greek is, perhaps, upon the whole, the best test of regular previous education. Mathematics are the predominant study of one of our Universities. Moral Philosophy is a principal subject at Oxford no less than at Edinburgh and Glasgow. An increasing class of persons receive a foreign or an English, in contradistinction to what may be termed a classical education. Some of the candidates again may be entered at Inns of Court. Lastly, it may be remarked that there are subjects, such as Physical Science and Civil Engineering, which, notwithstanding their immense growth in the last few years, have scarcely yet found their way down into education, and in reference to which the proposed examination may be made to operate usefully. These and similar considerations should enter into our scheme,

which, supported as it is by valuable prizes, must exercise a great influence on the higher education of the country.

3. The special requirements of the higher departments of the public offices appear to be chiefly two, viz. a knowledge of the principles of commerce, taxation, and political economy in the Treasury, Board of Trade, &c. ; of modern languages and modern history, under which last may be included international law, in the Foreign Office. In the offices which are principally offices of account, mathematical talent may with advantage be insisted upon. Whether immediately wanted for the daily work of the office or not, all such attainments tend to give an official a higher interest in his employment, and to fit him for superior positions. They may also be regarded as reflecting honour on the service. The requirement of these or any other qualifications would be determined by each office for itself, subject to the approval of the Board of Examiners, while the duty of the examiners would be to guarantee with the special attainment the general ability of the candidate. In the following scheme it has been attempted to carry out the views which have preceded :—

FOUR SCHOOLS.

1	2	3	4
Classical Literature.	Mathematics, with practical applications, and Natural Science.	Political Economy, Law, Moral Philosophy.	Modern Languages and Modern History, including International Law.

Note.—In the third of these schools political economy would supply the requirements of the Treasury, Board of Trade, &c., while the subjects that have been grouped in the last school are more especially adapted to the requirements in the Foreign Office.

The details of these schools are left to the examiners, with the single direction that original English composition should form a considerable element in the examination of all the candidates.

REGULATIONS.

1. Two examiners to examine in each school, and to form a judgement separately on all the papers.

2. Two schools to be required of all candidates, and none to be allowed to try in more than two.

3. The examination on paper in each school to last for three days.

4. Each candidate to be examined viva voce for one hour in any school at his option.

5. The successful candidates to be placed in order of merit.

6. A certain number of appointments to be appropriated to each examination. The choice to be given to each candidate (in order of merit) of what office he desires to enter, provided he has fulfilled in the examination the requirements of the office which he selects.

The order of proceeding would be as follows. Say, on February 1, the candidates (whose testimonials and references have been previously approved) have assembled, and pass the preliminary examination in Arithmetic and English Composition. Two or three days after, the examiners, as soon as they have had time to read their papers and reject those who were not qualified, would proceed to the examination in the first school. This would be carried on by two of their number, while the remaining six would be engaged in their different schools with the viva voce examination of the rest. The 'paper-work' of the first school would last about three days, and then would commence the 'paper-work' of the second school conducted by its two examiners, while the viva voce of the other three schools was also going on. At the termination of the whole, the names of the candidates, or rather of as many of them as there were appointments to be filled up, would appear in order of merit, with a notice appended to the name of each, of the schools in which he had been examined. Such a list would not be difficult to make out, if there were a uniform system of marking amongst the examiners, which might be such as to represent fairly the general ability of the candidates, as well as the more precise result of the examination. Such a system is already in use at the Education Office, and is perfectly successful.

E

B. The objection of impracticability will perhaps be felt to apply more strongly to the application of the scheme to the supplementary clerks, and in general to the humbler class of public servants, on account of their great number and dispersion through the country, and also on account of the difficulty of devising a mode by which such situations as theirs can be uniformly made rewards of merit. The experience of the Education Department of the Privy Council Office, in which as many as 1,800 certificates of merit have been given, after examination, to schoolmasters and pupil-teachers in a single year, shows that no numbers occasion any real difficulty.

First, let us suppose the whole number of the lower class of public servants to amount to 10,000, offering perhaps 500 vacancies annually. It would be, as you observe, unfair to subject the candidates for these small situations to the expense of a journey to London, Edinburgh, or Dublin. The examination must be brought to them. With this view the whole country might be divided into districts. A few assistant district examiners would be required for the superintendence of the examination, who might be furnished with the questions, and might bring the answers to London after each examination, and sorting them by subjects, determine on their merits, under the control of the Central Board.

The previous scrutiny of the moral character of the candidates would be conducted in nearly the same manner for all. (See *supra*, p. 45.)

REGULATIONS.

1. The examination to be carried on by the assistant examiners.

2. To consist of reading aloud in the presence of one of them ;

of writing from dictation ;

of arithmetic ;

of geography ;

of writing a letter or making an abstract ;

of viva voce on any subject calculated to test general intelligence ;

To which might be added a 'useful knowledge' paper of common questions about common things.

3. The examinations of all the different districts to be brought together at the central office.

4. The names of as many candidates as there are vacancies, actual or probable, to be published, either in order of merit or divided into classes, according to the nature or value of the appointments.

A smile may be raised at the idea of subjecting excisemen and tide-waiters to a competing literary examination, as there might have been thirty years ago at subjecting village school-masters to a similar test ; but it must be remembered, on the other hand :—

1. That such a measure will exercise the happiest influence on the education of the lower classes throughout England, acting by the surest of all motives—the desire that a man has of bettering himself in life.

2. That reading, writing, and arithmetic, a good hand, and the power of expressing himself in a letter, no less than the general intelligence tested by the examination, render the lowest public servant fitter for his position than he would be without them, and give him a chance of rising in the service.

3. That the examination will relate to common things treated in a common-sense way.

4. That no other means can be devised for getting rid of patronage.

A further objection may be made to the selection of candidates by a competing examination, that this affords no test of their fitness for places of trust, for which also their youth seems to disqualify them. But places of trust would not be given to youths just entering the service, but to those whose characters were long tried in it.

In this class of public servants there would be at least as much security for high character as at present. They will have obtained their situations in an independent manner through their own merits. The sense of this cannot but induce self-respect, and diffuse a wholesome spirit among the lower no less than the higher classes of official men. Appointment by merit would not impair, but would rather increase the unity of the public service, while it would tend to take away from promotion by merit the appearance of being favouritism in disguise. Permit me to express in conclusion my earnest wishes for the success of the scheme. If carried out it will relieve public men from the abuses and from the annoyance of patronage; it will raise the public service; it will give all classes a common interest in maintaining its rank and efficiency. Though a subordinate aspect of it, I cannot help feeling, as a College tutor, its great importance to the University, supplying as it does, to well-educated young men, a new opening for honourable distinction. The effect of it in giving a stimulus to the education of the lower classes can hardly be over-estimated.

Yours very truly,

B. JOWETT.

III. EUROPEAN POLITICS

On March 28, 1849, the German Assembly elected the King of Prussia Emperor of Germany, but he declined to accept the position, and owing to the influence of Austria the plans for the union of Germany broke down for a time [1].

To A. P. Stanley.

[1849.]

. . . —— thinks himself a prophet because it entered into his stupid, practical head a year ago that the idea of German unity was a dream. It seems to be a Christian duty to watch the mistakes of one's neighbours in politics, and all the mass of human misery produced by them, with a kind of complacent self-satisfaction. Seriously (you see I am taking the moral, thoughtful line as a humble imitator of Arnold), one cannot help being struck with the apathy and indifference shown about the fortunes of the world of Europe in the present day. Is it possible that we should ever feel a national enthusiasm again ?

I wonder whether the world is getting 'stale, flat, and unprofitable,' or whether oneself is becoming 'stale, flat, and unprofitable,' or both. As the old man in Cornwall said to you, 'partly both, but I incline to think the latter.'

To the Same.

35 Rue de la Madeleine, *Jan.* 7, [1851].

I have no news to tell you (having been, indeed, shut up to write answers to your questions), except that sort of indefinite

---

[1] See J. W. Headlam, *Bismarck*, p. 72 ff.

idea of things which is conveyed by the atmosphere of the place. France seems to have the most despotic Government it has ever known, not excepting the old Bourbon in some respects. Changarnier is the pillar of the State, though not apparently on good terms either with the President[1] or his Ministers or the Assembly[2]. Respecting the re-election of the President there seems to be a fix: a clear majority are said to be in favour of it, but as it is a violation of the Constitution, the consent of two-thirds of the Chamber must be obtained: this would not [be] given, it is thought, at present[3].

An Algerine triumvirate of Lamoricière, Changarnier, and Cavaignac, is suggested as a possible dénoûment.

On Monday we had 'une crise Ministerielle,' occasioned by the unknown individuals who were brought in fourteen months since feeling that they were not treated civilly by the Assembly. There is a strange anomaly in the present Government from the liability of the President elected by the people to quarrel with the Assembly, who are also elected by the people: the danger of which collision, as a philosopher explained to me a few days since, is avoided in America by not giving the Ministry of the President seats in the Assembly.

To R. B. D. MORIER[4].

September 2, [1860].

How I should like to have a good talk about foreign politics with you! You know I was always a Napoleonist, as far as is consistent with being an Englishman. The way I come to it is this; the map of Europe is badly settled at present in accordance with traditions of Vienna, rights of petty German princes, &c. In the next twenty years it must be resettled, and the

[1] Louis Napoleon.

[2] On Jan. 10, 1851, Changarnier was deprived of the command of the national guard.

[3] In November followed the *coup d'état*. Changarnier, Cavaignac, and Lamoricière were arrested. Louis Napoleon was chosen Prince-President of the Republic for ten years (Dec. 21, 22).

[4] Morier was now attaché at Berlin, and in Sept. and Oct. 1860 he acted as private secretary to Lord John Russell, when in attendance on the Queen at Coburg.

only person who can lend a guiding hand in the resettlement is N. I have been very much struck with his *Idées*, which I read lately, and also with what one of the librarians of the British Museum told me, that for years he used to read there daily. He is not scrupulous, and perhaps his Court may be a mass of immorality and his Ministers dishonest jobbers, but he is the only man who sees the end many moves on, and understands not only France, but Europe and the times. His programme seems to me to be a kingdom of Italy—an Empire of Germany—probably extension to Belgium and the Rhine (if in any juncture it can be done without the risk of a European war)—free trade—influence in the Mediterranean—with more distant visions of resettling Hungary and Spain. He will not fall into the error of his uncle (see the *Idées*) of doing things too rapidly. And he has the best plan of all—to have no plan.

The other day I saw a letter from one of your Berlin politicians named Bernhardi, which made honourable mention of you. It was full of dismal prophecies. I dare say you don't talk very freely to the gentleman who wrote it, for he appears to talk very freely to his friends. One thing he said amused me, 'that he had thought young Stockmar a dull, silly fellow, without anything of the paternal genius,' but that he had now arrived at the conclusion that he was a very deep fellow indeed, ' having the art of doing everything and appearing perfectly insignificant.'

The English people hate L. N. because they think he will take away the English prestige, and they are but faintly reconciled to him by the hope of improved markets, &c.; the English aristocracy, inspired partly by the same order abroad (who make diplomatic public opinion), also hate him because he has a piece of the popular fibre in him, and is the enemy of petty princes, feudal rights, &c., and because he is a principle of government, which is independent of them. If the two unite, they will force us into a war with France as surely as Pitt did in 1795. The press will help to unite them; a war would sell the newspapers, and they have to revenge the injury which L. N. has done to the freedom of the press.

I rejoice in Garibaldi's success more than in any public

event which has happened for twenty years. It will doubtless have a great effect throughout Europe[1].

Instead of oppressing Hungary and Italy and envying France, I wish Germany, with the help of L. N., would remodel itself into a German Empire. All might be winners then in Europe and no losers.

But I have given you enough of my crude fancies on foreign politics. I fancy, from M. Bernhardi's approbation of you, you are on a different tack. I may be utterly wrong, but I need hardly remind you that the only way to judge is utterly to disengage yourself from the feelings and prejudices of the people among whom you live. The logic of facts (with the precaution of *surtout point de zèle*) is the only kind of reasoning that points to the true tendencies of things.

To Miss Elliot at Florence.

FRESHWATER, *April* 16, 1861.

Where do you suppose I was on Sunday? among your relatives at Pembroke Lodge[2]. Of course I liked them because they were kind to me, but independently of this, it was impossible not to be pleased at their simple and unaffected ways. I was greatly interested in seeing and talking with Lord John. I fancied I could perceive how both his and her virtues in some degree interfere with their success as politicians. But I felt that there was strength underneath and more of a philosophical comprehension of things than in any other public man I ever came across. His high rank has had the opposite effect with him from what it has with most people: it has prevented his being a man of the world.

I have just been reading Gladstone's speech on the Budget, not much in point of eloquence, but I think right in its proposals, viz. a penny less of Income Tax and no Paper Duties, which means, I believe, the *Times* for twopence, also a denunciation of expenditure which is enormous and wasteful, and is the real cause why the rich man pays income tax and

[1] Garibaldi landed at Reggio on Aug. 18, and entered Naples Sept. 7.
[2] Lord John and Lady Russell.

poor and rich alike pay tea duty. The French Treaty seems to be an entire success [1].

Politics at home seem to be in a very ' stickit' state. They are all summed up in one word : 'the Upper and Middle Classes have got the power in their hands and are determined to keep it.' That is the reason why Lord John's political cards can make no way while Gladstone's do, because they unite the middle and lower classes against the aristocracy—trade and labour against land. Lord John's hope seems to me to be that foreign politics will eventually react upon home if the aspirations of Europe in this year are fulfilled.

I hope that you and your sister are enjoying North Italy, than which nothing is really more enjoyable. Pray let me hear from one of you when you are at Florence, and do not give up Rome and Naples, and, if possible, see the end of the Papacy and the beginning of the kingdom of Italy at Rome.

To R. B. D. MORIER.

FRESHWATER, *May* 10, 1861.

So you think me too much of a hero-worshipper of L. Napoleon. I have no objection to look at the dark side of him— Cayenne, jobbery of ministers, oaths to the Constitution broken. Still he appears to me to be the great political head in Europe, the only man who could have freed Italy, who can place Germany, Hungary, &c., on a better footing, who can prevent war between France and England, who can reform the Catholic Church. Did you ever read his works attentively? I quite admit the divergence of French and English interests. But I think that it is quite impossible to set up English interests against European ones. The state of things will perhaps be this—France will bear the expense; will give active help to the nationalities; will take the lead, will diplomatize, will be suspected. England will bear no expense; will give words which, at a particular juncture, may be of value; will be straightforward, will have fewer friends and fewer enemies. The position of these two countries in reference to Italy will probably be the relative position of them in reference to the

---

[1] See Bright, *History of England*, iv. 386, 388.

*E

politics of Europe generally, and Germany of 1865 will be
Italy of 1860, and the Rhine provinces will be Savoy and Nice
over again. The background of Russia it is very difficult to
make out; will it restore Poland in the Russian sense? or
support, as in 1848, the German powers against their subjects?
Let me propose to you, as the thesis for an essay, the Mediterranean in 1870.

There is a great Conservative reaction at present in England
—like the old High Church movement at Oxford. But I do
not believe it will last. 'The end of the wave' is, I think,
a true figure of speech. And the probable changes in Europe
will before long affect England, as always.

Lord John Russell and his wife have very kindly made
friends with me. I quite agree in your judgement about him.
I like his simplicity. Notwithstanding his shyness, he talks to
you on any subject of history or philosophy like a real man.
You can readily understand when you see him, how it has
come to pass that he has been 'bowled over' by Palmerston,
and yet is really the better and greater man of the two. No
one who is so deficient in social and external qualities can ever
have justice done him. Next year, I hope, a move will be
made to get rid of subscription at the Universities, in which
we shall claim his assistance.

You have no doubt heard of a great row about a book called
Essays and Reviews[1]. It seems to me that a great change is
beginning in the religious feeling of England, and that persons
are finding out that it is impossible to have one mode of
reasoning, evidence, &c., about religious facts and another about
all others. The reception of this book has been a remarkable
sign of what is going on in people's minds. You will think
that I lead an uneasy life. Having got used to this it does
not much trouble me, and I fear that it will never be otherwise.

To Miss Elliot.

2 Torbay Terrace, Torquay,
June 9, 1861.

If you are still in Italy, I suppose your thoughts are occupied
with one subject—the death of Count Cavour. Nothing of the

[1] Published in March, 1860; see *Life*, vol. i. p. 290 ff.

kind has seemed to me so sad since Sir Robert Peel. But if,
as I suspect, you are a real old Whig, the death of the latter
called up much the same feelings as that of Cavour in the heart
of the Pope and Antonelli.

I wonder what they think about it, and what part of purga-
tory or inferno they assign to him? and also, what is a more
serious question, where he really is? It makes one weep to
imagine a great man in the midst of his projects suddenly
called out of life into another world. It is, perhaps, well that
some instinct or good taste warns us from the speculation. He
was the only politician (except L. Napoleon) of our time who
had an indomitable will—that thing which in these degenerate
days seems upon the whole most worthy of respect in this
world.

The future of Italy is the most interesting thing in Europe,
and especially the future of the R. Catholic Church. I suppose
it will go on gradually changing; there seems to be hardly
sufficient faith in any other form of religion to supplant it.
When free trade is established and Germany set to rights, and
France has reached the Rhine, the Emperor will employ his
leisure hours in reforming it. The first step should be the
education of the Clergy and the permission of marriage to the
Clergy, if possible.

Why do you encourage the 'les évêques aux lanternes' pro-
pensities of the Italians? Indeed, it is by no means certain
that any moral improvement would take place in the people
of England, if all the twenty-four bishops were strung up of
a row. I desire no evil to any of them, and would have
nothing to do with such measures, except so far as giving
them rope enough if they are inclined to use it.

To R. B. D. MORIER.

1862.

What are you about, diplomatizing in that most unpolitical
country of Prussia, in which ideas are like air and froth, and
never seem to find their way into the minds of the people[1]?
I often think of their wayward highflown speculation in con-

---

[1] Morier was made second Secretary at Berlin in Oct. 1862.

*E 2

trast with the small performance in practice. Some persons say that they are giving up Metaphysics, and hope by so doing to find a short cut into practical life[1]. I wonder whether this is so ; it appears to me to be the greatest mistake to give up that in which they have shown real genius and may be said to have led the world.

To ——

March 7, 1865.

I think (1) that the Conservative reaction of the last three years has come to an end ; (2) that the coming event of the American War is likely to produce a great change of opinion in England, something like that of the War of Independence ninety years ago. Also that the anomalous state of the Representation, the existence of the Church of Ireland, and the present state of the Church of England, cannot much longer be defended. 'The bell of universal events' is beginning to sound. (Did you see Bullock's translation of Krasinski's remarkable poem, out of which I borrow this phrase[2]?)

To R. B. D. Morier.

December 26, 1867.

. . . What political idol hast thou not broken with me ? First, all the idols that sat in a row (not without a tendency to leave 'the sitting part of a man behind them[3]') on one side of the temple, and then all the idols on the other side of the temple. And now the only one that remained thou art for grinding to powder.

I dare say that he is no better than the rest; and I rather think that you may be right. But, my dear Sir John, what are you about, and whither are you going ? Not even a great man like you can expect to rule the world alone : without the help and countenance of my Lord G. or C. or S. or W. It appears to me that there is a certain time of life at which one begins to discover that all mankind, and especially *les hommes*

---

[1] Which they presently did in the matter of Schleswig-Holstein, and the Austrian War, 1863-1866.

[2] See *Life*, vol. i. p. 370. The poem, *Resurrecturis*, was published in Paris, second edition, 1862, and Mr. [Bullock] Hall's translation was published in *Macmillan's Magazine*, July 1864, also in a volume entitled *Polish Travels*.

[3] Sheridan.

d'état, are rogues or fools, or both. It is not certain that they are much worse than I myself am, but they are none the less rogues and fools for that. At this critical juncture all depends upon whether I am able to conceal my evil opinion of them. If I can, I may rule them, if not, they are my life-long enemies. It is the greatest advantage to see through other men (and most men may be seen through). But if they see that you see through them, then you are ruined.

Please to lay to heart this discourse of Parson Hugh[1]. And if you charge him with Jesuitry and Machiavellianism he will reply, ' These be fery honest knaveries ' when they are practised for the good of the public.

. . . Nobody can guess what the course of English politics will be. It seems to me that the Radicals, Bright and Mill, will sweep away Gladstone,

' Letting I dare not wait upon I will[2],'

who is troubled by ridiculous Ecclesiastical crotchets, after helping to let in the deluge which sooner or later will destroy the Church. Liberal politics, at least the Whig party, are at zero, and Dizzy, ' as men call him,' is proportionately strong. But how long this will last no one can say.

To the Same.

Inglewood, Torquay, *July* 18, 1870.

Where are you, and what are you doing, at this crisis of fate ? I hope not 'larding the earth with your bulk' before Frankfort, like your great prototype, even though you should come to life again after having performed similar heroic feats. 'This is the strangest fellow, brother John[3].' I suppose that our little plans for September will be disconcerted by these great events (but not if I can help it). I stay here for about ten days longer ; then to Tummel Bridge, Pitlochry, from August 4 ; then, September 7, Oxford[4].

---

[1] Parson Hugh Evans, with whom Jowett identifies himself. See Shakespeare, *Merry Wives,* iv. 4.

[2] Shakespeare, *Macbeth,* i. 7.

[3] Ibid., 1 *Hen. IV,* v. 4.

[4] For the election to the Mastership.

Did you foresee this[1]? How I should like to have a talk with you about the matter. It seems to me, considering the visits to Biarritz, that Napoleon was deceived by Bismarck in a way that he could not make public, and so that the *casus belli* is more real than has as yet appeared. The debate in the French Chamber was extremely unsatisfactory. I think that Prussia is very much to blame, as well as France, and that it is nonsense to say she had given no causes for suspicion, and having done so she ought to have been willing completely to remove them. ῝Ηδε ἡ ἡμέρα . . . μεγάλων κακῶν ἄρξει[2].

Supposing, according to the story, that the King had been treated with a slight want of etiquette, that does not justify the destruction of 500,000 men. This war seems to me to be detestable and cruel to the last degree upon the intermediate countries, Darmstadt, Baden, Frankfort, &c., whose country is to be the cockpit. Two consequences will probably flow out of it: 1. Republics: 2. International tribunals. The Ghosts of Frederic the Great and of Napoleon I. are rejoicing in the world below—What a pity that they can't get their heads out. . . .

Though I know that Sir John Falstaff ('Sir John with all Europe[3]') is sought after in the wars, 'prithee Jack,' send me a line to say that thou art in the flesh still.

If you are really abroad, or if you can say anything to anyone, do help us to preserve real neutrality. It will be fatal if we side with Prussia against France.

To the Same.

Inglewood, Torquay, *July* 25, 1870.

I wrote to you a week ago, but I dare say that you never got my letter, for which I shall not be sorry, for it contained some of the old jokes, which are not very appropriate at this serious time. You must be just hearing the first drops of the thunder shower. To us at a distance it is an awful thing (for nothing is really at a distance now), and you are in the very

---

[1] The Franco-Prussian War. France declared war, July 17.
[2] Thuc. ii. 12.
[3] Shakespeare, 2 *Hen. IV*, ii. 2.

midst, and will soon (probably) be among the dead and dying; I write to tell you that I feel for you and your wife (she is a brave lady), and that I shall often think of you during the next month. I hope that you will have opportunities of distinguishing yourself, which means, in this case, not only protecting British property but saving human life. My impression is that the French must be beaten in the long run— they go off too easily and have not the stamina of the Germans. The chances on the other side are (1) the great superiority in the weapons of war ; or (2) great superiority in generals.

I suppose that the French, i. e. the Emperor, have been cheated by Bismarck, in 1866 : the 'Projet¹' which appears in the newspapers to-day seems to show that they had some understanding. Do you remember the Thucydides which we used to read together at the Lakes ?—τὴν μὲν ἀληθεστάτην πρόφασιν, ἀφανεστάτην δὲ λόγῳ, τοὺς Ἀθηναίους ἡγοῦμαι . . . φόβον παρέχοντας τοῖς Λακεδαιμονίοις ἀναγκάσαι ἐς τὸ πολεμεῖν².

The Emperor seems to have lost his head. I fear that this will be the end of his dynasty and the ruin of France. And I don't want to see him ruined, for he has been the best friend of England, and though upon the whole my sympathies go with the Protestant power, yet we have need of both France and Prussia in Europe. These wars tend to make other wars, for although France may be too much weakened to continue, she will fight again as soon as she recovers her strength. The hatred of France to England from 1815–1855 will be as nothing compared with her abiding hatred of Prussia.

¹ In a draft treaty secretly proposed to the Prussian government by the French Emperor in 1866, but written down from Bismarck's dictation :

1. The Emperor recognizes the acquisitions which Prussia has made in the last war ;

2. The King of Prussia promises to facilitate the acquisition of Luxemburg by France ;

3. The Emperor will not oppose a federal union of the northern and southern states of Germany excluding Austria ;

4. The King of Prussia, in case the Emperor should enter or conquer Belgium, will support him in arms against any opposing power.

This was published in the *Times* on July 25, 1870.

² Thuc. i. 23.

What do Napoleon I. and Frederic the Great think about
the war of which they are in a certain sense the authors ?

The great danger for us is Russia. But I do not think
that she will stir : France will not allow her to go to Constantinople for recollections of the Crimea ; nor Prussia for
fear of offending England.

Might not this war have been avoided by a Congress ? Our
diplomatists are truly insular—they not only want not to
interfere in the wars of other people, but not to interfere to
enable them to make peace. . . .

May God be with you ! If you have a few minutes to
spare write to me, and I will write to you by return of post,
but I shan't expect you to write.

To THE SAME.

TUMMEL BRIDGE, PITLOCHRY, N. B., *Aug.* 1870.

I send you a line chiefly to say that I cannot help sometimes thinking of you and your wife, who are in the midst
of these terrible events. They are, of course, an opportunity
not to be lost, of seeing and learning and perhaps doing many
things. I hope that you will keep a journal if things of
interest occur.

We in England are a good deal balanced between the
combatants. The newspapers on the whole in favour of
Prussia, chiefly I think with the 'arrière-pensée' about
Belgium. If France greatly wins, which may be the result
of the Mitrailleuse and the Chassepot, she will of course take
Belgium. We shall and I think ought to let her, though it
would be very wrong and imprudent to say this. At a distance,
in wars, people are full of national honour and the like, which
if there are the armies to maintain them and the men to wield
them is quite right. When we approach nearer, ' commerce'
is the word, &c. . . .

That is the real point of Catholicism. It implies a powerful
motive in England, and a very weak motive to the rest of the
world. One cannot help feeling that the map of Europe
would have been better arranged if there had not been those
small kingdoms like Belgium and Holland which are a per-

petual temptation to their neighbours. I hope the ministry will not commit themselves about Belgium in such a manner as to compel us to fight under all circumstances. The contest may be hopeless and ruinous. One good result of the war is the withdrawal of the French troops from Rome. . . .

I suppose that you and your wife are anxious about the children, yet that is really imaginary: they will live and flourish through a great many wars.

To the Same.

Tummel Bridge, Pitlochry, N. B.,
Aug. 16, 1870.

. . . My dear friend, what a fierce epistle have you written to me! I am afraid to read it over again, and so I have locked it up for the present. When I think of you and the Crown Prince and the 'Princess dear' who kindly asked me to come and see them, and for whom I really feel a deep regard, I seem very guilty in being neutral in this war. But I cannot read the matter with your eyes quite. I think that it is a war between two great nations both determined to fight, and that either might have avoided the contest if they had pleased without dishonour. Of the two nations the Catholic France has done more for the liberal cause in Europe than Prussia which is much more moral, and respectable, and Protestant. In the interest of peace I do not want either of them to gain anything. You can't crush France, and if you compel her to make peace on disadvantageous terms, you necessitate another war as soon as she regains health and strength. The after effects of war are very little thought of. It seemed a fine thing for the English and the Cossacks to be in Paris in 1815. But it has kept this country in a perpetual fear of invasion from France since 1830, really meditated in 1842 (I think) and only prevented as I believe ten years ago by Louis Napoleon. A war to restore the oppressed nationality of Ireland was at that time a favourite French idea. In that matter and in the French treaty he has served us against the wishes of the French nation.

It is quite true that I have a feeling for the Emperor. He is

F

a dreamer—he has had corrupt ministers, from whose mal-administration he is now suffering—he has broken faith on more than one occasion. But he is a man of genius, who has had many great thoughts pass through his mind ; he has shown the greatest courage ; he is the real liberator of Italy, and would have been the liberator of Poland. I know he is spoken of in the language which Tacitus applies to the Roman Emperors. But I never read a book, or a speech, or a letter of his without being impressed by him. He is an unsafe politician, because he is too dreamy and too full of ideas, and he either cannot or will not choose suitable instruments.

You say that I do not consider the wickedness of the Emperor's doings in the matter of the treaty sufficiently from a politico-ethical point of view : (my dear friend, when you make a serious attack on my character, please not to use such long words). You are quite right about that I think. But are Bismarck and the Prussians, and their conduct to the small German states, and to Schleswig-Holstein capable of being justified by a ' politico-ethical standard ? ' And yet all this violence of theirs has gone to make up the idea of German nationality. The king and the nation have pro-fited by him though they do not like him. And France having been once outwitted by the Prussians is naturally irritated and apprehensive. . . .

I meant to have written you a long letter explaining why I desire England to be perfectly neutral. But it is very late and I will come and see you, and then you shall convert me if you can, for I always find your words have a good deal of effect on me. About Belgium I quite agree with you, I think that the treaty[1] was really meant to pacify the people and to commit the government to nothing practicable.

When the time approaches I will write to you again, and hear from you the best way of coming. Is there any difficulty in getting from France into Belgium ? I am afraid that I shall not have quite finished Plato. I have about 400 pages to print and about 100 to write out of 2,600.

It is late and I must finish. I am really sorry that we

[1] Treaty for the neutrality of Belgium between Prussia, Great Britain, and France.

differ, as we appear to do. But it is perhaps not a bad thing that you who breathe a German atmosphere should hear the other side, though I have stated it badly and hurriedly.

To THE SAME.

BALLIOL COLLEGE, *Sept.* 12, 1870.

I should like to write to you about public matters, as I cannot have the pleasure of talking to you. It grieves me to see the Germans at Paris as much as it would to see the French at Berlin. They have all they can really gain. And for the future they cannot be perfectly safe in any case, because they cannot exterminate the French, and they are of course creating in 38,000,000 of people sentiments of never-dying hatred which become the curse of the world in after generations. They might insist on an indemnity, reduction of the French army, (cession of the French navy?) levelling the forts of Strassburg and Metz, restoration of Nice. If they proceed they will carry on a war of vast proportions, which *must* take a form of unusual barbarity. And the sympathies of Europe, partly from fear, partly from humanity will quickly pass from the Germans to the French.

I don't want 'La belle France' or any other woman to be pained in her feelings. These are the things which make 'nations like individuals go mad.' A mad woman can be put in an Asylum, not a nation.

I was not really hurt at your letter, nor ever could be, my dear fellow, from anything which you wrote. There is no one of whom I think with more entire affection, although we are partly divided (I doubt whether so much as you suppose) upon this matter.

To THE SAME.

Jan. 2, 1871.

I wish that I could make you change your views about crushing France, which seems to me necessarily to lead to continuous or intermittent wars over the greater part of Europe. Shall I ask you a personal question? Do you think that you would have held your present views if you had lived for the last twenty years in France instead of Germany? That is not a fair question for another person to ask a man, but it is a question which a man should sometimes ask himself. The ground for carrying on war is self-defence, and I think that it is difficult to suppose that the Germans would be safer for having the line of the Vosges, because, even if the military advantage were considerable, it makes it a sort of necessity and point of honour to the French to go to war again as soon as they can, and they will still have 35,000,000 of people animated by a sort of Polish hatred against them. On the other hand it does not seem to me impossible that if Germany would accede to gentle terms, the rest of Europe might be got to aid in enforcing a peace.

Do consider the consequence to Germany of this military Aristocracy and German Empire and military glory—of the enormous conscription, millions instead of 100,000 maintained in peace, 100,000 instead of the 10,000 falling in war, and the system spreading by the necessities of self-defence from one country to another. Also think of the uncertainties of Germany—Austria and Prussia, Austria and its five nations, and the fruits of contact with Russia and Sweden, before you trust to consolidated Germany, and the probably underlying forces of peoples who may overthrow the arrangements of kings and diplomatists. Also reflect on the character of the King and Bismarck, which no one knows better than you (I always feel that the Crown Prince is a sunny spot amid all these horrid scenes). There is another element, the affinities (1) of Republican, (2) of Romance and Roman Catholic countries to one another, which has to be considered in the future of Europe.

As to the internal affairs of Germany I fear that the national has put off indefinitely the constitutional cause. These 'citizen' armies will always (1) have more of the military than of the popular spirit ; (2) they will always rather incline to so-called wars of self-defence, because no man likes to spend three years of his life in drill, and never to test his own qualities as a soldier. All that has taken place in France is the victory of the Junkers, and gives them political influence, just as Waterloo, &c. gave our English Aristocracy fifteen years of power.

I am writing at a strange house[1] while waiting for a fly. I fear you will think I greatly diverge from your views about European politics. Mine have no claim to authority. I only look on at a distance, and at present the French 'mourir pour la patrie' on the part of people who are not really responsible for the war touches me greatly. But though I am divided from you in opinion on these points, I must always feel that I cannot be divided from you in heart and friendship, and must always think of you as one of the best and dearest friends I have ever had. With best love to your wife and children. . . .

I am very happy in my new house—(while the world is in such misery)—and I shall send you the 4 vols. of Plato in a few days.

To THE SAME.

OXFORD, *May* 19, 1871.

. . . I suppose that you are very busy getting information and working at the hospitals. We are very much excited, as you will see by the newspapers, about Russia. It seems to me that these kind of treaties like the treaty between France, Austria, England and Russia[2] cannot be expected to be binding for ever, and ought to be periodically revised. (The old Greek fashion of making a treaty for a term of years was really more rational.) But there can be no revision of them unless there were more common action, and more European as distinguished from National feeling, among the several states. Russia naturally takes advantage of the occasion with a suspicion probably true, but which can never be proved or disproved, of complicity on the part of Prussia, and America in the background ready to press Alabama claims, and our ministers writing in the *Edinburgh* and making speeches at the Guildhall—never was a nation in a worse plight. If we do not go to war we shall lose prestige, and if we do go to war we shall lose prestige, and lose the game too, and therefore I suppose we shall not go to war, but shall 'eat the leek and swear horribly.'

I saw Sir L. Mallet to-day and had a talk with him: I always like talking with him, and get instruction from him. Yet I think his ideas of isolation are impracticable, if I understand

[1] Ockham Park.   [2] Treaty of Paris, 1856.

him rightly. Neither nations nor individuals who have no friends can get on. But it must be some time before the continent is in that settled state that we can make friends. Both in politics and in civilization generally, Europe seems to have gone back ten years in the last five months, and Germany, I suspect, as much, or almost as much as France in her internal improvement. For this generation we must have intense hatred between the two races. There is no real crushing an enemy unless you can stamp him out. . . .

To THE SAME.

Jan. 16, 1873.

. . . I suppose that you are surveying the politics of Europe with 'extensive view' out of the upper storey of a house in Munich [1]. The future seems to me dark. In England we have settled our American question with a great loss of money and some loss of prestige, but the country is not dissatisfied ; we have got rid of our most dangerous enemy, and have set a precedent for arbitration [2]. There is the Eastern question still, in which we shall be outwitted by Russia, who does not want India, but wants to make India the means of getting Constantinople. It sometimes seems as if it would be better to resign ourselves to what we cannot help, e.g. in the matter of Canada and of Constantinople. But then comes the difficulty that we cannot arrange the map of Europe and Asia beforehand. National opinion is not ripe for action until the time has passed.

If the map of Europe was once rightly divided we should be in little danger of war for the future. But now who can delay a war between France and Germany more than five or ten years? And who can interfere to prevent France from trying to recover what was once her own? Certainly not this country, whose interests both as a Protestant country and in regard to the East are clearly with Germany, and yet her sympathies are with France. I think that this is a true account of public opinion in England, and I hardly know how to account

[1] Morier was transferred as Chargé d'affaires from Stuttgart to Munich in 1872. There he remained four years.

[2] Settlement of the *Alabama* claims, Sept. 1872.

for it. Partly no doubt from jealousy of the conqueror and from a dislike of the taking of Alsatia, but much more I think from the charm of French manners which affects nations as well as individuals. The hatred of Germany in France is naturally much stronger than any other feeling towards God or man. And it seems to me not impossible that twenty years hence France may be at the head of a religious league against Germany, Protestants and Infidelity. . . . The Ministry are stronger than they were this time last year. They are going to attack (1) the Irish University Question, in which I expect that they will be impartial between Protestants and Catholics, but doubt whether they will carry their measure against the factiousness of both. This, however, would not ruin them. (2) Local Taxation, which means I suppose a paid magistracy; this is a question which may strengthen the Liberals ultimately, but will have to be fought. There is no likelihood of their dissolving before the end of the term, and this Parliament has still two years to run. The old quarrel with the Dissenters about education remains as bad as ever, or rather is getting worse, for the Wesleyans are now siding with the Independent Dissenters, and in my judgement they really have a serious grievance.

Gladstone talks about holding office too long, but he is hardly thought to be in earnest. Nobody knows what would become of the Liberal party if he did give up. . . .

To the Same.

July 21, 1873.

Politics are in a bad and muddled state. The Ministry weaker, the House of Commons more disorganized, the Church more Popish, the Dissenters more antagonistic, the House of Lords more obstructive, and every prospect that all this will be rendered worse by a dissolution[1]. Some organic changes in the matter of the House of Lords and the Church seem to be needed; but there is no strength to make them. It is a great pity that the House of Lords was not reduced within proper limits at the time of the Irish Church Bill. Led by such

---

[1] Which took place in January, 1874.

a man as Lord Salisbury it now opposes every useful improvement. It is a good thing that the abolition of tests at the Universities is already carried. I do not think that this state of things can continue, yet except by a *coup d'état* or a wholesale creation of Peers it cannot be prevented.

Gladstone has spoken this session as well as he ever did, but without seeming to raise himself or his party. The quarrel with the Dissenters about education is incurable, and they are the best organized portion of the Liberal party. In this matter I sympathize with the Dissenters. It cannot be right, in addition to imposing upon them an established Church, to take from them four-fifths of the education of the country. I think that the 'suprema lex' of politics should be how a country can be kept united, in a war, or in any other crisis, or how its divisions may be healed, not any lesser object of political expediency.

How do your New Catholics [1] get on? I am glad they have made a bishop, because that organizes them and commits them to the struggle. But I have no expectations from them. There is no fire in their bellies or in their veins: no real burning sense that the world requires to be made better. The 'Historic conscience' is really as much violated by a great deal of Protestantism as by the Jesuit infallibility. Where is the political or moral or spiritual force which can carry them on except as malcontents or nonjurors? They have no thought of placing religion on a really moral or even an historical foundation.

Bismarck's move [2] is another matter, and I heartily wish him success. I do not agree with some of the English newspapers —especially with the *Spectator*. 'Because a body is the most insidious and dangerous of all communities, you are to allow it free play, if it only meditates treason in the future and not in the present.' In maintaining this we are led away by an

[1] Jowett appears to mean by 'New Catholics' those who refused to acknowledge the infallibility of the Pope, though the name in use is Old Catholics. They elected their first bishop, Dr. Joseph Reinkens, June 1, 1873.

[2] A law for the expulsion of the Jesuits was published, July 1872; and the Falk laws (see below) were passed in May, 1873.

abstract notion of toleration of opinions. Of course there are
several things to be considered—we must not coerce if we
are only likely to strengthen our opponents: and we must
treat them with moderation—not send Jesuits to the galleys,
&c. But this is obvious.

I had a long and interesting conversation with our friend
Charilaus [1] the other day. Two or three things which he said
may interest you to hear: he thought that (1) the kingdom of
Italy was the best piece of political work done in our time:
(2) that there must be a war between France and Germany, and
that it would be a religious war: he attributed this necessity
as I do to the taking of Alsace and Lorraine: (3) he admitted
that freedom of commerce had not done all that might be
expected for the world, but thought that it had prevented two
wars during the last ten or twelve years—a war with France
and a war with America. He was very cordial.

To the Same.

October 14, 1873.

. . . It has often occurred to me to say to you, though I am
deterred by the extravagance of the words: 'You could prevent
a war in Europe if you devoted your whole mind to this object.'
But is this merely the extravagance of friendship? I am not
going to quote Shakespeare about 'authentic in your place and
person,' of 'great admittance,' and the like, for I am serious.
(1) Four years ago —— told me that you were 'the first man in
our profession'; (2) you are the personal friend of the Crown
Prince, who will be Emperor when the crisis comes: his
feelings are strongly against war, but he will want advisers
to show him how war may be avoided, and to fix the right
notes of the situation in his mind beforehand; (3) you also
know the Duc d'Aumale privately, and he will probably have
a great deal of influence on French affairs during the next five
years; facts about the German army, &c., communicated at the
right moment, may have an effect on the minds of the nation:
if not of the nation, of the leaders; (4) you are acquainted
with Prince Gortschakoff, and may improve the acquaintance

[1] Gladstone.

at odd times: there will be no war without Russia, and perhaps Russia may be satisfied ; (5) the Peloponnesians will not come for five years, and the delay will give you the opportunity of gaining influence and information, especially about France and Russia ; (6) the French are a mercurial people, and though pride is probably the most tenacious of national motives, they may get weary of large armies and continued taxation ; some concession might be made to them if they would consent to disarm, or possibly some democratic or industrial movement may supersede the war movement ; (7) the Catholic question, which is a great source of danger in Europe as in England, may be settled ; (8) Italy and Germany may be more closely united when the Alps are tunnelled, and Germany may come to a settlement with Denmark and Sweden ; (9) there may be a congress which, foreseeing a terrible future, more terrible than anything in the past, may readjust the map of Europe ; (10) as to America, you may be very glad at that being got out of the way, with a considerable loss of national prestige, and that you have had nothing to do with it ; (11) those who speak of war as certain, really speak under excitement: there is nothing certain when there are so many factors as there are in European politics ; they do not understand the nature of human affairs, nor the power which may be exercised over them by two or three resolute persons (perhaps as obscure as Bismarck or Moltke were fifteen years ago) who see the situation five years beforehand ; (12) if England appears to you to stand low in Europe at present, she does not stand lower than Prussia did fifteen years ago, or than she herself did at the beginning of Lord Chatham's administration.

I daresay that you will think this wild, yet please to think of it. If you cannot succeed in preventing the greatest calamity that can befall the world[1], your diplomacy is nothing and your life a failure, even though you are Ambassador at Paris or Constantinople. If you can succeed, you will be one of the most eminent men in Europe. Nothing seems to me worth doing or having in foreign politics which does not prevent war. If war breaks out it is 'Fold up the map of Europe,' and there

---

[1] The outbreak of a European war.

is an end. Any one who feels that he has this mission must be absolutely reticent ; he must have a sympathy with England and with English ministers or he will never gain an influence over them : he must make allowance for the difficulties in which a commercial country is necessarily placed : he must endeavour to influence English ministers through the opinion of foreign ones, for they will be more willing to follow than to lead. My strong feeling is that if you are to succeed you must take men as they are, not complaining of them over-much, and then you may raise them to something better. But if you become isolated from them you are nowhere : you are no longer a statesman but a critic, you see faults everywhere and necessarily become odious to those who commit them. My Oxford experience makes me repeat this ; I see so much idealism and so little effectual power.

Having read over this letter I am almost ashamed to send it. I had it in my mind to say this to you all the time that I was at Munich [1]. I wanted you to make the determination to avoid a continental war the motive—the religion of your life for the next ten years : to read and study, to take care of your health, to form political friendships with this view. You may seem weak now, but time is a long lever and every year you will gain influence. You say

οὐκ ἀξιῶ ’γὼ ’μαυτὸν ἰσχύειν μέγα [2],

but things as great have been done by persons who had not your ability or advantages of position. You would not forgive yourself if you had failed in doing anything and a European war broke out. Meditate on the consequences, either of the dismemberment of France (you are half a Frenchman) which is the more probable alternative, or of the other thing which, though improbable, is not impossible. I am not getting more rational, so I shall stop.

To the Same.

West Malvern, *January* 5, 1875.

I know that you do not mind my writing to you by the hand of another, which, as you will observe, is much more

[1] See *Life*, ii. p. 55.
[2] Aristoph. *Knights*, 182 (spoken by the Sausage-seller).

legible than my own, and I shall still lay upon you the
obligation to answer me a few lines within twenty-four hours.

So I hear from Mallet that you have declined the secretary-
ship at Paris. I daresay that you are right. I should not
have liked you to be placed under an inferior man; and it
would have been very expensive. I am only afraid of their
making your refusal an excuse for not offering anything else.

I rather hope that your controversial efforts are over, for
upon reflection I do not quite like them, and am doubtful
whether they will do any good except in proving your energy
and ability.

Are not Charilaus[1] and D.[2] really at the bottom of them?
And is not Charilaus Ultramontane and Ultra-Protestant in
one? wanting in his inmost soul to support the Ritualists who
are our enemies at home by attacking the Catholics who are
our foes at a distance; and do we not all know that the Pope
(or rather the Jesuits plus Archbishop Manning) are 'liars and the
fathers of it,' but that the mass of Catholics are peaceable and do
not wish to push things to extreme any more than Protestants,
and that it is the interest of the Liberal party 'to use and not
abuse' them. And has not D. a very poor sort of historical
conscience which he applies to forged Decretals but not to the
pretended prophecies of the Gospels?

All Christian sects are in a good deal of trouble when they
are confronted with history :—

'Scimus et hanc veniam,' &c.[3]

There is no harm in entering a little into religious controversy. You have had great opportunities of learning, and
no doubt the friendship of such a man as Döllinger is well
worth having. But I would rather write about great questions
of European policy or of social life. The New Catholic movement is nothing or very little, but Bismarck is a great deal,
whether the time has come for him to descend from earth or not.

What do you think of the Falk Laws[4] now? Will he

---

[1] Gladstone.   [2] Döllinger.
[3] Horace, *Ars Poet.* 11.
[4] The Falk Laws were the laws
against the Roman Catholics,

generally called the May Laws,
passed in May, 1873. Falk was
the Minister of Culture, and was
put in in order to carry them.

succeed or not? The difficulty in Germany and in Oxford is at bottom the same. How to have any intermediate between superstition and the negation of religion? The men of the educated classes are easily drawn one way, the women and the lower classes are apt to go the other. In England the Evangelicals and the Dissenters, or in Germany the Pietists, might have supplied the want, if they had had sense.

I sometimes feel that the want of religion is destructive to Idealism and elevation of character; but then again the disregard of truth seems to be equally destructive. I cannot tell you how this question presses upon me at times in reference to the Undergraduates and young Fellows in Balliol. I seem to see so clearly what is right, and to have so little power of impressing it upon others. . . .

The Diplomatic Service seems to have fewer chances than others, and there is more partiality. It appears to me therefore that a man should have some other object for which he is preparing, or which he is carrying out side by side with it. It has one advantage, which is leisure and opportunities of seeing mankind. I won't say 'Do not be disappointed,' but do remember that you have great abilities, and that for the right use of them you must rise to eminence, and that you must make ways of using them if you have none ready made for you.

The Ministry[1], as far as I can judge, are getting on very fairly. They make mistakes, but some of their blunders, like that on the Endowed Schools Bill, are really due to differences of opinion among themselves. They are trusted by their party, and there is no sign of the country wanting to get rid of them as yet. Nobody wants to have Gladstone again who, I am told, is to commence a crusade against the established church of Scotland, which is unfortunately the most liberal of the Churches, having succeeded to the old Moderates when the Free Church went out. Of course he will have the support of the Dissenters, who regard this as a first step towards the disestablishment of the Church of England. It is doubtful whether he means to take the second step, though he talks very freely against Church Establishments.

---

[1] i.e. Disraeli's Ministry, which came into office February, 1874.

There will be a great deal of trouble about Convocation and the Rubrics : they would be blown into space if the will of the English people had its way. But between them stand a number of influential persons like Gladstone himself, Lord Salisbury, Carnarvon, Northcote and others, who will try to prevent the explosion.

Gladstone's pamphlet[1] has produced a very bad impression among the Liberals, who think that he is quarrelling with the friends of the Liberal party, notwithstanding their perversity. They say truly that there are few reforms which could have been carried in this Conservative country without the help of the Irish brigade. But my impression is that when Parliament meets he will do all he can to conciliate the Catholics, and that his pamphlet will soon be forgotten, like his much more remarkable article in the *Quarterly* of four years ago.

To the Same.

September 25, 1875[2].

I am very sorry that you make such slow progress ; I had hoped that you would have been well long ago. But you are on the way to health, and six months of inactivity, though it is a trial and a great bore, does not make much difference in what a man is or is able to do compared with the whole of life. Most persons spend all their days in nothing, and you have been compelled to do nothing for a few months. . . .

The Herzegovina insurrection is the only interesting thing talked about in England, but nobody seems to know enough to make up their minds about it[3]. It appears to me that it must lead to something, because we can hardly allow the Turks to pound the Christians as they please with a view to

---

[1] *The Vatican Decrees.*

[2] In the summer of 1875 Jowett visited Morier at Munich (see *Life*, ii. p. 68). During his stay he had much conversation on theology with Döllinger. With Morier he discussed Bismarck and the Falk Laws.

[3] In July, 1875, the inhabitants of Herzegovina and Bosnia were driven to insurrection by the oppression of the Turkish tax-gatherers. This oppression and the severity with which the rebels were treated showed a disregard of the conditions on which the integrity of the Turkish Empire was guaranteed in the Treaty of Paris (1856). The Eastern question was once more opened.

putting down the insurrection. There is the difficulty of Christians and Mahometans being almost everywhere inter-mixed and being, to a great extent, of the same race. Also I suppose that there is a great doubt whether the Christians are any better than the Turks. It is a feeling which possesses me more strongly as I get older, that we ought not to allow the really iniquitous governments of the world to go on when-ever conveniently we can get rid of them. But then no government is worse than the worst, and therefore we ought to have some plan of federation or protectorate ready to come in ; no one seems to have such a plan.

I read a few days ago Gladstone's 'Is the Church of England worth preserving?' What a performance for the Liberal leader! The drift is: 'The Church is worth preserving if you keep the ritualists, not otherwise.' They had better provoke people as little as they can help ; and they should have no more trials for heresy, because they generally get the worst in them before the Privy Council ; also, they should keep on good terms with Dissenters, who are highly respectable people and very necessary to use in Politics. Of the real good of the Church of England he has not a conception, and its greatest evil he exalts into a benefit. . . .

To ——

WEST MALVERN, *Oct.* 17, 1876.

Public affairs seem to me to be in the worst condition I have ever seen them. We have been talking with levity about Herodian Massacres, then spouting about Bulgarian atrocities[1] (forgetting what we have done ourselves in India and Jamaica). Then lecturing the Turk, to whom we mean to give nothing but words, until day by day war gets nearer and Russia grows bolder and more openly treacherous, and all sensible men turn away in disgust from both parties and look, if anywhere, to Bismarck for help. Russia may be bankrupt and scattered now ; but ten years hence, with railroads and a fleet on the

---

[1] The Bulgarians were thought to have had some share in the rising in Herzegovina. They rose themselves in May, 1876. Intelligence of the 'Bulgarian atrocities' was published in the *Daily News,* June 23, 1876.

Black Sea, she will be enormously increased ; she will have her seat of empire at Constantinople, and will be mistress of the Mediterranean east of Italy. Never was there such a power of self-delusion in any man as in Gladstone. He impersonates in his own genius all the passing movements of the people. Whether Bismarck will move or not is the question at this moment. Bismarck is master of the situation because he is able and probably willing to act. It seems to me that even now at the eleventh hour Russia ought to be stopped by an armed intervention, and that all the efforts of English diplomacy ought to be directed to uniting Germany (Prussia and Austria) with England for this object. One is inclined to say, 'O for six months of Lord Palmerston!'

When the English people awake to the fact that for more than four months they and their government have been simply the dupes of Russia, their indignation will be great. But they will not know whom to blame—the opposition? the ministry? themselves?

To think of Lord Beaconsfield, that veteran in craft, speaking of the 'confidence' which he had in Russian intentions!

I write all this because you ask me what my opinion is, which, as I have no precise knowledge about these Turkish provinces, is not worth having.

To R. B. D. MORIER.

October 22, 1876.

Before I write a line to you I must remonstrate on your extremely bad conduct to me about two months ago. You promised to come down to Oxford on the Saturday before you left England, and Mrs. Morier promised for you. A room and a dinner were prepared, 'my oxen and my fatlings were killed,' but no sign of you nor any apology for your non-appearance. Is not this the extreme of faithlessness? What excuse hast thou, 'thou naughty varlet[1],' if I may speak so irreverently of his excellency, &c., at Lisbon[2].

Being of a placable disposition I shall forgive you if you

---

[1] Shakespeare, 1 *Hen. IV*, ii. 4.
[2] From 1876 to 1881 Morier was Minister at Lisbon.

write to me within twenty-four hours after receiving this letter. If you do not I shall cut you for two months, though in this case the cut will not extend to your wife and children. I should like very much to have a talk with you about foreign politics. I am at this moment what you always seem to be (and perhaps rightly) out of humour with all politicians. There seems to be no mind and no pluck in them. The intelligent part of the nation is beginning to feel itself humiliated. Do you remember a passage in the Thucydides which we used to construe together, μόνοι οὐκ ἀρχομένην τὴν αὔξησιν τῶν ἐχθρῶν, διπλασιουμένην δὲ καταλύοντες[1]. That is our case—we foresee no difficulties, and we do not attempt to face them until they have become insuperable. Our only idea of foreign politics is saying 'no' to everything, keeping out of the way and declaring to foreign nations that happen what will we shall not go to war. The English Embassy at Constantinople appears to have a traditional suspicion of Russia—not unfounded — but it all ends in making everything easy to Russia beyond her hopes. Lord Derby writes a moral lecture to the Turks, and does not seem to see that if the Turks make themselves disagreeable to their own subjects he is bound to do something for them in return. I should like to hear Bismarck's observations upon that letter.

I do not suppose that I can tell you anything which you do not already know. 'Ad nos vix tenuis famae perlabitur aura.'

Are these semi-barbarians who cut off the noses of Turks at all fit for self-government? Is there really a great Sclavonic movement in Russia which the ruling class cannot control? Everybody is talking of Russia being destined to get to Constantinople, and this is one of those prophecies which tends to fulfil itself. It is very convenient if we mean to sit (like Turks) with our hands folded to attribute the course of events to fate[2].

---

[1] Thuc. i. 69.

[2] In June, 1876, the Prince of Servia entered upon open war with Turkey. His army was largely composed of Russian volunteers, and led by the Russian general Tchernayeff. He was defeated, and an attempt at reconciliation was made by the Powers, but in vain. The war was resumed, and Russia was now almost openly a supporter

A curious element in the English part of the question is the attitude of the High Church clergy, who, having a good deal of sham Mediævalism, would like to have a sham crusade. . . .

Old Sandars [1] came to see me to-day. He was as friendly and jolly as could be. No one seems to me to be fuller of good conversation than he is. He makes remarks which influence your mind. But he has no ambition and never will have. He likes to write his article in the *Saturday* and talk with his friends.

To the Same.

Jan. 27, 1877.

This country has sunk rather low since I last wrote to you. The relative position of European nations at the present moment seems to be—

> Turks,
> Prussians,
> French,
> Austrians,
> English,
> Russians.

The Italians if, as is said, they intrigued with Russia for a slice of Austria near Trieste, ought to come between the English and the Russians, but they do not much matter. Is not the *renversement* extraordinary? The Turks, if they will behave properly to the Christians (and this seems not unlikely from Midhat Pacha, who was a good Governor of Adrianople) may last another generation or two. At any rate, the Russians, by their premature attempt in Servia, have lost the chance of getting to Constantinople. It is clear (1) that the Turks will fight; (2) that the Russians are regarded with the greatest jealousy by Western Europe. Even the French, who have something to hope from them, will not side with them. Also

of Servia. In 1877 (Jan.) there was a conference at Constantinople in the hope of averting war, but it failed, owing to the obstinacy of the Turks. Further proposals on the part of Russia resulted in the protocol of March 31, 1877, but Turkey refused to accept them, and on April 24 Russia declared war on Turkey.

[1] T. C. Sandars, sometime scholar of the College, editor of *Justinian.* Cp. vol. i. 126.

it seems as if Bismarck's interest was to maintain Austria at the head of the southern Sclaves and Magyars, partly because he would destroy the balance of power in Germany, if Austrian Germany separated from them, and also because he would wound the pride or self-love of all Germany, if he dethroned her from her imperial position. I often think over these things and tell you my guesses; I wish that we could have a talk about them. I suppose that the humiliating conduct of Russia has sprung from three or four causes: (1) the corrupt state of their army; (2) the bankrupt state of their finances; (3) the certainty that another dog would come and take the prey out of their mouths; (4) the discovery that the Turks were much more formidable than they supposed.

This is just the time when a great ambassador might do much with the Turks, occupying the same position in relation to them which Sir James Hudson did in relation to the Italians and Cavour. Midhat Pacha wants to be friends with England, and would like to have the help of such a man in carrying out his reforms. The Turk is safe if he can be made to see that his interest is to treat the Christians properly. Of course Midhat has great difficulties, but he can be schooled, and they can be schooled into seeing their own interest. Can you provide an ambassador as you provided a consul for Belgrade? (By the way, let me tell you that I hear the highest account of your consul from C—— who has been staying with him—he speaks in the strongest manner of his sagacity and knowledge and power of dealing with all sorts of persons.) Any one who could do so might prevent the bloodiest war between two fanatical races, which has taken place in modern times. (This, like some passages in Thucydides, is not grammatical, but the meaning is plain.)

To THE SAME.

BALLIOL COLLEGE, *March* 14, 1877.

I have long intended to write to you, knowing that you must be, as I am, intensely interested in the state of Europe.

This morning brought a new pamphlet of Gladstone's— 'damnable iteration' about Bulgarian horrors, which are horrid enough no doubt, but not to be weighed in the balance against a European war. I am not unwilling that he should raise the standard of public morality : but why did he say nothing about India, about Jamaica, where the horrors (with the exception of the outrages on women) were probably as great and as inexcusable by necessity as these Turkish horrors, the Jamaica executions and floggings of about 2,000 natives being even less excusable, for not one soldier was killed, and we had complete military possession of the island. Governor Eyre, beside the subscription made for him, had his expenses paid by the public —non dissentiente Gladstone.

These are little and personal matters compared with the great issues which are looming in the distance. The central facts of European politics seem to me to be : (1) That two years ago Bismarck was going to war with France and was stopped by Russia ; (2) That it is certain France will go to war with him in two or three years time ; and therefore he is perhaps justified in anticipating, or rather would be so, if there were not a way out of war by giving up Lorraine. (3) But then arises the question whether the pride of Germany will allow her to give up a yard of ground which she has once taken (the pride of nations like that of individuals is often their destruction, but though they foresee the consequences it is the last thing with which they will part) : cf. for a smaller instance of national pride, Spain and Cuba, which has already cost the Spaniards 70,000 soldiers. (4) It is possible also that the pride of France will be satisfied with nothing but retaliation on the Rhine. War is more and more an affair of money, and France is yearly becoming richer and Germany poorer, perhaps. (5) Turning to another corner of European politics, two fanatical races are ready to fly at each other's throats, and fanaticism, like pride, is not controlled by the ordinary motives of interest. (6) Although one part of Russia, including the Pan-Sclavic societies, hates Turkey, another part, including the Emperor, and still more the Czarewitch, hate and fear Germany, and therefore incline to France, which (I suppose) is the solution of the political enigma of the last few weeks. (7) There is yet a political factor of importance in the game, Austria, which is said while in the hands of Count Andrassy to be entirely under Bismarck's influence. 'J'ai ne politique que Bismarck.' (8) Italy is a forward child, growing up, but rather pert, which need not as yet be taken account of in European politics. (9) John Bull is old and very fat, fonder of talking than of moving about. He has greater difficulty in making war than any other country, because he will suffer more; and as Thucydides says, 'People are readier to risk their lives than their money in war.' He has no clear idea of what he would do, nor ever can have, for his brain is full of cross currents, love of money, national vanity, a speech of Gladstone or Bright. The monied classes and those who fear political change are generally for peace, the newspapers, like the army and navy, upon the whole for war, because it is for their interest. (10) In a European war between French and Germans, America can take no part directly or indirectly. Her sympathies and her Irish vote would probably be with France, her 5,000,000 of Germans—a very important factor—make neutrality absolutely necessary.

If Bismarck engages in war with France, he will probably fail :—(1) Because it will be a great crime at which Europe will shudder, though not so great if the question is only who cuts throats first; (2) The poor old weak Pope, who blesses the Turks, who hate the Greeks, who hate the Roman Catholics, will be a very potent adversary: for he will have some effect both in uniting France and in dividing Germany. (3) I am inclined to think that England, whether it be prudent or not, will be forced into the war. Scotland and Ireland would be ready to join as one man for France, and the High Church party and the upper classes of society have also a strong sympathy with the French. (4) On the other hand the Germans are disliked partly for their bad manners, and also by the middle classes, because they compete with us in trade ; nor do we much like Germany taking the position in Europe which England had for ten years after the peace in 1815. (5) Belgium and Holland will be indisposed to allow themselves to be made the last mouthfuls. (6) The royal families are a very important element in European politics: even our own. But these are mysteries of which I do not venture to speak to you, who are 'well known for your many learned and

warlike and courtlike preparations [1].' Forgive me for this last
joke, and acknowledge that I have learned to treat you with
the respect due to one who is 'Sir John with all Europe.'

To return: people minimize the power of Royal Families,
because they can only act with great effect at special crises.
But surely it is not too much to say that Louis Napoleon while
he lasted equalled half of the political power of the French
nation: as the Emperor of Russia equals half of the Russian
nation: the King of Prussia equals one-third or plus Bismarck
three-quarters of the Prussian political power. Even the
Queen of England, according to this fanciful way of measuring,
would not be less than one-sixth, because she can always touch
the scales when they are nicely balanced.

I cannot help asking the question—whether civilized Europe
at the end of the nineteenth century has no means of preventing universal war: and war too, which will not clear the
atmosphere, or place European politics ultimately on a better
basis. No one can foresee where it will stop, or what the
conditions of peace must be. People sometimes talk of the
benefits of war, of carrying out the designs of Providence, and
the like, of the virtues called forth by war, of the 'canker of
a long peace'; but in future wars there will be less and less
of virtue and heroism and more of money, and God will be
more and more on the side of the great guns. Improvements
in war, as they are called, tend rather to extinguish the human
side of it—the individual courage and chivalry, as well as the
long endurance. I do not expect to see any great result upon
character produced by war in the future.

Some persons suppose that we might have prevented the last
French war by announcing that we would declare ourselves
against either of the two parties which declared war first.
I think that this would have failed for two reasons: we should
have made enemies of both parties. Neither of them in their
inflammatory state would have believed that we acted for their
interest. Secondly, if we had made the announcement it would
have been impossible to determine which of the two made war
or moved troops first. Might not our action have been like
that of a child attempting to separate two men fighting?

[1] Shakespeare, *Merry Wives*, ii. 2.

A greater military power than we are was required. But it seems to me possible that a league might be formed now between England, Russia, Belgium, and Holland for preserving the peace of Europe. But would France join in such a league —not I suppose if it contained a stipulation that Germany was to be protected in the status quo. And if not, Prussia may exclaim, and say, 'You are in effect reserving for France the power of attacking me whenever she is better prepared, and preventing me from anticipating the attack.' I do not see any way out of this unless the rest of Europe could settle some terms for the restoration of Lorraine: and this it is possible that the French would as much resent as two parties of Irishmen would resent the interference of constables in their own proper quarrel. There are similar difficulties about disarmament; nobody will disarm when they are expecting a battle, and the expectation of a battle cannot be got out of their heads.

If the Germans go to war they will strike suddenly. 'Quinze jours à Paris.' They will probably succeed at first, and win battles: but what will be the end? They must build forts over a great part of France, or take military possession of Paris or some large city. And after all, the beaten nation will be too much for them. It cannot be permanently kept down or partitioned like Poland. The best thing would be for the French to gain just so much advantage as to enable them to recover Lorraine: but this is not likely at first, though it might be the ultimate result. The French appear to be wanting in military commanders and to have made insufficient preparations during the last two years. On the other hand they would fight for the life and death of their nation, the cause would be holy to all of them: for the one party in the national, for the other in the religious sense. They would merge all differences, and Gambetta would be a formidable War Minister.

Would there be equal unity in Germany? Would the whole Catholic population be still loyal? Would the national feeling continue to prevail over the social and democratic? Would the middle and lower classes give their money and shed their blood to maintain a political order of things in which they have but a small share and an army in which they never rise to be officers?

If the view of politics which I have been attempting to
sketch has any truth in it the first thing would seem to be that
we should have an 'entente cordiale' with Russia. At the same
time we have to guard against Russia's plans in the East.
I suppose there is a difficulty about anything 'cordiale' with
Russia, because of the intriguing character of her statesmen.
She may be bought off either by Turkey or by Germany.
We can perhaps rely most on the Czar and the Royal Family:
then we must try and reconcile Turkey and Russia, and see
what can be done by all three together for the amelioration of
the Christians. Their condition must not be lost sight of for
many reasons, and amongst others because philanthropy is
a great power in politics. At the same time no plan of
assisting them has been suggested as yet which is likely
to be successful. We should have a powerful man, such as
Sir James Hudson was in Italy, at Constantinople, and
numerous Russian and English consuls throughout Turkey,
who shall report the conduct of the Turks: we might stipulate
also for some local self-government, and for not allowing Turks
to carry arms in the street, and perhaps in some extreme case
the population ought to be protected by a mixed force of Turks,
English, and Russians. But these things can only be conjectured about by persons at a distance. Even Lord Stratford,
to judge by his letters in the *Times*, seems to be a very un-
trustworthy guide in Turkish politics. Possibly some territorial
rights in Egypt, protecting the route to India, might be got
out of the present situation.

I have inflicted a long 'screed' upon you, and feel that I am
the better for this κάθαρσις τῶν παθημάτων: though I do not
suppose that you will be equally the better for reading it.
I daresay that you are thinking of these things day and night.
The first shell that bursts will fall in a powder magazine.

Let me tell you an historical fact which is interesting and, as
far as I know, never published. A friend of mine, Mr. Keene
of Swyncombe, has the papers of his great uncle, Sir Benjamin
Keene, who was the English ambassador in Spain in the reigns
of George I and George II. Among these papers is a letter
from Lord Chatham offering to give up Gibraltar if the
Spaniards would make war on France and assist in retaking

Minorca. The Spanish minister was an Irishman named Wall : the negotiation went off: but the fact of Chatham having offered it is very curious. I read the letter and the answer marked 'most secret.'

Write to me when you can, if possible within twenty-four hours.

To the Same.

Oxford, *Dec.* 28, 1877.

Within forty-eight hours of receiving your letter I write to answer it. I remember the compact, and shall keep the letters safely for you, whenever you want to have them.

I was delighted to hear of your success in the Indian business: and take it as an earnest that your merits will one day be appreciated generally, as they now are by a few. Don't let us complain of things or persons or of the nineteenth century, or of the indifference of the country occupied in making money, but simply say to ourselves: These are the things or persons through which and with which we have to work, and by influencing them, or managing them, or forcing them, the end must be attained or not at all : I admit all that you say about Lord G., Lord D., and several others, which I feel now to be much more true than formerly, still I maintain that though it is necessary to be aware of all this, it is not good to dwell upon it ; it is not the attitude of mind which is likely to succeed ; it is querulous ; it has not the patient hopefulness of genius.

You always seem to me to have the best ideas and the greatest knowledge of foreign politics of any person I have ever known. . . . But you need a ποῦ στῶ with the outside world, which it is very hard for a diplomatist to obtain, because he can never lift up his voice in public. He is forced back on secret ways of influence, the influence of ideas, private letters to important persons in England, political friendships, 'temple of friendship' with Lord C., Lady D., and others, and these he cannot cultivate too assiduously. He must make to himself friends of the mammon of unrighteousness for honest purposes. . . .

What you say about the political situation seems to me too

H

true. Nothing can exceed the imbecile conduct of the Ministry: I suppose that if they were to defend themselves they, or rather Lord D., would say: How can we trust Bismarck who is the accomplice if not the original contriver of the war? we shall be forced by him to do what he likes. Of course they will or would have been unless they could have made the English alliance or opposition of importance to somebody. If you do not intend to fight under any circumstances, why, you had better say nothing and quietly withdraw from foreign politics: but, as you truly say, something else was expected from this Ministry: they were to make England respected—and now they have made England neither respected nor feared but only hated and despised. . . .

Some things can be judged of better by us at home than by you abroad. (1) Nine-tenths of the people you meet at dinner or in a railway are anti-Russian—they have forgotten Bulgarian atrocities; they are nervous about English interests; they feel some honest indignation at Russian perfidy—they remember the Crimean War. (2) The lower classes are also anti-Russian, but they are against war, fear the lowering of wages, &c. (3) Gladstone is distrusted by all the leaders of the Liberal party; Goschen speaks of him in a very different way from formerly: he is more and more diverging from him. (4) The effect of the humiliation in Europe on India is difficult to calculate; to some persons our loss of prestige appears to be a very serious matter, even though we may be quite able to protect the Suez Canal. (5) They also tell us that a large army of 100,000 men can be easily conveyed from India, and that 50,000 men could be sent every six months; 'if we lose credit in Europe, a larger force will be required in India:' This is soldier's talk (οἶσθα γὰρ τὸν τρόπον τῶν ἀνδρῶν) and there is probably something in it, though not so much as they in their desire for war pretend. (6) Upon the whole I don't think that we shall go to war, or that the country is willing to submit to any sacrifices for the Turks. (7) Is it not possible that a firm, i. e. a belligerent attitude on our part, and Bismarck's dislike to see Russia greatly aggrandized, for which aggrandizement she has no equivalent to offer him, and Austria's jealousy of Russia's neighbourhood in Servia and Bosnia may induce the three powers to reconsider the interests of England because they really coincide with their own ? . . .

Don't you think that Cobden and Bright have done us great harm ? No one can tell whether their peace speeches did not cause the Crimean War by creating the impression that we were not going to fight, and they and the ideas which they have inspired in the English people, are the reason why that impression remains still, so that no words of ours will convince the world that the British Lion will come out of its den. I was *désillusionné* of their notions about fifteen years ago by a sentence of Mazzini's, ' non-intervention is political suicide ; ' our friend Goschen appears to me very sound about all these questions.

I want you to consider the annexation of Egypt[1] in one other point of view—its bearing on the future of Africa. Must not that ' greater India ' be one day ours, and is not the colonization and improvement of it a great national concern of ours ? But, if so, can we afford to give up Egypt ? If it is just ; and if France is not to be feared, to take it seems to me expedient, and one element of justice is the improvement of the trodden down and industrious population, who at present have not even the hope which war gives of possible change in their condition. Looking forward, this is not to be lost sight of : βαρβάρων Ἕλληνας ἄρχειν εἰκός[2].

One more thing occurs to me to say : I think in foreign politics we should work towards ten years or five years hence and not be too much impressed by the events of the time. There are some things irreparable ; other things pass away. One of the things which passes away is the national humiliation, if not accompanied by material loss. A great deal of dirt, (perhaps more than was necessary) was eaten on the American question, but the result has been good ; the humiliation is forgotten and the friendship cemented with America, just for that reason (because we were humbled), which if we manage well will be lasting and stand us in good stead in some European crisis. Therefore I don't object to humiliation as a weapon of diplomacy and should be the first to suspect going

[1] See on this Bright's *Hist. of England*, iv. 553–556.
[2] Euripides, *Iph. Aul.* 1400.

to war for the national honour.   But on the other hand one
of the things irreparable for the future of the civilized world
is the possession of Constantinople by the Russians.   They
will never be got out again ; they will increase enormously in
power and population, and may become masters of the Mediterranean in ten years.   It will be an outrage on the civilized
world to have the least civilized of the great powers of Europe
at the head of it.

All these European questions are complicated by religious
questions.   In any future great struggle is France and (sham)
Catholicism to be arrayed against Germany and Infidelity ?
The progress of opinion seems to tend that way.   It is difficult
for a person who has a conviction of the necessity and truth
of religion to be wholly on either side in such a struggle.
Whither is the world tending ?   Backwards or forwards ?
Lord Odo [Russell] whom I met at Woburn gives a most dismal
picture of Germany ; he seems to fear that religion will so
entirely pass away that political subordination will be lost.
At any rate there must be a very great degradation of life.
American cuteness and materialism seem to be the two great
elements working in society.

Now I have prosed long enough : I wish that you were here
to talk to me : write as soon as may be convenient to you :
Farewell.

To the Same.

OXFORD, *Feb.* 16, 1878.

I write one line to say that I have read your most interesting letter, and am forwarding it to-night to Goschen.   I entirely
agree with you as far as my opinion is of any value on
a question of foreign policy :—although I do not remember
that I entertained or expressed the opinions which you seem
to attribute to me (or to some unknown person).   The situation changes constantly—to-day, Sunday, we are informed by
telegrams that a conference is to meet at Baden-Baden.

'Ad nos vix tenuis famae perlabitur aura.'

All that I know about foreign politics comes from you.   I am
a very faithful disciple, and will promise never to 'preach'

any more. The passage from Mazzini I saw more than twenty years ago, and it has remained in my mind ever since.

Some principles which I try to impress upon myself are the following (suited to present circumstances) :—

1. That neither Bismarck nor Lord Beaconsfield are the Devil (though the last is an *esprit faux*).

2. That the Russians have acted very much as we should, if we had been in their place.

3. That Frenchmen no longer hate Englishmen, and therefore that they need not always hate Germans.

4. That we have made terrible mistakes, and therefore that we must eat a certain amount of dirt and humiliation, and that for six months at least, if we are capable of continuing in the same mood of mind for so long, we ought to be deeply ashamed.

5. But that it is a long lane (in politics) which has no turn. We are not yet so deeply humiliated as Prussia was after Olmütz or France after Sedan. Two or three years of a great minister like Lord Chatham or his son might restore us to our place among first class powers. All this is not to be said, but may be thought.

The influence of the masses, the influence of the Court, the influence of the peace party who will be greatly weakened (they are chiefly the Dissenters who hope by the help of Gladstone and Bright to get rid of the Establishment), have been almost equally mischievous during the last year.

I am delighted to find that you take such a strong interest in these great questions. The time is shortly coming when, as I believe, not 'from the partiality of friendship,' you will have a great part in them. No one knows so much about them or has as clear ideas of them. The peace of Europe, the national honour of England are themes about which, if a man deeply feels them, he will become inspired to say and do what he thinks. A great deal may be done by writing private letters when an opportunity offers. . . .

I am not indisposed to echo your curses on the newspapers with whom all patriotism is lost in party spirit. This is a reflection suggested by taking up the *Daily News* of this morning, which cares nothing for the good of Europe compared with a possibility of injuring the Ministry. The Liberal party have been the best friends of Lord Beaconsfield ; especially Gladstone, for by their personal mode of carrying on the conflict they create a reaction in his favour. And whatever his faults are, and they are very great, he is not weak and does not mind what is said about him. The public heartily enjoyed that passage in his speech 'That he thought there were few greater charms in a statesman's life than *not* to make speeches and write letters :' Dizzy is a curious combination of the Archpriest of Humbug and a great man. But I must not run on any longer.

I hope 'loud whispers' are going on : and indeed there is no other way of accounting for any moderation which the Russians may show at Constantinople.

To THE SAME.

Feb. 28, 1878.

I write one line as you kindly wish to hear from me, but I have not seen anybody likely to know anything since I last wrote.

There is a general sympathy with the Turks in England, and a general enmity against the Russians. The only importance of this is, that, in home politics, the Ministry gain and the opposition lose ; though the Ministry are at least as much to blame because they are responsible. But it is thought that Dizzy would have acted differently, if some of his colleagues would have let him—the resignation of Lord Carnarvon has been an advantage to him. People would not have supported him in going to war, but now that they have not they regret that they did not. If at this moment there were a dissolution the Government would retain, perhaps increase, their majority [1].

[1] When Parliament met in Jan. 1878, the Government (Disraeli's) asked for a supplementary grant of £6,000 000 for the army and navy. While this grant was being discussed the news came that the fleet had been ordered to the Dardanelles, upon which Lord Carnarvon and Lord Derby resigned office. When the news was found to be false, Lord Derby returned to the ministry, but Lord Carnarvon did not. The grant was carried, and for a time 'Jingoism' was rampant.

Those who trace events to remote but real causes might ask, 'How many Turks and Russians have been slaughtered because High Churchmen in England love the Greek Church and hate Mahomedans, and because Dissenters desire the disestablishment of the English Church?'...

One of the worst influences in politics during this whole business, as far as I can learn, has been the Court . . . The *Standard* of to-day, which was brought me since I began this note, looks very warlike. And unless Russia will show some moderation war looks like a necessity. For how can Austria allow the N. of the Danube to be taken from her and the Dardanelles to be closed to her, and how can England simply resign the East to Russia, that semi-civilized intriguing power?

Would Lord Derby have been so badly off if, at any previous moment from the Berlin Memorandum [1] onwards, he had interfered?

It is to be feared that war will anticipate the Conference. France will begin to sing 'Partant pour la Syrie.' . . .

March 1.

Since I wrote the above yesterday events are getting on very fast. About this time last year I met Lord Derby at dinner, and thought that upon his sense or want of sense the lives of some hundred thousand human beings depended. What will have happened this time next year? Will 50,000 Englishmen be lying dead on Turkish and Russian battle-fields? We cannot tell how rapid the descent of England may be entering on a war only half prepared. It is, of course, possible that the pressure of Austria and England, and the more distant influence of France, may deter Russia. Loud whispers are needed.

One thing occurs to me. If we manage to insert ourselves and extricate Turkey from the grasp of the Sultan, then Gladstone and all the Russophils will declare that the good

[1] In May, 1876, the Ministers of Germany, Austria, and Russia met at Berlin and issued a note to Turkey on the Eastern question. But Lord Derby refused to accept the note, as his government had not been consulted. The note was not delivered owing to the insurrection in Bulgaria.

honest Russian has been driven from the path of moderation by our interference. And it certainly is a very difficult part that a British minister has to play because he has to get his ally out of the hands of his jailor, who can bowstring him at any moment.

I want to see the higher civilization of Europe combining against the lower, whether Czar or Pope, and offering something like paternal government to Egypt and the East. It is a dreadful thing in the world that countries whose inhabitants are hardworking inoffensive people, should be governed for centuries as Syria and Egypt have been. But then there is such a danger of taking away the government which they have and substituting only 'Chaos.' This might be avoided if the European powers would jointly take up their cause. The fairest countries of the ancient world are now the most desolate, the Egyptians are as badly off as they were under the Pharaohs. How long is this to go on? Will no saviour ever hear the cries of these Eastern peoples? That is the real Eastern question.

To THE SAME.

March 7, 1878.

Things have greatly changed, and I think for the better, since I wrote to you three days ago [1]. It seems that the Russians are showing considerable moderation, which I suppose means that they have difficulties first with Roumania and other 'home rulers,' secondly with Austria, thirdly with England. We ought to give them credit for moderation, whether they deserve it or not: at any rate not to swagger about the effect of our Ironclads. I hope that the lesson will not be lost upon us, and that we shall keep ourselves better prepared for war.

The home result of the affair is that the Ministry have gained greatly on the Liberals :—all except Lord Derby, who is a good deal discredited with his own party.

Cartwright came to see me a few days ago. (I like him.) He said that he heard, 'you were greatly excited ;' I replied, 'not more than we all are.' He thought (this was before the terms of peace were known) that Constantinople would be like

[1] On March 3 the Treaty of San Stefano was concluded between Turkey and Russia.

Cracow, and that Turkey would feebly exist administered by Russia. But I don't see how Russia can secure this when her army once leaves the country. She may be engaged in a war with Germany, or England and France may combine against her in some contingency a few years hence. W. C. C. thought that Bismarck had become unenterprising with the advance of years; that he had given up, if he ever entertained, the idea of invading France; that he was haunted by a nightmare of France and Russia uniting and crushing Germany in a vice; he believed that there would be a religious war against Germany, and that France would supply the physical, to which the Pope would add the 'moral' force. But I dare say a great many such speculations are very trite and familiar to you. . . .

To THE SAME.

WEST MALVERN, *April* 4, 1878.

This is my week of holiday: I cannot employ a morning better than in writing to you.

How the scene has changed since I last wrote, and how it changes, like the weather, day by day. I guess about matters rather than know about them. (I wish that I could have your view of them.)

(1) At this moment I have no doubt that four-fifths of the country are for resisting Russia, though the proportion would have been very different a year ago.

(2) Gladstone is nowhere in general opinion, but his wonderful power of speech, and a sort of *clientèle* among Dissenters and in manufacturing towns, will always make him formidable.

(3) The country is pleased with the appointment of Lord Salisbury and with his circular—he has interpreted their instincts to them[1]. Now about Lord S.:—he is an able speaker, and an able writer, will industriously get up any

---

[1] Lord Derby resigned on March 28, 1878, partly owing to difficulties arising from the Treaty of San Stefano, partly owing to the warlike policy of Disraeli. His place as Foreign Secretary was taken by Lord Salisbury, who at once issued a circular to our representatives at foreign Courts reviewing the Treaty. (See Bright's *History*, iv. 529 f.)

subject—his bodily presence is great, and he is a very considerable man at any moment. But there is no coherence or continuity in him—remember this if you have to do with him. . . . He is powerful and impulsive—trusted a good deal by those who know him at a distance, not much by his nearer allies. This character of distrust certainly affects the whole ministry. Even their own followers say 'Upon whom can we rely?'—though they are not at all disposed to rebel.

(4) The court feeling, the P. of W., &c., are all for war: Lord Salisbury is *not* and will do all that he can to avoid it by European combination. He told a friend of mine, about a week since (Coleridge), that there was nothing the Ministry less meant than war.

(5) The country feel a difficulty in knowing how war is to be carried on unless Austria joins, of which they are now beginning to entertain good hopes. They are also embarrassed by their relation to Turkey and uncertain whether to regard her as an ally or an enemy (under Russian influence).

(6) One element in the situation is the condition of the Russian army, which is said to be very bad, and will become worse when the snow melts.

(7) Altogether we are getting out of our depressed state (the depressions of nations do not last long), and inclined to think that we shall not go to war; if Austria does not join we shall be unwilling to go to war isolated; if she does, Russia will seek peace.

Lord Salisbury has a great opportunity if his imagination can be fired, and he can at the same time be kept prudent and consistent. Notwithstanding his bulk and size he is really as much under the influence of public opinion as Lord Derby. But he can still produce a great effect by judicious words addressed to England and to Europe. I was struck in reading Lecky's account of Lord Chatham (in his new book); I forget the words, but they were to the effect that with all his failings he had *idealized* the politics of the nation. This is what Lord S. might do for foreign politics: get people to take higher views of them—pluck the flower 'safety' out of the nettle 'danger'—make the country understand its own place in Europe. This might be done by an imaginative and eloquent statesman. But I doubt whether he has in him the idealism which is required. Idealism like humanitarianism is a tremendous power in politics if people only know how to use it. Gladstone might have done it (but his political teaching has been rather lowering to the country) or Lord Russell might have done it, but he was not strong enough and had too little idealism in himself, though not without a touch of philosophy.

It seems to me that we shall with common prudence escape war. We must be patient—war is to the interest of no one. But there is the chance both of Austria and of Turkey being betrayed to Russia. There has been some justification of our conduct hitherto in the unmanageableness of the Turks. But ought we not to insist that they shall have fair terms of peace for our own sakes as well as theirs? Are we simply to leave Turkey in Europe and Asia Minor in the hands of Russia? She is already hated as much as the Turks by Roumanians and Bulgarians. . . .

So I sum up my notions in the words of Thucydides[1]: μήτε πόλεμον ἄγαν δηλοῦντες, κ.τ.λ. I am not one of those who like my friend Miss —— shriek for peace, which is very natural in her, but I don't disapprove of the 'in utrumque paratus'; whether the sending the fleet to the Dardanelles (where naval men say they could not get out in the face of an enemy without some loss) or the calling out 20,000 or 30,000 reserves is prudent or necessary is another question. . . .

To THE SAME.

OXFORD, May 22, 1878.

The Northcotes stayed with me last week. They seem to be very confident of peace, and this is now the prevailing feeling. If so, it is the result of 'si vis pacem para bellum.' For had the Russians been let alone, they would, ultimately, have demanded terms from which English feeling would have recoiled, and we should have been forced into war unprepared. Lady Northcote said that Count Schouvaloff[2] had said to her,

---

[1] i. 82. [2] The Russian Ambassador at London.

' I might as well try to dance upon your Turkey carpet as get a decision out of [Lord Derby].'

Nevertheless I venture to think that [Lord Derby's] exclusion from politics would be a loss when this crisis has passed away, but he should never be Foreign Minister again. I agree entirely in your diagnosis of him with one exception. He is as you say impressible—by the sensible part of the people of England—by Manchester and Lancashire, and in this instance the impressions derived from Manchester and Lancashire were too strong for the others. But though I have not much sympathy with him, he appears to me to have more reflection and knowledge than you would attribute to him. . . .

Mallet has been staying with me. . . . He has one of the most important positions in the country, but surrounded by difficulties, and there is always a danger that either from want of health or want of spirits he will throw up the game. I want a man to say: ' The world, and especially official life, is full of obstructions ; I mean by caution, by reticence, by force of character to get the better of them in a course of years ': whereas most men of ability get no further than the stage of criticizing them. I hope you fire his imagination from time to time. He is a really able man, but wants practical energy. He told me that you stood well with Lord Salisbury : and he thought that you were sure soon to have some considerable position. . . . Salisbury is a man of great ability and perhaps even genius, but impulsive, forgetting one day what he did the day before and imprudent to the last degree without being aware of his imprudence ; he will settle off his own bat things of which he knows nothing and is very reckless of consequences. Mallet told me that hitherto he has been deeply impressed with the necessity of avoiding war, on account of the danger likely to ensue to the crown and aristocracy (this is probably also Lord Derby's feeling)—now he is beginning to take an opposite view. . . . . Let me impress upon you that the High Church influence in England has become a very important factor not only in home but also in foreign politics, chiefly through the influence of four or five distinguished statesmen.

Dizzy will be covered with glory if he succeeds in making

peace[1]. And there can be no doubt that he has gained much during the last year, from his ' backbone' and from the people having come round to him. Charilaus has lost in the same proportion: he is given up (though with regret) by all sensible people.... He came to see me the other day (which I felt to be an honour), and talked about a German who had written a valuable treatise upon *Rhyme* in Homer.

Mallet thinks that Lord Lytton has not made a bad Governor-General, though at first unpopular. M.'s views about Russia to me seem unsound: I gather that they are Gortschakoff's views. He wants Russia and England to arise and inherit the East: Mahometanism can only be kept down by force, and Russia and England can keep it down: Russia to do the rough work. I doubt the doctrine of keeping India down by force, and besides that there are 200 millions of Mahometans in the world, not lifeless or decayed, but capable of being roused into considerable force and energy. I detest this crusade against Mahometans, who are as useful in their part of the world as Christians are in ours.

How I wish that there were any chance of seeing you this summer and of talking over this and many other things : M. Arnold writes to me, ' Ecce labora et noli contristari ' (that fellow with all his levity has something of the great man in him), and I hand it on to you.

To THE SAME.

TORQUAY, *Dec.* 23, 1878.

I am grieved to find among my letters a very interesting one from you which is either unanswered or a request of yours contained in it has been neglected. I send you a short inscription. I am very pleased to do anything of this kind for one whom I so greatly respected as your dear father and for you[2]. We can talk it over when we meet, and I will try to alter any word which you think inadequate. The style of

---

[1] The Berlin Conference was opened June 13, and the Treaty of Berlin was signed on July 13. The Articles will be found in Haydn's *Dict. of Dates, sub voce* Berlin.

[2] See *Life*, ii. p. 112.

Latin inscriptions should be subdued rather than exaggerated. Not having a Latin bible here, I have not given the exact words of the Vulgate.

Public events have moved quickly and been very interesting, since you wrote. There is a degree of bitterness in English politics, especially on the part of the Liberals, which I do not remember since the Reform Bill. People are really quarrelsome over the dinner table. The distress in the country has been against the Ministry, and they would probably lose a few seats on a dissolution[1]. But after five years of office they are not materially shaken ; and the country is grateful to them for having given us a better and more tenable position than we held this time last year in the eyes of the world.

The climate and resources of Cyprus[2] are matters of fact about which people are simply divided accordingly as they happen to be Liberals or Conservatives. If I may believe Sir M. Lopes who has just returned, it is a great success—not much illness, a first-rate harbour, inexhaustible fertility. He thinks that we shall set an example of the way in which the East should be administered, which will soon spread to the Asiatic continent. It seems to me a soluble problem, not to make the Pachas honest, but to govern Turkey by European support, and to nurse something like European institutions. No country is utterly corrupted in which the mass of the people are not corrupted, and in which there spring up occasionally great military and political leaders.

The question of the Ameer[3] seems likely to settle itself easily. I incline to think that English influence, perhaps annexation, will do something towards the civilization of that part of the world ; that we shall have a better frontier ; that we had a sufficient technical reason for going to war ; and that it was a good thing to get rid of the fear of Russia. England and Russia must be conterminous in the course of

---

[1] The winter of 1878-1879 was very severe, and the numbers of the unemployed were great. Trade was also much depressed.

[2] Cyprus had been ceded to England June 4, 1878, under the terms of the Anglo-Turkish convention.

[3] Invasion of Afghanistan, flight and death of Shere Ali, Nov. 1878–Feb. 1879.

the next ten years. Is it better that Afghanistan should be a part of Russian or of English territory? The 'thorny hedge' doctrine does not really hold, for the uncivilized people between the two great powers are always being intrigued with by one or other of them—hence armed embassies and wars. Nor is there much really in the theory held by Lord Lawrence and others, that in case of a war with Russia we had better have a friendly than a beaten Afghanistan. For it seems pretty clear that the Afghans do not care about the expulsion of their ruler. Little can be made of our duties towards the native princes, especially when like Shere Ali they are only *de facto* sovereigns who have fought their way to the throne. But as a civilized nation we owe a great deal—all that we can accomplish—to uncivilized peoples. And if we can pacify the hill tribes and put down plunders and robbery we shall have done something for that part of the world.

Gladstone is not heard for his much speaking and writing; yet his speeches are said to be as good, if not better than ever. He is believed to have a great hold on the masses. But he cannot really bring them into play without a revolution, and his age, his conscience, and his connexions with the upper ten thousand would prevent his trying that. Nor has he the courage for it—yet it is difficult to say what he will or will not do: when he is beaten he becomes a fanatic—he blows the trumpet of morality. All the devils in hell are not so black as Dizzy. (Let me remark what a mistake the Liberals make in their ineffectual attempts to blacken Dizzy, who is a very great man with great faults.) Peace at any price and disestablishment and disarmament are his battle cries. But the majority of the country are of another mind. One of the most dishonest things which the Liberals do is the imputation of the distress of the country to the expenditure of the ministry. As if the country could have felt as yet an increase of taxation on its income of 800,000,000 of half per cent., of which not a quarter per cent. has as yet been imposed. . . .

Such is my 'essence of public opinion' as far as it can be reduced to two sheets of note paper. Are we to have the pleasure of seeing you in January as you intended? I wish you were in some country in which I could get at you and in which you could have a real political sphere[1].

To THE SAME.

OXFORD, *Oct.* 23, 1879.

I am sitting alone after dinner and the thought occurs to me, why should I not write to you? Long vacation has come and gone and six months have passed without my hearing a word about you: I suppose that you have been doing something, either at Goa or Delagoa, or in some other part of the world. I hope that wife and children are well. Give my best love to them. . . .

I do not know that I can supply any private lights about Politics beyond what you see in the newspapers. I doubt whether the Liberals who are extremely violent have made much progress in the country, though they have a little, and may gain, perhaps, twenty seats, which will make Parliamentary government almost intolerable. There are two reasons why I do not think that they can come in. 1. They are united only in enmity to the present government and the desire to get into office: 2. They cannot simply undo all the foreign policy of their predecessors. 3. I may add they have the whole force of the Court against them, a formidable make-weight when parties are nearly divided. The bad harvest and the financial deficit are in their favour; but the Ministry will hardly be made responsible for the harvest, though it may put men's minds into a more susceptible state, and the deficit must be paid under either Ministry. It is the direct consequence of a policy which the country on the whole approves; though unwilling to pay the bill. The great fault of the Ministry is that they are not stronger. My old friend, Northcote, though a clever and very honest man, is not able enough to be leader of the House of Commons, though he is an excellent administrator, and has great command of his temper. Mr. Cross seems to win very favourable opinions: so, more than any of the young men, does Edward Stanhope. The ability of Lord Salisbury (a kind of inconsecutive ability) is acknowledged, but his

---

[1] Morier was now at Lisbon.

judgement and temper are much doubted. He is more damaged than any one in the Ministry. Lord Derby is getting up again, and it is supposed that he is going to join the Liberals. But he had better not do this : his rôle is the sensible peace-loving Conservative. The speeches he makes are just suited to the *homme intellectuel moyen*, who is a great power in England.

I try to keep myself as much a Liberal as possible ; for I really am a Liberal in home politics, Church, Education and Free Trade. But I cannot help feeling that the Liberals by their violence and exaggeration have done great harm. Their conduct on the question of ' Flogging in the Army ' was very discreditable [1].

One person who appears to be very influential with them now (Sir W. Harcourt who is supposed to dominate Lord Hartington) was perfectly detested by them six years ago. He is a very clever fellow, but not really a public spirited man or a statesman.

It seems to me that Foreign Politics are in a better state than a year ago. Turkey and Russia are fortunately both beaten. Austria is well placed ; the remaining difficulties, though great, are such as must necessarily arise from the conflict of semi-barbarous fanatical and partially degraded races. The accounts from Eastern Roumelia seem to be satisfactory ; I wish you could go to Constantinople, get into the Sultan's confidence and drive away the Pashas and the Harem. . . .

Indian questions are becoming more important in English politics. Fawcett deserves credit for this. About the Afghan question Indian opinion generally supports the Government, I think, notwithstanding the great names of Lord Lawrence and Lord Northbrook. If India is not to be bankrupt there must be either increase of taxation or diminution of expenditure : increase of taxation at present seems impossible (though in the future there is a possibility of it from an increased land-revenue) and therefore there must be diminution of expenditure which means reduction of the army. And if we could reduce the native armies this might be possible without danger to India.

[1] This subject was discussed in Parliament, May, 1879.

K

It would be much for the advantage of India, if we could get the native principalities into our hands.

I do not think that this Ministry will go out as long as Dizzy lives, or perhaps, as he expresses it, as long as it pleases Providence to spare Mr. Gladstone's life—then I should expect a coalition under Lord Derby, at any rate for a time.

Take care of yourself and bid defiance to the gout. When are you coming to look us up in England?

To THE SAME.

WEST MALVERN, *Dec.* 29, 1879.

I send a few lines at the end of the old year and the beginning of the new one. Best wishes to you and yours: I should like to hear from you, if you have time to write.

I am afraid the year closes rather darkly and hopelessly for Europe. (Though I also believe that nations quickly recover and that one's opinions about them are apt to take the colour of one's own circumstances.) But at present it seems to me that besides the commercial distress, there is great reason for anxiety in the three chief countries of Europe—France, Germany, and Russia; France, after seeming for a time settled, falling into the hands of the left, which means war with the clergy and the old regime, whether Napoleonist or Legitimist, who may perhaps ally themselves with the army, and will hardly give up all without a struggle. The problem is how two entirely opposite elements can be made to live together happily in the same country: I fancy that Imperialism has much deeper roots than we suppose, and was much more based upon the necessities of the case. I believe it is 'scotched' not 'killed,' and that in some form it is very likely to revive, notwithstanding personal difficulties: not that I can wish this. The saying of Macaulay, 'France missed the Reformation and gained the Revolution,' is applicable to French politics of other times. It always has the Catholic Church too strong for good government and for the well-being of social life, and is always breaking out into violent measures against it. Then there is Germany—poor, military, divided by caste, impoverished and oppressed by the conscription, the most educated country in

Europe and yet having no share in its own government, hanging on the life of one man, and looking forward to the possibility of a desperate war. As for Russia, it may any day fall through the crust into the volcanoes beneath. Everything needs to be reformed, and there are no means of reforming it : the natural instruments of reform are in Siberia, and there is no middle party on which to work. There must be great force of character and self-devotion in Russia among these mad patriots, but there is no power of union and concert.

At home, allowing for the bad state of trade and harvests, I do not believe that our condition is so bad. The Liberals are furious, and headed by Gladstone grow more and more exasperated ; but I do not think that they make a great impression. The real enemy to the present Ministry is the depression of commerce and the bad harvest, which throw the minds of people into a sensitive state and make them desire change. 'We are badly off ; let us try Gladstone, who promises so fair.' The general opinion is that the result of the Election will be almost a tie [1]; and that after the next Election another will soon follow, probably with a coalition Ministry. It seems to me that the sooner this last comes the better, for neither party will have a decided majority ; they will hang upon the Irish members, perhaps even upon a Tichborne vote—and half the Liberal party are more akin to the Conservatives than they are to their friends below the gangway. It seems to me that politics are not so great or patriotic or chivalrous as they used to be. Either I see things nearer, or they have really degenerated. Gladstone does not appear to me to have gained so much with the mob as he has lost with the upper and educated classes, who after all are still the greater part of politics.

I read Mr. Bright's speech the other day about America with great interest. (What he and Fawcett say is real and simple— G. is sophisticated.) But I should like to set against his account of the greatness of the New World, the greatness of the Old, which contains nine-tenths of the intelligence, art, mind, population of the whole. I wish you and others who have to think about foreign politics would seriously consider

---

[1] In April, 1880, Gladstone was returned by a large majority.

the duties of the West towards the East, of civilized to semi-
civilized race (there is no real question of savages ; they die out,
and unless by some natural process they can pass into Hindoos
in India or into Mahometans in Africa, are not worth considering).   But the case of the semi-civilized races is otherwise ;
including the Mahometans they are two-thirds of the world ;
they are within a few days of us and we must have a *modus
vivendi* with them.   It is doubtful whether these terrible,
barbarous governments ought to go on ; or whether, if they do,
they may not become dangerous to us all : we ought to have
staffs of residents at their courts and get all the information
possible about them.   They have to be treated in different
ways from Turkey downwards.   For Turkey with all its
brutalities is really the first of them, the nearest to civilization.
The civilized part of the world (not Russia) must take upon
itself this work with some sort of European concert.   We are
getting so very near them that the question must be faced in
the coming generation ; therefore, though I have formed no
opinion of the Afghanistan war, I am not so averse to it merely
on the grounds of bloodshed as the Liberals in general are.
I doubt whether the semi-civilized world can be much ame-
liorated without a good deal of bloodshed, unless you suppose
a miraculous change to take place in human nature.   On the
other hand war in Africa or India may be promoted by the
worst motives—greed of colonists, desire of promotion, the
imperious or timorous character of the dominant race.   But
I do not see that we escape from responsibility for all the
dreadful things which are done in Turkestan and China (e. g.
a whole province, during the last three years, has had its
population, about 3,000,000, exterminated in China) by standing
aside for them.   It strikes me often how little power or will
nations have to help their 'poor relations' in extremity : do
you know that more than 5,000,000 of persons perished in the
last Indian famine ? ·

I wish that I could consider these subjects with your larger
knowledge and experience of them.   If I were in your position
I should keep my eyes steadily fixed on the Eastern Question.
I do not believe that the reform of Turkey is utterly hopeless.
There are two chances, the assembly and personal influence

over the Sultan : there is always the fear, I suppose, of the
Pachas and the Sultan supporting the Russians to save themselves for the moment. When we speak of the difficulties of
Turkey it should always be remembered (1) that we could not
in centuries raise the natives of Bengal to the position of most
of the Turks: (2) that Turkey must be reformed or exterminated,
and you cannot exterminate 2,000,000 of Turks in Europe and
10,000,000 in Asia. . . .

When are you coming to England, and when are you going
to Vienna ? I hope that will be before long, that I may come
and pay you a visit there.

I have not read over this rigmarole which I have been
writing to you. Notes to Thucydides are printing—a tedious
and hardly satisfactory business. I am reminded of them by
the appearance of Forbes with the proof ; and now must
break off.

To the Marquis of Lansdowne.

West Malvern, *April* 4, 1880.

The utterances of some persons both Liberals and Conservatives are very provoking, especially 'Sit down : don't
stir : and I will dissect you. You will be dead at the end of
the operation, but that does not matter.' I do not wish to see
a landlord spirit; indeed it is the first business of every landlord,
Irish or English, to repress and conceal this (not to destroy the
weight of his words by pleading the cause in which he is
personally interested). But if the landlords go about saying
' that they are a doomed class,' they will be doomed and a good
deal more doomed with them.

The state of Ireland is no doubt worse than it has ever been
in this century. But this rebellion is not so giantlike as it
looks : if the loyal Irish are encouraged to organize and severe
blows are struck at the leaders, neither the sufferings of the
landlords, nor the disquiet of the country are nearly so great as
[in] many of the European countries during the last fifty years.
The most dangerous symptom is the foolish half sympathy of
English Liberals not looking forward to the consequences. For
I think that we may be sure that the English (working men

and all included) will not part with Ireland, or allow Ireland to part.

To THE SAME.

OXFORD, *May* 8.

This is the greatest crisis in politics that I can remember [1]. It is difficult to see any light.

The English, if they mean to keep Ireland, must be prepared to reform the law, and they must be prepared to spend a good deal of money. If it be worth while 'to double the national debt in order to prevent a French invasion' (Cobden), it must be worth while to spend a hundred millions in civilizing and pacifying Ireland by emigration, liberal assistance to the Catholics, and the like. The Irish landlords must not be thinking too much of their rents, but of the country. They have not suffered so much as they would have done in a civil war. And though they will lose considerably, yet if they can succeed in restoring order, their properties will be as valuable as they were thirty or fifty years ago. I know that there are great difficulties, but might they not have done something more for themselves and for the defence of the country than they have done?

To THE SAME.

WEST MALVERN, *July* 23.

I feel very strongly the mischief that Gladstone is doing, and that he probably will do, as long as he lives, for the future. But whatever we might wish I do not see that his hold on the middle and lower classes is shaken, and therefore he is the master 'until this tyranny be over-past.' Had Dizzy been alive, or had the Conservative party been stronger or better led, the result might have been different.

To THE SAME.

BALLIOL COLLEGE, *Nov.* 29, 1883.

I am glad that you are not disappointed with Canada [2]. I see no reason why the Governor-General of a great province should be a *roi fainéant*, or a mere figure-head. He cannot descend

---

[1] The assassination of Lord F. Cavendish and Mr. Burke on May 6.

[2] The Marquis of Lansdowne was Governor-General of Canada from 1884 to 1888.

into the arena and knock, and strike, but he can always act through others, if he knows how to choose them ; he can make good appointments ; he can have a clear line of policy about education, about land, about public improvements, about credit and banking, which in four or five years he may be able to carry out. If he knows more about these than anybody else, he will have the greatest weight, though he never utters a word publicly or says very little about them (and probably the less he is perceived to do, the more he will be able to do).

He can make himself beloved, and his kindnesses and courtesies are valued ten times as much as any one else's. He can raise the tone and ideas of the whole community by occasional speeches, but he must speak not like a popular orator, but like the Governor of a Province.

There are some questions in colonies, e. g. the land question and the credit question, which seem to be always attended to when it is too late. Shall I add a favourite sentence of mine ? 'Measures of precaution are never justly appreciated, because when most effectual they are never seen to be necessary.'

I am afraid that I get rather more conservative as I get older. I feel that the coming democracy is a necessity, not a good, or rather partly a good, and partly an evil. But it is mere weakness to complain of the time in which one's own lot is cast. The country is not lost and never will be lost. It is a curious question, not much discussed, what should be the attitude of those who naturally belong to the old regime towards the new. A radical who lives in a castle appears to me a mistake ; he (or she) fancies himself to be full of noble ideas, but he is enjoying two kinds of life at once. The old French noblesse fell into this error, I suppose, and when the Revolution came they were nowhere. Nor do I quite like [the] aristocratic patronizing of democracy in De Tocqueville. No man should give up his own position, which is a sort of lever helping him to move the world, and pretend to be what he is not. The old regime have the advantage of good manners which are a great political force under any form of government. They may be the leaders of every real social and philanthropic cause. They may be truly liberal, if they would only 'forget some things,' e. g. the game laws, and 'remember others' such as the miserable homes of the poor in town and country. They may get hold of the better mind of democracy and set it against the worse: ἔχοντες καὶ πρὸς ὀργήν τι ἀντειπεῖν. They may oppose abuses and corruptions of all sorts. They seem to be the men most needed in the world, and therefore I conclude there must be a place for them in the politics of the future. The fear is that they will become isolated and so powerless. It is hard to combine the necessary force of character with the balanced position which they hold. All this has to be carefully thought out.

I have given you enough of these commonplace reflections. Yesterday I had a long talk with Mr. Gladstone, who happens to be at Oxford. He said, he thought we were tending to a sort of mild socialism, but that he was not at all afraid of democracy. I tried to interest him about middle class education, but though he said he was glad to talk about it, I found that he had endless powers of getting away from the point. He looked aged and rather tired, said he did not like moving about, thought that Cambridge men were beating Oxford in the political race, that D. would leave a mark on the history of his country, &c. There was nothing really remarkable in his conversation, though anything which falls from him seems important. I think he has long since unconsciously learnt that speech is a mode of concealing thought.

To R. B. D. MORIER.

Dec. 11, 1884.

I am delighted to hear of your appointment to one of the first posts in Europe[1], and I think—when the strange internal development of Russia is considered, its proximity to us in India and its perpetual threatening of Turkey and Asia Minor—one of the most interesting of diplomatic positions.

I read your letter and rejoiced in it. I quite understand that the feeling of doing great things comes over you, and quite believe that you may accomplish some of them in the next ten years. Russia is a mysterious power, because there is a hidden though disorganized strength in her—physical,

[1] Morier was appointed Ambassador at St. Petersburg on Dec. 1, 1884.

religious, and to some extent moral. Imperialism or revolution are her alternatives, and in either form she may yet have the future of Europe in her hands. This negative idealism, which is called nihilism, shows that her people are capable of any insane fanaticism : and nations, like individuals, may go mad.

If I might advise (positively for the last time) on this joyful occasion, I would urge upon you once more 'caution and reticence.' I do not mean as to keeping of secrets, and I know that there must be a give and take of information. But what you do not appear to me to see, is, that you cannot speak indiscriminately against Gladstone, Harcourt, and other persons, who are for the moment influential, without raising a great deal of prejudice against yourself, and creating unnecessary drawbacks in the accomplishment of objects, which you have at heart. Every one knows how another speaks of him and cannot be expected to love his assailant. Everybody acknowledges your ability ; but I believe that the persons, whose opinion you most value, feel that this defect of which you never seem to be aware, has nearly shipwrecked you. . . . May I give you as a motto for a diplomatist my favourite sentence out of Fielding : 'I forgave him, not from any magnanimity of soul, still less for Christian charity, but simply because it was expedient to me.' Or to put the thought in a more unworldly phrase, I forgave him simply because, having the interests of England and Europe at heart, I have no room for personal enmities or antipathies.

As you have not shipwrecked let us rejoice together. Like you I shall be always full of schemes, some of which I have now the opportunity of carrying out, but they are not of sufficient interest to make it worth while that I should give an account of them. I suppose that you will be coming to England on the way to St. Petersburg, and we can talk about these and many other things. I quite understand the pleasure of doing, and of carrying out ideas, especially when they take time and are part of a line of policy : and I think when one is appointed to a great position he may legitimately indulge in some day-dreams in the hope of making them realities. . . .

As you suppose, I am deeply grieved at the death of Grant. He was a true friend and a fine fellow who did a great work. No one ever did so much for the University of Edinburgh.

Looking forward as the greatest pleasure of the Vacation to seeing you.

To THE SAME.

WEST MALVERN, *Jan.* 1, 1885.

I send you a welcome—every good wish for the new year.

I will not discuss in writing, or perhaps at all, the latter part of your letter. But I should be very sorry if you supposed that I did not sympathize with your work or rejoice in your success, especially in this last matter of the Spanish Treaty[1], which is a great result of diplomatic perseverance and skill. . . .

I quite agree with you that foreign affairs seem to be in as bad a state as they can be: Gladstone has drowned everything in a sea of democracy. And I can always bear witness to your having said that we must not occupy Egypt[2], that we must settle the Congo question, that the Boers must be made to lay down their arms. And now the question is how to meet new difficulties which need never have arisen.

To THE LADY ABERCROMBY.

OXFORD, *March* 30, 1885.

Politics appear to me increasingly wearisome and disgusting: war is a serious matter, and nobody seems to know with what intention or prospects we are at war in the Sudan or commencing a war in Afghanistan: everything is to be set aside for the redistribution. And all because the country is mesmerized by this great demagogue and rhetorician. I am beginning to think that anything is better than this. I made friends with Lord Rosebery since I saw you: he appears to me to be a man of very uncommon powers, if he has force of character enough to be independent.

[1] From 1881 to 1884 Morier had been Minister at Madrid.
[2] See *supra*, p. 91.

To THE SAME.

BALLIOL COLLEGE, *April* 28, 1885.

Public affairs look bad, and we seem to be on the eve of war. I try to keep my mind free from the influence of news-papers, but it is not easy. The way I put the matter to myself is this : If we are prepared for war, then fight (for there is abundant cause). But if we are not prepared, then eat any amount of dirt that we may live to fight another day. Or to put the same idea in more befitting words : What king having 10,000 men does not consider whether he is able to meet him that cometh against him with 20,000 men ? Or if not, when his enemy is a long way off, he sendeth an embassy, &c.

I am desirous that neither self-glorification nor self-depreciation should prevent us from seeing hard facts : e.g. especially the difference between 10,000 men and 100,000 men, or between 100,000 and 1,000,000. The best thing that can happen to us is that we shall go to war, shall be beaten, shall be helped (after we have bled sufficiently) by Bismarck, who will see that now is his time for crushing Russia and seizing the Baltic provinces. The necessity for our going to war seems to me to arise out of the necessity of supporting the Ameer, and the great chance of success is the desperate courage of the five millions of Afghans fighting for their liberties, if they can be persuaded that we are their friends. I have been reading Von Busch, and like especially Bismarck's contempt of oratory. Tennyson says, ' O Lord Bismarck, come and govern us ; we will give you a million a year.'

To R. B. D. MORIER.

FARRINGFORD, FRESHWATER,
Jan. 7, 1888.

I have a sort of feeling, that from tiredness caused by over-exertion and travelling, I did not do justice to all the interesting things that you confided to me, and that you might be dis-appointed in such a want of friendship and sympathy at a trying time of your life.

You know that I do not pretend to know anything about

foreign politics. I glean a little from you; otherwise I only judge of them from the most general point of view, and my confidence in my own opinions is greatly shaken from finding that I have changed two or three times backwards and forwards under the impression of the hour during the last twenty years.

I am very much struck by what you have told me, and it seems to me that St. Petersburg is probably the place at which this awful European war is most likely to be prevented, and that you are the person most likely to be able to stop it [1].

I quite agree in thinking that the possibilities of danger in India, or even of the Russian occupation of Constantinople and Asia Minor, which means the next generation, is not to be weighed in the balance against the European conflagration which means next year, and which means no one can tell what calamities to Europe, to the world, and to civilization. Besides, twenty or twenty-five years give a breathing time, during which many changes may be made and many preparations taken against the unknown Russia of the future.

You suppose Bismarck to feel himself subject to an irresistible force, which he may in some degree turn aside by striking the first blow. But you are not absolutely certain of this; and as old men are necessarily a little uncertain about their course, it may be that the man of blood and iron, who has a piece of religion or superstition in him, may shrink from going down into Hell leaving Europe in a blaze. And the best way to keep his conscience alive is to make it appear to all Europe that he is the true author of the war. They should be invited to infer from what he did at the commencement of the first French war, what he is doing in the prospect of another. 'I speak peace with my lips, but my newspapers and my armaments go to war.'

I quite feel that your position is a tremendous responsibility. There is no post in Europe more important or more honourable. It is no matter whether you are appreciated or not by ministers or others, except in so far as it conduces to the success of

[1] Towards the end of 1887, much excitement was caused at Vienna and Berlin by the movement of troops on the Galician border, and this was increased by an article in the *Invalide Russe*, declaring that Russia wished for peace but was prepared for war.

your efforts to have their confidence. . . . You are placed at St. Petersburg (by God, as Carlyle would have said) to preserve the peace of Europe, and no private anxieties, or fear about the result should be allowed to weigh upon your mind for an hour, while such great things are entrusted to you. The temper of the Duke of Wellington before one of his battles is the example to be followed, the temper which leaves nothing undone, and can go to sleep for an hour or two before the battle begins.

You sometimes appear to think that I do not sympathize with your political views and aims as a friend should do. Shall I tell you the truth? I do not doubt your ability or courage or insight. But I am afraid sometimes of your want of self-control, which strikes others as well as myself. And yet I should despair of making you see this. You would say, ' Who can be different from what nature made him? who can be wise and valiant in a moment?' 'It is ungracious of you to say this because I talk freely to you.' And so it is very ungracious, but will you think of it? Because it may be a real impediment to action at St. Petersburg, at Berlin, at home in some important crisis.

For example, is it wise to show antipathy to Bismarck? The idea that you are antipathetic to him is held to be the explanation of your political line with those who are opposed to you. . . . Besides, it makes it impossible for you to approach him, if in any of his moods it should be desirable that you did so. Even Bismarck looks differently from the inside; and inside views, and 'put yourself in the position of your opponent,' have to be considered by the diplomatist. He needs the absolutely 'dry light' free from sympathies and antipathies, though he works through both. Besides, you have to avoid the appearance of pitting yourself against Bismarck, which, though very possible in fact, would do you no good in the eyes of the public.

My dear friend, your career will be one of the greatest interest to me in the remaining years of my life. I am only telling you what you already know, and will agree in (except, perhaps, some part of the last paragraph). I always feel deeply grateful to you for your unshaken friendship now more than forty years old. I hope that you will be appreciated as you deserve: but much more than that—whether appreciated or not—you may (be) able by God's help to do a great work for the peace and good of the world.

I might have inflicted upon you a longer letter, if the postman were not waiting.

IV. LETTERS ON INDIA

(1) LETTERS TO THE MARQUIS OF LANSDOWNE.

To the Marquis of Lansdowne[1].

BALLIOL COLLEGE, *Feb.* 20, 1888.

I am rejoiced to hear that you have accepted the Governor-Generalship. To me it seems to be the highest position which an Englishman can attain. There is more opportunity of doing great and permanent good in India than in any department of administration in England, and the office having more power is also more free from the disagreeables of home politics. The routine work appears to be very severe—the first object of any one who has to govern a great country should be to cut it down that he may keep his head clear for more important matters.

I see a good deal of the old Civil Servants. The subjects about which they chiefly talk to me are:—(1) The Afghan Boundary question, which they generally regard as settled not for ever, but for the next ten years: (2) Much more serious to them appears the relation of natives and Europeans, especially crowds and congresses, which are so unmanageable and for which railways afford greater facilities than formerly. 'India for the Hindoo' is like Ireland for the Irish, and universal suffrage in England will not allow them to be coerced. They say that there would be a great risk in any increase, however small, of the land tax: (3) They have a trouble of their own—the depreciation of silver; they admit that silver purchases as much in India as formerly, but they lose one-third in their

---

[1] The Marquis of Lansdowne was Viceroy of India from 1888 to 1893.

pensions and home remittances. Their wives ask pathetically, Will silver always be going down? (4) They naturally talk to me about admission to the Service, and they are generally of opinion, as I am, that the Civil Service Students are sent out too young. The age at present is nineteen; it used to be twenty-one and twenty-two. This question, which I only regard from the point of view of the interests of the service, is mixed up in the minds of many with the other question of the admission of the natives, to whom the later age is somewhat more favourable: (5) They speak hopefully of the financial prospects of India (not this year or next, but five years hence), while they lament the want of continuity in the management of it. The improvement of it is expected to arise from the development of trade, the working of mines, and the improved revenue of the newly assessed districts, now beginning to accrue. (6) They give wonderful accounts of the increase of production in India partly stimulated by the fall of silver, and the best authorities, like Sir William Hunter, think that when railroads are more developed in India, Indian wheat may be sold in England at 20s. a quarter, as it can be produced on the spot for 7s. a quarter—a lower depth for the English agriculturist. (7) There is no small war between the lovers of economy and the lovers of reproductive improvement, about sanitation (a work which seems in India to be practically inexhaustible), about irrigation, extension of railways, &c. In matters relating to health I am very much afraid of 'the ignorant impatience of taxation.' (8) Of education I hear from Sir W. Hunter that it cannot be stopped and will double in a few years. (9) They wish to preserve native institutions, but they say that the power to do so is a good deal impaired by the personal rights which the English government confers on the natives. They also approve of municipal government, where the party spirit of race or religion is not too strong to make it practicable.

I have written down these few remarks thinking that they may possibly interest you and at any rate be as profitable as the wrongs and crimes of Ireland. They are the impressions which I have gathered in conversation from persons whose opinion I trust and who have great knowledge of India.

To the Same.

Balliol College, *May* 1, 1888.

We are delighted to hear that you are coming to us on June 22 [1].

Shall I venture to send a few more remarks upon Indian subjects, as far as I can collect what appears to me to be the best opinion about them?

. . . .

The native character is a very curious subject of speculation, not that it is unfathomable, but it is so different from European, that we hardly understand it. The native is extremely open to kindness—a few words showing interest—and he is at once overpowered by the appearance of strength ; and he knows himself to be safe under the protection of the English. Of course he does not like aliens in blood, in language, in religion, but he is substantially loyal from other motives (I am speaking from information which I get chiefly about the South of India). Then he is puzzled by the conflict of Caste and Western ideas, and wants to be a clerk instead of a peasant and to have a share in the rewards of the Civil Service ; and our education of the natives is to a great extent the cause of this—it is a real difficulty which we have to look in the face, and must settle peaceably before it becomes exasperated. In India as in England we are apt to do things rather too late—so in Ireland.

· The word Ireland suggests many parallels, if I may go off upon a word. There is fixity of tenure, good for the Ryot, if he can be prevented from selling his Tenant Right. There are small freeholds, as I believe in Madras, good again for the cultivators, if they are not saleable to the money-lender. Ireland has to be governed with an English Liberal party over the water, India too has to be governed in the presence of an English Liberal party (though at a greater distance), who will be easily got hold of by the native agitators, and will apply English words and symbols to India—and there is India and the India Office.

Agriculture seems to be the occupation of an immense

[1] See *Life*, vol. ii. p. 304.

M

majority of the natives, yet we have done little for the improvement of it, and we have left it in the hands of the Collectors of the Revenue, which has made our attempt to improve it suspected by the natives and distasteful to them. (We are trying at Oxford to give the civilians some little interest in agriculture.) We seem in India to be sometimes too much afraid of at all increasing the expenditure, however great may be the return, e. g. in Railways and Irrigation, as seems to have been the case. This 'ignorant impatience of taxation' may do a great deal of harm in an undeveloped country, if it leads to the discontinuance of public works required for health or agriculture. Saving money by any means is a barbarous finance.

I suppose the secret of finance in India is the keeping down of the military expenditure. Unless this is done, all kinds of improvements must be starved. Money cannot be got from taxation, and it must therefore be got from the reduction of expenditure—'parsimonia.' And then comes a Russian scare : I do not venture to balance between the conflicting claims; but any one can see that the Anglo-Indian feeling will be in one direction, native feelings and interests in another.

It is certainly very disagreeable to know that money intended to provide against famine is directed to the payment of military expenses. These famines occur on the average about once in eleven years. Their extent is very great, but in these days of rapid communication they can be met by an expenditure of money, so as to prevent any great loss of life. The state of the finances, the spread of railroads, and of canals, and especially of cheap roads and railways, are of course great safeguards. I am afraid it is very probable that you will have at least one (greater Irish) famine in the course of your viceroyalty.

Local government appears to be an extremely difficult question. In the towns it is said to do very well, but in the villages there are not sufficient materials. The point seems to be to combine what remains of the old village organization of India with Government supervision. Nothing is more important in India than sanitation from the point of view, not only of health, but of wealth, and there is nothing of which the natives are less intelligent. They need to be stirred up about it, and made to co-operate. When left to the Collector there is no executive, and this, speaking generally, is one of the great evils of India.

I have written this in great haste. Will you kindly consider not the style but the subject?

To THE SAME.

BALLIOL COLLEGE, *July* 31, 1888.

I went yesterday to call on —— who is spending a few weeks in Oxford. As I told you, I try to pick up information from old Indians. I said: 'What do you suppose to be the number of persons who are agitating the cause of the natives in India?' Reply: 'There are, at the utmost, about 25,000 educated persons among the natives. The agitators are just the fringe of these.' He added that this small body were in many respects very remarkable persons, and that in India you could not tell what a day would bring forth: example, the Mutiny, which, he said, was considered by all well-informed persons to have had no other cause but the greased cartridges. I said: 'Then you are doubtful about native education.' 'Why, no,' he replied, 'education makes the natives better aware of their own relation to one another and to the English.' . . .

I can't help seeing how difficult a game the Viceroy of India has to play, between the hopes of the natives and the suspicions of the English. He may do a great deal by reticence and by universal kindness and attention, which is the best basis of popularity; also by constant thought about the wants and possibilities of India. He may hope that having so great a duty to perform, the temper of a great man may govern his life and actions.

To THE SAME.

BALLIOL COLLEGE, *Jan.* 27, 1889.

I should be glad to hear that you are well and you do not find the work too much for your strength. No part of the Viceroy's duties is more important than the social ones, and it is impossible for an overworked man to fulfil these properly. Who can be genial, witty, good-humoured, gracious, hospitable, when he has been reading blue books for twelve hours before?

I do not believe the congresses are really dangerous, because they consist chiefly, if not entirely, of educated men, and educated men in India are not more than $\frac{1}{10,000}$, and $\frac{1}{10,000}$ are not really to be feared, even if they have the support of the extreme Liberals in England, and are themselves, as they probably are, the most active and energetic of men. We may do a great deal in India, (1) by securing the allegiance of the native princes, (2) by conferring benefits on the masses, such as sanitation, irrigation, and the prevention of famine, by the improvement of agriculture, by admitting them to a somewhat larger share of administration. But whenever we admit them to Representation they will flood and drown us.

To THE SAME.

BALLIOL COLLEGE, *April* 16, 1889.

—— came to see me the other day. He was of opinion that the congresses in India would do no harm: 'let them talk.' He seemed to fear nothing in India except an explosion caused by Radicalism in England. At the same time he thought this so dangerous that he would advise none of his friends to put money in the Indian Funds.

I hear that the India Office are likely to raise the age of the Candidates for the Civil Service of India to twenty-two-and-a-half. I hope that they will not do away with the University probation. This would be a great mistake considering what a heterogeneous body the Candidates are, with or without homes (?) or schools. They require to be brought together before they go out. And under men like Markby and Toynbee they gain a great deal of good.

To THE SAME.

BALLIOL COLLEGE, *Jan.* 4, 1891.

May I send you a few remarks on some Indian subjects which interest me?

First: The Marriage question, about which a Parsee, Mr. Malabari, has been stirring up the English people. My first thought is, that I do not like exciting English opinion against native customs any more than I should approve society in Calcutta addressing us about the ways of the fashionable world in England. But I also feel that we must give and take, and accept any good influence which comes from either, in order to carry out necessary reforms. England would like to make great social changes in India, and if young India aspires to have representative institutions, and to be protected in them by a British force, we must not grumble at either.

The Marriage question appears to be difficult. No one supposes that the age of marriage, though in practice not so low as is sometimes supposed, can be considerably raised in India. It is determined by custom. Nor is it possible for the government or the law really to protect a young maiden or a widow who is married again against the effects of public opinion or ecclesiastical penalties. The proposal to raise the age of consent would be unmeaning in India, where the consent given is really that of the parents. I am told by a native lady who resides in Oxford, that it would raise a great storm, because the natives would think that in transferring the consent from the parents to the maiden we were tampering with their marriage customs. There seems to be no great proof of criminal abuse of the girl ; nor would such a crime be easily discovered in the interior of an Indian household, or easily proved or defined.

What then can be done or ought to be done?

Not much : because anything that we do, unless supported by public opinion, will either be ineffectual or hurtful.

But something can be done :

1. On such subjects, the best natives should be consulted, and their point of view appreciated. They will have a good deal to say on the feeling of the people and something on moral grounds also.

2. It seems to be generally agreed that suits for the restitution of conjugal rights, a figment of English Law which has been introduced in India, might with advantage be abolished, because they may sometimes enable a bad husband to tyrannize over his wife. The natives do not care about it, and if abolished it would leave the parents free to protect their daughter if they had the courage to do so. Did you ever hear the saying of a native, 'I would rather go to war with the Governor-General than with my mother-in-law'? Very amusing, and it also contains a truth.

It would be an excellent thing if some learned Brahmin would prove out of the Vedas that the prohibition of the marriage of widows, like Suttee, did not exist in primitive times.

We must get the consent 'of my mother-in-law' before much improvement can be made.

3. I think that it is much to be lamented that we know so little of what the natives think or feel. We are acquainted with them chiefly through the Civil Service, who have inherited for more than a century the traditions of the 'conquering' race. I do not deny that the first duty of the English rulers of India is to maintain themselves. But can nothing be done to conciliate the natives without offending the Civil Service? We have never managed to adapt the one to the other. There are many things which we cannot do for the natives, and therefore they must be allowed to do for themselves. Have we ever heartily endeavoured to co-operate with them or trained them to co-operate with us? I do not mean to depreciate the Civil Servants; they are an admirable body of men, but I think also that any one placed at the head of them must keep his mind above them. The commotions which were raised among the English about the so-called Ilbert Bill show how very difficult it is to place the relations of the natives to their rulers in any degree on a better footing. The English and native tempers can never harmonize. The Englishman has no sympathy with other nations. He cannot govern without asserting his superiority. He has always a latent consciousness of the difference of colour. And hence a native would rather be under the capricious sway of one of the native princes, than under the equitable administration of a Civil Servant. And yet there have been some Englishmen who have been greatly beloved and revered by the natives of India.

I wonder whether you find the congresses troublesome or dangerous. To me it seems that a good-humoured ignoring of them is probably the right policy. 'The mother of India' is glad to hear that her subjects amuse themselves at a debating society, &c. They should be treated with the greatest courtesy and even compliment, but of course, if they go beyond their tether, they have to be stopped. I hear that —— gave great offence by some attack which wounded their self-respect. There may be some reason for not allowing government officials to attend them. But it should also be considered, that if they are excluded, the tone of the congress is lowered.

4. I suppose the question which interests native Reformers more than any other is Representation on the Governor-General's Council. I hope that this will in some form be granted them, not merely by nomination but by election. I think that this would greatly tend to gain or recover the good will of India. It would greatly increase our knowledge of the feelings of the natives and would take away the bitterness of being subject to a master. It can hardly be delayed more than a few years in the present state of English politics. And it is dangerous to delay it at all, because it supplies a basis for agitation about India in England. And is it really dangerous to grant it? The precedents of the French Revolution or of the English Reform Bill are out of place in India. While we have native princes, and a large English and native army, we shall never have universal suffrage in India. In a country which has a free press, the right of holding public meetings, hourly communication with England, English education and all the latest novelties in politics and religion, to refuse any degree of representation is the height of inconsistency. And it is impossible for us to govern India well, without a much larger infusion of the best natives. Is it too much to hope that the question will be settled in the next three years? It would be grievous to have it deferred till it was forced upon the Indian authorities by the English democracy.

The military expenditure seems to be the financial curse of India. Is it possible to reduce the expense and have the same or a greater number of troops fit for service, after the manner of the Prussians or the Swiss?

Will you occasionally take a look around at some things which are not much talked about in the English newspapers— e. g. the Native Police, and their corruption and oppression, sanitary improvement, for which the native and even the English official have not much nose, Indian agriculture and irrigation, which is the staff of life, and the protection against famine to the native? The question of the hour is, as I suppose,

Representation. English public opinion would easily lend the force to carry it.

I feel rather ashamed of having written you this letter upon a subject of which you know so much and I so little. I fear that I have presumed too much on the old relation of tutor and pupil. But I know that you will not be offended. I thank you beforehand for having read so far.

To THE SAME.

BALLIOL COLLEGE, *March* 17, 1891.

Many thanks for your most interesting letter. To me it seems that the highest aim of the Government of India is to promote a better feeling between the English and their subjects. They and we must cease to think of us and them as conquerors, and try to have a common feeling of the good of India. The native has always shown himself very appreciative of kind words and of beneficent rule, such as Lord William Bentinck's, sixty or seventy years ago. It would be a great thing to become personally acquainted with those whom the natives most respect, whether native princes, or soldiers, or sages, or prophets. If they can be made to understand the better mind of England towards India, the people would gradually understand it also. There is a wisdom beyond the traditions of the Civil Service, though these are not to be undervalued. Time presses, and the Indian Council and a Conservative Government are apt to delay. Two years have passed and you have the promise and opportunity of nearly three still before you.

To THE SAME.

BALLIOL COLLEGE, *May* 24, 1891.

I am very sorry that you have had trouble in India [1]. Before this reaches you there will probably have been a debate upon it in the House of Commons, and all that party malice can say is, in the present state of English parties, likely to have been said. It does not seem to me that much can be made of it. People will soon understand that a Durbar does not mean

[1] On March 24, 1891, Mr. J. W. Quinton, Chief Commissioner of Assam, and four others were treacherously murdered at Manipur.

a private, but a public assembly. I know that this Manipur disaster, as it is termed, will not deter you from proceeding with important reforms. It is certainly desirable that the impression should be effaced (that is true if you have only broken a pane of glass) and that India should go on to something else. Some Indian reforms can be made more safely when a Conservative Government is in office, but this may also be the impediment. Having now the experience of things and persons necessary to any successful action, it is well not to lose time, for things move slowly, and the measures which one Governor-General sees clearly to be desirable may have to be left to take their chances with another. This little contretemps—if it be one—is of no consequence. The phases of politics are like the changes of weather, and are always being forgotten.

To THE SAME.

BALLIOL COLLEGE, *July* 15, 1891.

I was very glad to see that you were going to remain in India for the whole term. The first two-and-a-half years were necessarily tentative and experimental. You have now 'better opinion, better confirmation,' and know whom to trust and what to do about the Representation Question, about the Native Princes, about Public Works, about Education, &c., and many other things, of which I only know the names. I am sure that you will not leave undone anything that is desirable and possible, and no one can have greater opportunities. If considerable changes require to be made in India, they ought to be made in the next two years, because at the end of that time we may have democracy let loose upon us, who from sympathy and from mere party motives may use India as during the last ten years they have used Ireland. We are naturally scared at the notion of Universal Suffrage for India. But might not some beginning of Representative Institutions be given which would strengthen English interests in India partly by nomination of some of the best Natives by the English Government on the Council, partly by election of the Provincial Council—so it appears to me ? The increased

N

knowledge of the feelings of the natives would be a great gain.

I hope that you do not allow yourself to overwork. I think I must have told you when you were an undergraduate, that overworking is not energy but weakness. There is nothing so important to a statesman as the condition of his nerves, especially in a hot climate.

To THE SAME.

Dec. 16, 1891.

I had a visit from —— a day or two ago. He thinks that admission to the Legislative Council will soon be carried, but not to the Governor-General's Executive Council, at present. I am sure that it would be better to give the boon at once.

You will find England very much changed in the political situation whenever you return home. It has passed out of the old political parties into a sea of some sort of which Mr. Gladstone is the old man with powers of mind and popularity apparently undiminished. In some respects I sympathize with the change; there is clearly manifested an interest in the mass of the people and their wants, which there never was before.

I cannot tell you how much I feel the great kindness of friends, who have certainly not been wanting to me in affection beyond what I could ever have expected. May I be able, if I am spared a few years, to make some return to them!

To THE SAME.

BALLIOL COLLEGE, *March* 11, 1892.

—— was paying me a visit last Sunday. We talked about the social relations of the English and the natives: he said, although admitting that this was a dangerous doctrine: 'they will never mend until the natives are more able to assert themselves and become respected.' It seems to me, though I always feel in writing to you that 'Ad nos vix tenuis famae perlabitur aura,' the difficulty of India is social rather than political, as in England; and that if the natives of India were treated with greater kindness and consideration by soldiers as well as by civilians, and that we could be regarded as their friends and not merely as their masters, the dangers of the Indian Empire would be sensibly diminished.

I was very ill indeed last October, but am now better, and hope to see you once again on your return home and to entertain you in Balliol Hall. I cannot tell you what a comfort my friends were to me in illness.

To THE SAME.

BALLIOL, *May* 8, 1892.

I am glad to see that the India Council Bill is getting through Parliament and is, I suppose, in the form in which you desire to have it. I am very glad that the measure is now to be passed. It will do something to conciliate the natives, and a great deal to make their wants better understood by us. I wish that you would some day give the English a good lecture on their ways of behaving to them.

I hope that you have your health, and that you are not overwhelmed with the fatigues of business. In another two years we shall look forward to the pleasure of seeing you at home again. May your last years be the most successful of all, and may you leave India with the feeling that nothing has been left undone, which could have been done.

(2) ON THE TRAINING OF THE INDIAN CIVIL SERVANTS [1].

To THE MARQUIS OF SALISBURY [2].

BALLIOL COLLEGE, *December* 27, 1874.

MY LORD,

Having heard that the mode of selection and training of candidates for the Indian Civil Service is again under consideration, I venture to trouble you with a few remarks on a subject in which I naturally take an interest, having been

[1] See *Life*, vol. ii. c. 5.
[2] From Blue Book [C. 1446] *Civil Service of India—The Selec-*   *tion and Training of Candidates,* &c. 1876.

one of those who were engaged in drawing up the original regulations.

The remarks which I have to offer fall under three heads:

I. The examinations for first appointments.
II. The limits of age.
III. The training of selected candidates.

I. Under this head the evil which is at present complained of by the head masters of public schools and others is chiefly that the system is too favourable to the 'crammers.' I am far from saying anything against the gentlemen who are thus described; they are admirable teachers, who make a study of the papers, and appear to possess the power of communicating a great variety of knowledge in a short time.

But still it seems undesirable that a youth should be taken away from Harrow or Rugby and sent for six months or a twelvemonth to a tutor in London. He is interrupted in his studies, and at the age of eighteen or nineteen he is exposed to a good deal of danger from the temptations of a London life, especially when not under the care of his parents. There is another objection. The masters of public schools are set against the service, and are naturally indisposed to send up their best pupils as candidates, because, besides other reasons, they gain no credit from them. They complain that the youth who knows a little of many things, which are learned at the 'crammer's,' will beat another, who is far superior to him in ability and solid attainments, but has confined his attention to a few subjects only. They remark that no such previous preparation is required in order to enable their pupils to obtain scholarships at the Universities, and hence they infer some defect in the arrangements of the examination.

I have stated their objections as far as I have been able to gather them from conversations which I have had with some of the most eminent of them. The objections appear to me to be well founded, and I think that they might be met—

1. By limiting the number of subjects which a candidate is allowed to offer to four.

This is as many as a boy at school or an undergraduate at college ordinarily studies.

2. By diminishing the number of marks allowed for English literature and history to 500, or (including English composition) giving to English subjects altogether 1,000 marks. This again would more than represent the proportion which the study of English bears to the study of other branches of knowledge at Schools and Universities. In respect to the subjects of the first examination, I would offer another suggestion, viz., that political economy and the general principles of jurisprudence should be included in them. Since the report of Lord Macaulay's Committee was framed, they have been added to the University Course both at Oxford and Cambridge, and are taught at the Scotch Universities. If it be objected that they form no part of the usual curriculum of Schools, it may be answered : Neither do the Moral Sciences, nor Sanscrit and Arabic. Admitting fully the principle on which the original report was founded, I see no reason for excluding from the first examination subjects which form a part of general education, because they are specially required of the selected candidates.

II. Respecting the age of candidates, I would argue strongly that we should have the widest limits consistent with the requirements of the Indian Service. At present the number who offer themselves is smaller than might be expected. The fears of parents, the terrors of an Indian climate, the hope of getting some employment in England, are strong deterrents. But if the age were reduced from twenty-one to eighteen or nineteen, I should expect that the number of well qualified candidates would be diminished by at least one-half. Fathers and mothers do not make up their minds 'to part with their children' at that age. The Selected Candidates would be all schoolboys, and it is much more difficult to form an estimate of their real capacity at seventeen or eighteen than at nineteen or twenty.

The comparison of Woolwich or Sandhurst is out of place here.

During the first ten years of the present system the age was fixed at twenty-two, and about two-fifths of the competing candidates were selected from Oxford and Cambridge. Since the limit of age was reduced (in 1866) to twenty-one, the number of University candidates has proportionably diminished. I am inclined to think that this is a loss which has not been compensated by the arrival of the candidates in India a few months sooner. The service has probably been deprived of some of the best men who would have offered themselves.

As the Government of India desire that the candidates should not be more than twenty-four years of age on their arrival in India, I would propose that the limits of age remain as at present (seventeen to twenty-one). But with the view (chiefly) of including as many University men as possible, I would allow candidates to compete up to twenty-two who had previously passed an examination in law, political economy, and some Indian language, such candidates being required only to undergo a year of special study. In every case they should proceed to India before attaining the age of twenty-four.

The problem is, how to attract the greatest number of highly educated and able young men. Any unnecessary restriction diminishes the number. The lowering of the age to eighteen or nineteen would probably give as many candidates as now present themselves who are below those ages, and a very few more.

III. The scheme of 1854 was defective in leaving the selected candidates too much to themselves. The Commissioners were right, I think, in proposing to abolish Haileybury, which had not the social and educational advantages of a University, and which could not supply the necessary instruction in law. They wanted to make the service as open as possible. Of the English Universities at that time no use could be made, because they were confined to members of the Church of England, and because, at least at Oxford, students would have been obliged to reside within the walls of a college at an expense which, to many of them, might have been inconvenient. At that time there was no regular training in law and political economy, such as is given now, not only in the University, but at some colleges.

The change which has been made in these respects naturally leads to a reconsideration of the subject. If the selected candidates could be brought to Oxford and Cambridge, the service would greatly gain in popularity and in prestige. It would be much more attractive both to young men and to their parents. The name of a University degree and education would counter-balance the objections to India, which are generally felt by those who have no Indian connexions. The candidates would also have the more solid advantages of society and increased knowledge of the world. Without becoming a clique they would make the acquaintance of one another. Many of them at present are rather friendless and isolated ; their college would be a home to them, to which they might look for help and support when needed. There could be no difficulty in some college tutor superintending their studies, or in their finding the requisite instruction in law, political economy, and the principal Indian languages from University teachers.

In making this proposal, I would remark :—

1. That the best colleges would be quite willing to receive them, and make arrangements for them, and would be proud to take part in training the future governors of India.

2. That the proposal involves no risk or expense, and if found to be a failure can easily be given up.

3. That there would be nothing invidious in it if a similar proposal were made to all colleges and universities which were willing—

To provide the requisite instruction in law, political economy, and oriental languages ;

To undertake the superintendence of the students and make reports of them ;

To give them a degree on passing an examination in their own subjects.

Most of the candidates would probably come to Oxford and Cambridge. A few would attach themselves to King's College or to University College, London. Their residence at some College or University might be made, not absolutely com-pulsory, but only the condition of their receiving the usual allowances.

I am aware that several objections may be made to this proposal :—

1. It will be said that clever young men having the temptation of scholarships and fellowships before them will easily be seduced into another career. I do not agree to this.

The appointments in the Indian Civil Service can compete with scholarships and fellowships, leading in most cases only to college tutorships and under-masterships of public schools. Among University men, the strongest motive for throwing up their appointments is the desire to finish their University course. But, as they are public servants, I strongly agree in thinking that they should be held to their engagement, and, in addition to refunding their allowance in case of withdrawal, be required to give a bond of £500, which they should forfeit if they failed to pass their examinations and proceed to India.

2. It will be argued, that if the greater number of them are located at Oxford and Cambridge, they cannot attend the Law Courts. But they can be taught law, and the university terms only last during about twenty-four weeks in the year, so that twenty-eight weeks would remain for attendance in London at the Courts. They might be placed under the superintendence of a professor or teacher of law, who could also direct their studies in London.

The same remark applies to the study of some Oriental languages, such as Tamil and Telugu, in which it might be impossible to give instruction at the Universities. For all such exceptional acquirements the vacations would give ample opportunity.

3. A more serious objection in the case of students whose time is short, is the length of the vacations both at Oxford and Cambridge and at the Scotch Universities. To meet this objection it might be made a condition with the colleges which receive them, that they should allow them to reside and provide for their instruction during the vacation.

4. It will be objected that as they can only reside two years, and a degree at Oxford cannot be obtained in less than about two years and eight months (in Cambridge I believe that the time is somewhat longer); and as some of them will be unacquainted with Latin and Greek, which are at present required in the first public (or previous) examination, they could not, according to the regulations which at present prevail in the University, receive a degree.

This is true, but the Secretary of State for India, if he wished, could probably make an arrangement with the University (I am.

speaking of Oxford\, that they should be admitted to a degree if they resided for two years, and passed with honours in law, political economy, and in Indian subjects.

None of these objections are serious. On the other hand, the gain of a University life to them would be very great. They would be better cared for than at present ; they would have the pleasure and advantage of mingling with their con- temporaries in every rank of life ; they would have college recollections and interests, and the opportunity of forming friends and connexions. In most of these respects, and in some others, the plan of bringing them to the University appears to be far superior to that of collecting them in a single college, which would have no *genius loci*, and to which they must be compelled to go if such an institution were called into existence. I believe that a University education would greatly help to meet an invidious objection which is sometimes made against ' Competition-Wallahs,' that they are not always ' gentlemen.' It is not in the interest of the Universities that I urge this view of the subject, but in the interest of India, which should also be considered.

Annexed is a short summary of the changes which have been suggested :—

1. That in the first examination no candidate should offer more than four subjects.

2. That the number of marks assigned to English Literature and history should be reduced to 500.

3. That law and political economy should be included in the first examination.

4. That the limits of age should remain seventeen to twenty- one ; but should be extended to twenty-two for candidates who, previously to competing, had passed in some of their special subjects.

5. That as a condition of receiving an allowance every can- didate should be required to reside at some College or University to be approved by the Secretary of State for India, or the Civil Service Commissioners.

6. That only such Colleges or Universities should be approved as offered the advantages of instruction and superintendence, and (perhaps) of a degree.

I hope that your Lordship will excuse the freedom with which I have submitted these suggestions to your better judgement. I have not spoken of them to any one in Oxford.

I remain, my Lord,

&c., &c.,

(Signed)   B. JOWETT.

(3) INDIA AND THE CIVIL SERVICE.

To C. P. ILBERT[1].

CAMPERDOWN, *Sept.* 17, 1882.

... Without rushing into every newly hatched scheme of philanthropy, there must be many things of the first importance, which any one who has the requisite knowledge and ability may accomplish. According to my notions a good deal more secrecy is required in managing the world than is generally supposed. Some things have to be done through others, and the mover should disappear. It is necessary to make everybody a friend and nobody an enemy ; above all, not to be suspected by any class of being a great Reformer who is going to upset their traditions, but to do things without being found out. There is another process, that of gaining the confidence of every important person, and at the same time picking their brains, which is one of the great arts of administration.

.   .   .   .

The whole question of the future of the East is full of interest, and is, perhaps, the greatest political question in the world. It seems to me that the Eastern must always be dependent on Western powers, on England above all, then on Russia, and possibly on some new power fixed at Constantinople. They will never have the ability to resist, and their only chance would be the assistance of one Western power against another, but France or Germany has nothing to gain by this. I do not think that India will materially progress in self-government in

---

[1] C. P. Ilbert sailed for India in April, 1882, as Legal Member of the Executive Council.

our time, but it may improve enormously in other ways. Its trade and agriculture may treble and quadruple. Its old religions like the Old Testament may remain, but added to them may be a purer morality. And slowly, as public opinion improves, laws may be passed greatly affecting the social state of the country; e. g. about marriage, which, as well as betrothal, might be forbidden before a certain age. Notwithstanding the poverty of the soil and the want of minerals, the wealth, and the revenue, and the public works may immensely increase. Instead of saying that by great efforts we may just keep things from getting worse, I believe that within a century there are the makings of a new India. It is true that the character is persistent, but even this may be greatly changed, in some degree by education, and much more by material causes. We may get rid of famines by a system of insurance against them, such as the famine commission recommends. . . . It seems to me that in the East generally, whether Turkey or India, there ought to be a good deal of Western supervision of Eastern officials, the one supplying honesty and justice, the other knowledge of the natives and aptitude for dealing with men.

To THE MARQUIS OF SALISBURY [1].

BALLIOL COLLEGE, *July* 17, 1882.

MY LORD,

I venture to lay before you once more my reasons for thinking that a change is required in some of the regulations relating to the age and training of the Indian candidates. My excuse for troubling you is that the subject is naturally brought before me by the circumstance that more than half of them during the last three years have been members of Balliol College, and nearly two-thirds of them have resided at Oxford.

The change in the age of the candidates which was made a few years since had two or three principal objects :—

1. It was hoped that the best boys from the public schools would be attracted to the service. This hope has not been realized. The number of candidates has fallen to less than one-half; and the candidates under the new system are

---

[1] See *Life*, vol. ii. p. 348 ff.

decidedly inferior in quality to those who were elected under the old.

2. It was also thought that youths would be chosen direct from school, and would thus be saved from the temptations of a life in London with private tutors. This aim also has not been fulfilled. For a proportion of the candidates larger than was formerly the case receive a part of their preparation in London, and are exposed to temptation at an age when they are less able to take care of themselves (i.e. between seventeen and nineteen instead of between nineteen and twenty-one).

3. It was a third object to enable the Indian Civil Service candidates to obtain a degree at the University, a privilege which appears to be much valued by them. But the University of Oxford (at least) has definitely refused to grant this privilege to the Indian students unless like other students they reside for three years, a condition which places the degree out of the reach of most of them.

The failure to obtain these objects would seem to make it right that the whole subject should be again considered. Other considerations which appear to me even more important are the following:—

I. The candidates are too young and immature. They are often overworked by the first examination, when they are set to prepare themselves for the second. Their minds are tired and need rest, when they suddenly find that they are called upon to learn new subjects of great difficulty such as Sanscrit, Law, Political Economy. They are not strong enough for the task. There is also a great difference between a young man of twenty or twenty-one and one of twenty-two or twenty-three in good sense, good manners, knowledge of the world, conduct of life, as well as acquirements, and in their powers of learning. The difference is especially seen in the management of business and in the capacity for dealing with persons. A young man is sent to India under the present system at twenty or twenty-one or sometimes even earlier, yet he would never think of commencing practice in a profession in England at that age. He is not less but more likely to adapt himself to the country when he has seen something of society and of the world at home.

II. The preparation for the Indian Service is at present very imperfect. Too many subjects are crowded into a short time, and it is difficult to lay a solid foundation in any of them. There are also other subjects of which it is desirable that the Indian candidates should have some elementary knowledge (such as Agriculture and Engineering of roads or waterworks), which will enable them to use the experience gained on the spot. They are not going to be farmers or engineers, but they will often have to judge of agriculture, irrigation and the like. It would be a great misfortune in England if landlords knew nothing of such matters; it is probably even a greater misfortune to India that the Civil Servants should be wholly ignorant of them.

III. The greater number of the Indian candidates now come to the University. It is very desirable that they should amalgamate, as far as the difference of pursuits allows, with the other students, that they should receive the impress of the place, and that they should reside a sufficient length of time to take a degree. But the present period of two years' probation is too short for the attainment of these objects. I believe that nearly all of them would desire to remain three years, if such a length of residence did not interfere with their professional prospects in India. They come from nearly every rank in society, and such a residence would greatly tend to improve them socially and to unite them among themselves.

In order to carry out these views may I venture to submit the following proposals to your better judgement?

1. That the limits of age should be from eighteen to twenty. The average age of the candidates would then be about nineteen, the average age at which Undergraduates come up to the University. They would still be in most cases elected from School.

2. That the time of probation for all of them be extended to three years. The term of a University course at Oxford (though not necessarily longer than three years) is found in practice to extend to four years. The Indian candidates would therefore complete their preparation for India about a year sooner than their fellow-students at Oxford ordinarily begin their professional studies. The same payment which is now made to them for two years might be spread over three years.

If the time were lengthened, the training in some additional subjects might then be possible, and I think that the University would not be unwilling to undertake both the teaching of these and the examination in them.

In conclusion, let me draw your lordship's attention to two points which seem to prove that a change is imperatively required, and should be made without delay.

1. The number of candidates at the open competition has fallen from 350 to 147. The greater number of these are not of the class who obtain scholarships at Oxford and Cambridge, yet it must be remembered that they are chosen for their literary attainments.

2. The professors and tutors who are brought into relation with the Indian candidates are unanimous (as far as I know) in saying that they are too young and immature: inferior to the candidates elected under the old system. This is the complaint of Dr. Markby, the Reader in Indian Law, of Professor Nicholl, of Mr. Toynbee, the tutor of the Indian students at Balliol, of Mr. Platts, the teacher of Persian (an eminent scholar), and of many others. To which I may add the testimony of Mr. Wren, who has had greater experience of both systems than any one else, and who is in every way entitled to attention.

The great error or defect seems to me to be the youth of the candidates. No advantages to be gained at the University or anywhere else can compensate for this. If they are selected after a literary competition and required to study after the selection has been made, the age should be somewhat later and the time allowed for study longer.

The character of the future Civil Service of India depends on the rigid selection and training of the candidates. If we wait for the results of Indian experience the mischief will have been done. I venture therefore to ask your Lordship once more to consider this question for the reasons which I have given.

I remain, &c.,
(Signed)   B. Jowett.

To Sir M. E. Grant-Duff, Governor of Madras.

March 25, 1883.

I write to thank you for your letter and also for your kindness to my young friend ——. I hope that he shows himself deserving of your help.

.   .   .   .   .

I should like to know what you think of the Indian Students. It was supposed that they would be more manageable if they went out young. But to me it seems that their youth is a very great misfortune ; they are too weak, inexperienced, unformed. Why any one should suppose that a young man of twenty-one is superior to a young man of twenty-three is to me quite unintelligible. Certainly, as a fact, they are not equal to the candidates when the age was late, and this, as far as I know, is the opinion of all their teachers.

I had a conversation with Sir James Caird about India the other day. He was desponding : population increasing five per cent. per annum, land decreasing in fertility and incapable of improvement, because there was no capital which could be laid out on it. He had two remedies : one, which he himself acknowledged hardly practicable, a great colonization of Queensland ; the other the establishment of land Banks to lend capital to the cultivator at reasonable rates of interest.

We shall be glad to welcome you to England again. You must come and see me at Balliol, if I am living.

.   .   .   .   .   .

A very intelligent Armenian has been talking to me of the subject races in Turkey. Their condition seems very hopeless —two-and-a-half millions of Armenians, eighteen millions of Turks, the Armenians fearing the Russians and hating the Greeks almost more than they fear and hate the Turks. I asked him if there were any good Turks : he said, ' Yes, sometimes whole villages far superior to Christians, who practise virtue and are wonderfully hospitable to strangers.' Christians want equality, but it is difficult to see how they can have it unarmed against four times as many armed Turks. I wish I could meet with some one who would speak hopefully to me of the East.

You have been absent from England at a time when it was fortunate to be out of politics. It seemed to me that the Ministry was a good deal shaken at the time of the assassination of Lord F. Cavendish. The War and their better management of Irish crime has restored them, and there is for the present nothing to resist them. The great blot on the Ministry has been the undetected crime in Ireland, which for a time it was affirmed to be impossible to detect. The country was getting demoralized by the notion that 'practical politics' meant dynamite. Now the tide is turned : but for more than a year it was seriously maintained that nothing could be done—that we must go from bad to worse. Lord Spencer and Trevelyan deserve the greatest credit : and though the Tories say with truth, 'Why was not this done sooner ? ' the country will not allow them to rake up an error which has been in a great measure [the result of their neglect ?].

To C. P. Ilbert.

WOBURN ABBEY, *November* 14, 1883.

I take the opportunity of a holiday at Woburn to answer your letter : I am sorry that I have not done so sooner.

The present regulations for the admission of Indian civilians appear to me faulty in principle, because on the average a young man of twenty or twenty-one years of age is very inferior to men of twenty-two or twenty-three years of age. He is less mature, that is to say, he knows less, and is less formed in manner, he has less experience and less force of character, and less strength of body. I am confident of this, which is really the main point, from long acquaintance not only with Indian probationers, but with young men generally. The Civil Service Commission are, I believe, agreed on this view of the question : and have urged it from time to time on the Secretary of State for India.

I have been told that the real objection to raising the age is the facility which would be afforded to natives of India. I think it very likely that increased numbers of natives will find their way into the Service through the open competition (owing to the greater ease of travelling and opportunities of education in India), but I should doubt whether more will come if the examination is thrown open to older candidates. The native is probably more on a level with the European at eighteen or nineteen than at any later age, and therefore better able to compete with him.

I am not certain whether you are likely to obtain the best kind of native through the competition. I have no means of judging. The three native civilians who have been at Oxford are very good specimens. But it may be worth considering whether it would not be better to have a competition of native candidates in India, who should be nominated as at the Foreign Office, for their character and position. The native civilians thus elected would be partly, but not wholly, students of Universities. A certain number of places might be reserved for them, say one-sixth of the whole number. They might be also required to have a time of study and probation in Europe.

There are two ways in which the present system might be altered for the English candidates. Either (1) the age might be retained (or raised again) and three years' residence required at the two Universities or at some other place of teaching. This plan has the advantage of enabling the candidates to take a University degree (which they seem greatly to value), or to be called to the Bar, or both. It would also allow time for more satisfactory study of law, languages, and other subjects, such as agriculture or forestry, which it might be desirable to introduce into their course.

(I do not think that it would be worth while to send the candidates to Oxford for a year only.)

(2) The other plan would be to extend the age to twenty-one or twenty-two, and retain the two years' probation. Twenty-two was the age originally fixed for admission, afterwards, I believe in consequence of representations from India, reduced to twenty-one. But I do not think that the representations made from India rested on a good ground, because at that time there was no adequate provision made for the training of the probationers. A majority of them in those days were University men.

The Civil Service Commissioners are in favour of the first

P

plan—I mean Walrond, who has several times urged it on me. It is certainly the easier to carry out. I do not think that more of the candidates come from Public Schools than formerly: some persons in humble circumstances still find their way into the Service; one whom I have known at Balliol during the last three years was the son of a carpenter, another of a milliner. The lower age is unfavourable to students of Scotch Universities, and their exclusion is certainly not an advantage. But upon the whole I believe Walrond to be right. I am confident that what I am saying represents his views as expressed to me in conversation, but it would be better to elicit them more directly.

The average age at which a degree is taken at Oxford is about twenty-two-and-a-half. But there would be no difficulty in making the curriculum of the Indian students enter into the University course, as political economy, law, and the Indian classical languages are already included in the final examination. We are likely to make a further change in Responsions and Moderations, which will admit natives to a degree with a classical Oriental language substituted for either Greek or Latin. But this change would not affect Indian civilians. There are several natives now at Oxford, and they seem to derive considerable benefit from their residence there. I am of opinion that it would be a good thing both for Oxford and India, to assist them in coming to England for education by Scholarships and Exhibitions, a practice which prevails to a considerable extent in the Colonies. I quite agree in the desirableness of teaching the Indian probationers Revenue, Law and Agriculture. The difficulty about the first is that there is no text-book, and the subject, as I am informed, could only be got up out of Blue Books. But it would not be impossible to find a competent lecturer. That would mean money, and in providing a Readership in Indian Law, a teacher of Hindustani, of Persian, of Tamil and Telugu and of Indian Geography, the University has spent as much as it can afford. Would the India Office be willing to supply the necessary payment ?

With respect to Agriculture, the Indian civilian ought to have a knowledge of land, similar to that which an intelligent country gentleman has.

If possible, he should be something both of a civil engineer and of a land agent (I am speaking chiefly of those who become collectors). The best way of giving them this knowledge would be through lectures. I believe Brandis, the late Director of Forestry, would be willing to give lectures on one part of the subject. If three years were allowed for the course, it might be possible to send the candidates to Cirencester or Salisbury for a few months. This might be too great an interference with their other work : I should rather trust to a good lecturer creating an interest in the subject. We might begin by allowing some knowledge of Indian agriculture to be included with the geography of India, and offered as a voluntary part of the examination. I very much approve of getting eminent persons who have Indian experience to lecture at Oxford, and shall endeavour with Markby's help to get this idea carried out during the next two years. We made a faint, but not unsuccessful, beginning with Sir G. Campbell two years ago. It is a good thing to bring the young men into contact with Indian experience. There are at present fifty-four Indian probationers at Oxford, and we have a joint committee.

I believe that I have answered your questions. Excuse the somewhat unconnected style in which this letter is written.

To the Same.

July 21, 1884.

I think as I have always thought about the candidates for the Indian Civil Service, and can only express myself in the same way.

I have nothing to say against them personally. Some of them are excellent. But they are too young and immature. They have two years less strength of body and mind, less stamina, less moral character, less knowledge of the world, less power of standing alone than they ought to have. They are boys when they should be men. No one would thrust youths of twenty into the medical or legal professions. Why should they be thought better qualified for the responsible duties of the Indian Civil Service?

There are other ways in which the early age tends to

deteriorate the Service. The competition for the first examination is a greater strain upon the candidates; the parents are less willing to part with their sons than they would be a year or two later; and the youths themselves are less able to judge what they would like or what they are fitted for in life.

To meet these evils I should recommend either (1) that the age for the first competition be raised to twenty-two, which was the age originally fixed, and that there should be added the special training of two years at some College or University, which was forgotten or omitted in the original scheme. The effect of such regulations would be to bring some of the candidates to India as late as twenty-four, but the average at twenty-two or twenty-three.

Or (2) to raise the age for the first competition to twenty; and add a probation or training of three years at some College or University, i. e. practically at Oxford or Cambridge. This plan compared with the former has the advantage of enabling all the candidates to take a degree, which they seem greatly to value; and it has the disadvantage of a lower age for the first competition. Whichever plan is chosen I would allow no candidate to try under eighteen.

Either proposal would work well I think. The main point, which is the *sine qua non* in my opinion, in my judgement is gained. The candidate would be sent out to India later, i. e. at twenty-two, twenty-three, twenty-four, instead of twenty, twenty-one, twenty-two.

The change which is proposed by the India Council is an improvement upon the present system, because it enables the candidates if they please to take a degree, and gives an opportunity for a more complete training. But it is expensive and not satisfactory.

1. It bribes a certain number of the candidates to go out to India at the later age, if they think it for their interest. But a great many immature youths of twenty and twenty-one would still make their appearance.

2. It leaves the age for the first competition as at present. If it were raised to twenty the competitors would be on the average of the same age at which young men come up to the University, and there would be more of them. I think

also that the examination itself would be less exhausting, especially if the provision suggested above were added, that no candidate should be allowed to try under eighteen.

To A. GODLEY[1].

BALLIOL, *March* 14, 1889.

Hearing that the Public Service Commission have reported in favour of raising the age of admission to the Indian Civil Service, and that the Government of India agree in the opinion expressed by them, I venture to trouble you with a few remarks on the subject.

Those of us in Oxford who have had to do with the Indian students are generally of the same opinion. We think that they are too young, too unformed, too deficient in moral and intellectual strength, and have too little experience of the world to be equal to the duties which will fall to them soon after their arrival in India. There is no time of life in which two or three years makes so great a difference as between the ages of eighteen and twenty-four. The extreme youth of some of the candidates, and the youthfulness of all of them, seems to us the blot on the present system, which in most respects has worked well.

We think that if an alteration is made (1) a term of probation to be passed in preparatory studies should still be required of them in England. (2) They should be encouraged to pass their probation at some University. This would be a great advantage to them, especially to those among them who through circumstances have not had much opportunity of social intercourse. (3) That the candidates should be selected from an area, at least equally large, or if possible larger than at present. There is a danger that if they were taken only or chiefly from Universities, we should lose the schools. It would be better to retain both.

May I ask you to consider a plan which would, I think, carry out these principles and meet some objections. The proposal is :—

That the candidates should be divided into two classes, one

[1] Now Sir A. Godley, Permanent Under-Secretary for India.

limited to the ages of seventeen to nineteen, the other to the ages of nineteen to twenty-one, at the beginning of the year in which the examination is held.

They should all be examined together at the same examination.

The first class should have a probation of three years to be spent in study and preparation at some University or College, which provides instruction in their special subjects. The whole term of their stay in England after the first examination would be about three years and a quarter. The second class, who would mostly be University men, should have a probation of two years only, to be passed in a similar manner (in all two years and a quarter).

The first class (from seventeen to nineteen) should be examined as at present, in the ordinary subjects of a liberal education. From the second class (those for whom the age is extended) some portion of their special work, such as Law, Political Economy, a Classical Oriental Language, Indian History, or some out of these, should be required as a preliminary to the rest of the examination. The marks thus obtained to be added up with the marks assigned to them for the rest of their work and to be included in the total. There would be no more difficulty in combining the special and general examination than in similarly combining the different subjects of the general examination.

All candidates would go out to India not later than at twenty-four years of age.

The objects aimed at in the proposed plan are briefly the following :—(1) to raise the age of the candidates to about twenty-four, in accordance with the recommendation of the Commission and the Government of India. (2) To extend, rather than diminish, the area of selection so as to include University men, as in the English Civil Service, without excluding youths from school. (3) To give to all candidates the social and other advantages of a University education, and to nearly all of them the possibility of taking a University degree.

It may be argued in favour of the proposal that no vested interests are much disturbed by it either of private teachers, of schools, or of Universities. It might therefore be carried out at once.

It may be further remarked that candidates would be less likely to be taken away from school and brought up to London and sent to other teachers, in order to receive special preparation for the examination.

The proposed alteration would not make any material difference in the cost of the candidates to the Government.

I am requested by Sir William Markby to state that he agrees with the above proposals.

To Lord Cross [1].

My Lord,

Mr. Walpole's letter of June 11 in reply to that sent by us on April 8 last, whilst inviting an expression of our views upon the subject of Probation of Selected Candidates for the Indian Civil Service, suggests that until the question of the limit of age for competition has been settled by your Lordship the question of probation cannot be satisfactorily dealt with.

There is no doubt an inconvenience in discussing the question of probation independently of the question of age, but as we do not understand that your Lordship intends to deal with the two questions otherwise than simultaneously, it appears to be necessary, if we are to lay before your Lordship our views upon either subject at all, that we should do so now, and we think it will be found that most of what we have to say applies to candidates of any age.

It is desirable in the first place to point out that the period spent by selected candidates in England prior to their departure for India, and which is usually called the period of probation, has in reality two aspects—that of probation (properly so called) and that of preparation.

As a period of probation (properly so called) it enables your Lordship to ascertain much more accurately than can be done without probation, whether the selected candidate is physically, morally, and intellectually capable of performing his duties in India.

---

[1] Secretary of State for India.

The Examinations of the Civil Service Commissioners subsequent to Selection and the Riding Examinations are by no means very strict ; we are not sure that they might not be made somewhat stricter with advantage. Still, according to our experience, they have been most useful in weeding out of the Service men who would be unlikely to do good work in India. The men so got rid of, easily, and without expense, would have been far more difficult to deal with if they had finally entered the Service and received appointments in India.

Important as this consideration appears to us to be, the period spent in England possesses still more importance as a period of preparation. We assume that at whatever age men may be selected for service in India, they cannot perform efficiently any duties until they have learnt something of the laws and languages of the people of that country. And the question which we suppose will have to be considered is not whether there is to be any preparation at all, but whether the necessary period of preparation can be better spent at home or in India.

We do not presume to offer any final opinion upon this very important question. But we desire to lay before your Lordship certain considerations which we hope will assist your Lordship in comparing the advantages of the two methods of preparation.

We have before us a Manual of the Rules and Regulations applicable to the Members of the Covenanted Civil Service of India, which contains the Rules relating to the Departmental Examination of Officers by the Lower and Higher Standards. We conclude that these rules indicate the course of study which an officer specially preparing himself for the performance of his duties in India should pursue, and we see no difficulty whatever in a system of education being established here which would enable him to pursue this course of study with advantage. There will, of course, always be some languages spoken in India which it will not be possible to study in England, but the more widely spoken vernaculars are already taught in this country, and it would not be difficult to teach others. All the other subjects, namely, Civil and Criminal Law, Revenue, Police Regulations, Surveying and Bookkeeping, appear to us to be undoubtedly capable of being studied in England.

Moreover, not only can these subjects be studied in England, but it seems to us to be very doubtful whether in any proper sense of the word they can be studied in India, unless it be by men of exceptional leisure and exceptional ability. We do not understand it to be intended that there shall be any institutions in India for imparting systematic instruction in any of the subjects which an officer is required to learn. Each person will have to get up the subjects as best he can with the casual assistance of any chance teacher that may happen to fall in his way. Now we are clearly of opinion that, as regards all the subjects required, systematic teaching of some kind is highly necessary. The knowledge of the vernacular languages which is required is not a bare acquaintance with the spoken tongue, but such a firm grasp of them as can only be obtained by a contemporaneous study of the Classical languages such as these rules seek to encourage. Knowledge of this kind cannot be picked up anywhere. All that can be picked up without systematic teaching is the barest and most illiterate acquaintance with the language of the people with whom the learner happens to mix.

Still less is it possible to acquire without systematic instruction a knowledge of the principles which underlie the various codes of law in which an officer has to be examined. Without some explanation from a competent teacher he might learn by heart the words of the law, but he would be sure to misunderstand them, and therefore, in practice, to misapply them.

The same observations apply to the study of the revenue and land laws of India. An officer who had simply learnt by heart the actual rules in force in his own province, knowing nothing of their previous history and the economical and social principles which they involve, would be unable to cope with any but the very simplest problems of administration.

There are also subjects not mentioned in these rules of which Indian Civil Servants ought not to be entirely ignorant, but which cannot be learnt in India—such, for example, as Indian History, Political Economy, and Agriculture.

No doubt the special knowledge required for an Indian Civil Servant cannot be obtained except at a considerable cost. This must be so, whether the period of preparation be spent in India

Q

or in England. But inasmuch as a probationer receives in England less than half of the lowest pay which an officer receives in India, and inasmuch as there is a readiness on the part of some of the Universities to provide at their own cost a considerable part of the education required, there can hardly be any doubt that the expenses incurred for preparation in India would far exceed those incurred in England for a similar period.

There is another aspect of this question which we also venture to think deserves your Lordship's serious attention. Whatever be the age determined on, there cannot be any doubt that some at least of the successful candidates will be men with little or no knowledge of the world, with no knowledge of their fellow-civilians, and (from want of experience) with hardly that courtesy of manner which is so often insisted on as essentially necessary in dealing with natives of India. These are just the defects which are likely to be removed by residence in a University, where a considerable number of selected candidates associate with each other and with other young men of their own age.

It has been suggested that a single year instead of two years might be spent in England by the selected candidates on probation. A similar plan seems to have been under discussion in 1876. We gather from a minute of Sir Henry Maine that he was then of opinion that the older Universities would at that time have declined to receive the candidates for so short a period. We are of opinion that they would be equally unwilling to do so now. The large expense necessary for keeping up the required staff could not be justified if the period spent in the University were so short. There are many general considerations which seem to us to lead to the conclusion that the education of Indian Civil Servants ought to be completed here. It does not appear to us that the circumstances in which a young civilian finds himself placed on his arrival in India are either conducive to study or such as are likely to make study fruitful. The climate is, we should suppose, not altogether favourable for the purpose. It cannot be interesting to these young men to have to study alone, without even a companion ; and it must be very disheartening to them to have to work without assistance. It must also be disappointing to a man who is nominated to an office to which active duties are attached, to find himself, instead of performing those duties, still preparing for an examination to test his fitness.

We do not desire to discuss the question of age, but we may observe that if the maximum limit of age be fixed at twenty-two, the average age of successful candidates at the open competition would be twenty-one. If two years were allowed for probation they would be ready to go out to India at twenty-three—the age at which most Undergraduates take their degree.

Lastly, we would draw your Lordship's attention to the fact that a system of education has been established in this University expressly to meet the requirements of Indian Civil Service Probationers. This system has been built up at great expense and no little sacrifice of time and labour by many persons with the sole object of enabling these young men to fulfil efficiently the duties required of them. Teachers have been appointed and are still holding office who have devoted many years of their lives to their work here, and for this purpose they have abandoned other avocations. It will be a great hardship upon these teachers if they are now all to be dismissed, and it will be a great disappointment to the University if the arrangements which they have so carefully made are all to be broken up.

We have, &c.,

(Signed) JAMES BELLAMY, Vice-Chancellor.

H. G. LIDDELL, Dean of Christ Church.

B. JOWETT, Master of Balliol College.

FROM A. GODLEY TO THE MASTER OF BALLIOL.

INDIA OFFICE, *February* 11, 1890.

REVEREND SIR,

I am directed by the Secretary of State for India in Council to inform you that the letter which you addressed to me on December 29 last, on the subject of the probation to be undergone by candidates for the Indian Civil Service, has been laid before the Secretary of State in Council, and has been carefully considered by his Lordship.

You are aware that on September 12 Viscount Cross addressed to the Viceroy a despatch, in which he intimated to His Excellency his decision that candidates should, under the new system, be allowed to spend only a little more than a year in this country after their selection.

That decision has now been very carefully reviewed; but his Lordship in Council has arrived finally at the conclusion that it must be maintained, as it appears to him that the disadvantages of allowing candidates to arrive in India at the maximum age of twenty-five-and-two-thirds would more than counterbalance any advantages which might be gained by extending the period of probation.

I am directed to express to you his Lordship's great regret at finding himself unable to adopt the course which you recommend. The Secretary of State in Council has already acknowledged the debt which he owes to the Universities of Oxford and Cambridge on account of the trouble and expense which they have incurred for the benefit of the probationers, and he fully appreciates the important part which your College has taken from the first in training and preparing these students for their Indian career. It is, therefore, with much reluctance that he has arrived at a decision which, he fears, must interfere with many of the arrangements which the Universities and Colleges have been good enough to make for this purpose; but he is satisfied that the curtailment of the period of probation is an inevitable consequence of the recent change in the limits of age.

I am, &c.,
(Signed)   A. GODLEY.

To A. GODLEY.

BALLIOL COLLEGE, OXFORD,
February 14, 1890.

I write to acknowledge your letter, and will ask you to express to the Secretary of State my sincere gratitude for the kind and courteous manner in which he has spoken of the University of Oxford and of this College in particular.

May I be allowed to say that I view his decision with regret, and not without apprehension for the future of the Indian Civil

Service? The change will probably put an end to the staff of teachers which have been maintained for many years at the expense of the two Universities. But what is more important is that it will be a serious blow to Oriental studies in Oxford, and we fear that the Oriental School will have to be given up.

I will not repeat the reasons which lead me to think that the two years' training of the probationers in England is very important to the efficiency of the Service.

But may I be permitted shortly to suggest a mode of carrying out the decision of the Secretary of State and his Council which would, I think, minimize the evil?

The plan will be as follows :—

(1) To require of all probationers that they should have arrived in India before they have attained the age of twenty-four-and-a-half years ;

(2) that before going to India they should reside in this country for a year at some place of education where they could receive instruction in their special or necessary subjects ;

(3) that there should be a Pass Examination in those special or necessary subjects ;

(4) that there should also be a higher examination, including a wider range of Indian subjects, in which those who desired might compete with one another for seniority in the Service, as at present.

The plan suggested would have the advantage of maintaining the standard of Indian knowledge in the Service. It would also encourage them to offer in the First Competitive Examination subjects specially adapted to their profession, such as Sanscrit, Law, Political Economy ; and these can also be offered in the Schools at Oxford. It would thus be possible to preserve Oriental studies at the Universities. The greater number of the candidates, though only a year's probation is required of them, having been elected at twenty-one or twenty-two, would have time for a more liberal study of Indian subjects ; and even those who are restricted by the limit of twenty-four-and-a-half years would begin their Indian work as a part of their preparation for the First Competition.

I may observe that the principle of throwing open the Service to all persons who have received a liberal education, laid down by Lord Macaulay's Commission and generally approved, is not at all infringed by this proposal. The Examination would still be open to all persons who may be thus described, though to some of the candidates an option would be given of offering subjects which are likely to be useful to them in their profession, as is done already. And, indeed, the two classes of subjects do not admit of being accurately distinguished.

The alteration or addition is a slight one, though not slight in its effects. It is no more than this:—Instead of requiring all candidates to go to India at the end of their year of probation, to require them to arrive in India not later than the age of twenty-four-and-a-half.

Excuse my troubling you once more on this subject.

V. MISCELLANEOUS

To B. C. Brodie.

Teignmouth, *Oct.* 15, [1844].

I heard a day or two since that the Moral Philosophy Professorship was vacant. Stanley and Temple, who wrote to mention it, urged me very strongly to become a candidate. I said that there was no chance of success, and that I was unfit, &c., but that if Donkin and Clough wished it also, I would not object. It appears that they approve, so that my name has been sent in [1]. Εὖ γὰρ εἴη [2].

I promised to advertise you for Vaughan [3], and heartily wish that he may succeed. If he comes forward and is not supposed to be excluded by his former rejections, I shall certainly withdraw, not liking the appearance of measuring myself against him. The other candidates are Wilson of Corpus, Eden, and one who must be nameless for the present. If Vaughan wishes to be a candidate he should send in his name immediately, as they are about to fill it up.

My chance of success is so small that I may be considered a disinterested person, and therefore I will venture to suggest to you one thing about Vaughan. I once asked you an unfair question about him, 'what his religious opinions were,' and forget the answer, but remember the impression. I never mentioned it to any one, even to Stanley, but find that other persons are aware of it, as indeed it must be impossible for any thoughtful man, however cautious, to conceal his religious opinions, if he talks with others on serious subjects. I do believe myself, without undervaluing the particular truths of

---

[1] The chair was given to H. G. Liddell, afterwards Dean of Christ Church. See *Life*, vol. i. p. 92.

[2] 'May it be for good!'

[3] Henry Halford Vaughan. See *Life*, vol. i. pp. 97, 123.

Christianity, that there is a common ground of conscientious-
ness, without which no set of men can work together, but in
which other differences might exist suspended while each fulfilled the different parts and sides of their whole duty.   But
I doubt whether Oxford is exactly the place to try the experiment—suspicion is too rife and charity too weak, and the
chasm in general too wide to be filled up, and then come the
difficulties of subscription, which it is hard to say is absolutely
unmeaning.

I only mention this to you as a matter worth thinking of—
not as absolutely excluding Vaughan.   I have no doubt that an
honest and truthful mind, like his, although I could not agree
with his views about religion, would do more real good than
those whose highest ambition is to throw up a new dyke in
defence of Church and State.   I should be glad that such
influence should work upon Oxford, but in Oxford I do not
think that his views upon any subject would be fairly received
on account of a general prejudice against his tenets about
religion.   I may be mistaken about what these views are, but
it would be surely painful to him to find not merely that he
was at open war with the 'malignants,' but that such men as
Stanley and Liddell thought it right to stand apart from him,
which might possibly be the case.

These matters are for him to consider, if you think it worth
while to suggest them to him.   For my own part personally
I would much sooner hear him than teach myself.   Stanley
assured me that he was not standing, and if there is the
slightest probability of my interfering with his success I will
give it up.   I am induced to stand because others urge it, and
because I feel it would suit me better than any other chair,
however imperfectly I may be able to perform its duties.

To A. P. Stanley.

Bonn, *Jan.* 1, 1849.

... I hope you will write to me. Nothing will give me greater
pleasure than to hear from you.   I am working at the constitution of the University, dragging [through] Huber, which is but
a bad book.   He seems to fancy that he has a true notion of

English Society, because, as a foreigner, he has gone out of his way to learn some of the worst English prejudices respecting it.

Shall I name one or two things which have struck me about your part of the book [1]? They are sufficiently obvious, and will no doubt have struck yourself. I desire that Hussey, *et hoc genus omne*, should have no pretence for saying that we wish to make the Universities a mere professorial system. We must express, I think, as strongly as possible, our sense that education at the Universities does not consist in the mere teaching or learning, but in a thousand undefined things—associations, place, amusement, &c.—in what makes England to differ from the rest of the world. The Universities are not a system of education, but a life—a particular sphere of English life, which we want to raise by introducing a popular and intellectual element. This is all very obvious and not new, but I feel that in writing there is much difficulty to avoid becoming one-sided when a particular part of the work is entrusted to one. We should guard also against the notion that we want to make the Universities what F. Newman calls 'transcripts of our own minds.' I want also to have the objection answered, 'Why do not the present Professors, Hussey, Ogilvie, &c. succeed?' For the more out-of-the-way branches of knowledge some provision should be made, I think, to train up a school by means of scholarships, &c. A sufficient number of scholarships might be infallibly made to create a School of Physical Science, considering how much ability of this sort is scattered about, which only needs to be drawn to Oxford as its centre. Also will you touch upon the fallacy of confounding Physical Science as an instrument of education with its after study? Also a strong τόπος in your part of the book should be, I think, that the basis of all moral influence is good teaching, in short, an attack upon 'chappies' as out of place in a University.

I desire chiefly to see the thing well knit together, so as to explain clearly that neither Reform of the Constitution nor opening of the Fellowships, nor a body of Professors, but all together, combining energy, good sense, and experience, are the means by which we propose to raise Oxford to a different level.

You have had enough of this prose. I ought to have some-

---

[1] The projected work on University Reform. See above, p. 43.

B

thing else to write to you about. When I was in London I went to hear your friend Mr. Brookfield preach (where I thought I saw your mother—'if, indeed, it was your mother, which I doubt,' for she vanished into thin air as I went to speak to her coming out). It was very good: he preaches like an apostle. Temple told me that he represents the ecclesiastical section of that distinguished body[1]. In the afternoon I was seduced by the love of music into again hearing the worst of English theologians, the Rev. Dr. Thomson, 'und, Ach meiner!' I will not go again to hear the finest English anthem. The 'poor beast' was cruelly handled by the way. But what offended me most was the assumption that the Book of Revelation could not be understood unless we agreed that St. John wrote it as the end of the Canon of Scripture:—this lie, which he picked up out of writers of the fourth century, and says 'has been providentially preserved to us.' In thinking of all the possibilities of lying and believing lies that there [are] in Theology, one almost wonders that any truth should remain. And any lie on one side of the question would be more gratefully received even by good and so-called impartial men, as for example even our friend Jacobson[2], I fear, than many truths on the other.

The boy Cruickshank is with me here[3]. Except for a kind of self-conceit, he is a very good boy. At present he is so thoroughly satisfied with the side of the question into which he has argued himself that there is no prospect of his being argued out of it. You might as well endeavour to make Jacobson tell you what he thought of the Athanasian Creed as make him tell you why he has become a Roman Catholic.

I have read Macaulay's *History* with the greatest delight. The best history, I think, that has been written since Gibbon ; rather wanting, perhaps, in philosophical power, but abundantly making up for this in freshness and vivid descriptions of places and characters. It is, moreover, a well, regularly written book, without the dullness of Hallam or the grotesqueness of Carlyle.

And so the year is gone—upon the whole a happy year to me as, I hope, it has been to you, notwithstanding the molesta-

---

[1] The Cambridge 'Apostles.' See Tennyson's *Life*, vol. i. pp. 42 f., 85.

[2] Regius Professor of Divinity.

[3] See *Life*, vol. i. p. 21.

tion and solicitation of Professorships. If you had had a Professorship I do not think you could have been more useful
than you are. As to *position*, unless one wanted to marry,
I see nothing more desirable than that of a College Tutor.

To THE SAME.

BORROWDALE, 1849.
[*July* or *Aug.*]

'Der Ewige Jude,' Dr. Wolff[1] has been here. Last Sunday
I went to hear him preach. He is not fit to be at large.
I wish the Lunacy Commissioners would sit upon some of
the clergy. He and W. Palmer[2] might be first tried. (The
latter hero is up in Scotland and about to appear at the Synod
of our dear friend Argyle and the Isles, who, notwithstanding
he is fortified by certain hints we wrote down on a card for
him, will, I fear, be torn in pieces with all his flock by this
ravening wolf.) To return to Dr. Wolff:—I doubt not you
have seen him, and therefore I need not describe the vast,
shaggy monster. He began his sermon as follows :—' Friends,
I may as well tell you at once what I am going to preach
about—the restoration of the Jews to their native land.'
Then a pause. 'Now for an objection or two.' Another
pause. 'Not only common people but very sensible people
come and ask me, What do the Bishops say to it?' This
objection, which must be confessed to have some weight, he
answered by a long story of an argument with the Bishop
of Ripon[3], whom he completely floored by the assistance of
Bishop Bootler, notwithstanding the aforesaid Bishop had read
Bootler six times through and not discovered the passage.
This objection, which was put in the forefront of the battle,
being disposed of, he proceeded to other minor ones, such as
the fact that the doctrine in question was not held by the
Primitive Church, which he denied, affirming that it was so
held by Irenaeus, *Melancthon*, Tertullian, and others. I have
not room to tell you all the nonsense he said. It was a curious
scene to see the country people, with whom the church was

[1] Known for his travels in
Bokhara, &c.

[2] Fellow of Magdalen College,
Author of *The Patriarch and the*

Tsar, &c.; see *An Appeal to the
Scottish Church*, p. 526 f., Edin.
1849.

[3] The Right Rev. C. T. Longley.

B 2

crammed, gaping and wondering at this madman. There was a method in his madness too, and granting his premise that Scripture was to be taken, not in a metaphysical, but in what he termed a grammatico-historical sense, everything legitimately followed. After all, it was only an exaggeration of the common opinions and fixed ideas of people, greatly tending to confirm the theory that 'all the world is mad.'

Myers[1] kindly came to see me at your instigation. I liked him very much. He is free from the twists and obscurities of Hare and Maurice. Moreover, he has two noble children with him, with whom Morier and I struck up a friendship.

Morier answers your questions—

(1) by saying that he does not suppose Sir S. Canning's knowledge of the East to be of that wonderful description narrated by Sir T. A. ;

(2) that he has a cousin, who will gladly undertake for you the conveyance of the Firman.

I shall be very glad if Johnson will join in our book[2].

To the Same.

Oct. [1849].

. . . I have forgotten the purpose with which I sat down to write—to give you an account of Vaughan's Lecture.

Imagine the room in the new Taylor Building crammed with hearers :—Vaughan, with cap on head, surrounded by a bevy of ladies and of Heads of Houses (Soapy Sam in a corner) ready to burst, 'das zwanzigjährige Geheimniss.' It reminded me of another inaugural lecture delivered about eight years since[3] : that of yesterday was more speculative and poetical, not at all wanting, I think, in moral grandeur, yet not putting topics of this sort so prominently forward. It was a kind of intellectual sermon, written in the spirit of one who felt the nothingness of human knowledge, from which you went away a 'better and a wiser man.' I do not attempt to do justice to the richness and originality of language with which it was written. It began with a comparison of ancient and modern society : ancient society more simple, modern society more complex :

[1] The Vicar of Keswick.
[2] G. H. S. Johnson, afterwards Dean of Wells.
[3] Dr. Arnold's Inaugural Lecture on Modern History.

yet, after all, this superior simplicity in ancient society turned out to be a sort of clumsiness: many laws, languages, religions, &c. doing the place of one, the simplicity of a first invention, in short, the simplicity of clumsiness compared with the more perfect machine of modern society, complex only to the eye, with infinite movements, wheels, springs, harmonized and ordered by a common principle.

He went on to dwell on the idea of Society as distinct from Nationality. We are sometimes misled by a figure of speech to think of nations dying like an individual. Although this was a mere illusion, yet all nations have hitherto come to an end. Notwithstanding the greater continuity of modern than of ancient nations (which had long passed the fated Saecla of the Roman Empire), yet the real thing which was continuous, which gave us the idea of continuity, was Society. There was a meaning in European Society: it was a most complex effect with causes numberless—the Roman Church, the Civil Law, 'the ghost of the dead Roman Empire,' a monk, a nun, a crucifix, &c. (you must supply the rest for yourself). Lastly, after concluding the idea of Society, he went on to look upon history in another point of view, in relation to the world of science without it—and especially to Geology and Physiology.

Geology, too, was a history: it would have remained for ever descriptive and never have asked about the past, but that man had an instinct which made him ask after his own past, which he transferred to the world around him. These sciences seemed dark and lifeless, but in the point where they meet with history they too are touched with the feeling of humanity. Vast and grand as they are, the first ray which shone upon those unknown worlds was reflected from the history of man.

I have told you enough to show that I have spoiled a good thing, which was all I expected to do when I began. The style was eminently suggestive : single words conveying floods of light and meaning. Objectors say that it was too abstract. I thought it combined very happily great comprehensiveness and great powers of expression.

It was all cast in a mould, no patchwork or figments in it.

The next lecture will be on Tuesday at 2 o'clock, on the 'Critical Changes of Modern Society.'

To THE SAME.

[1849.]

I ought to have answered your note sooner. My work in the Schools has begun [1], and I have pupils in the evening, which makes letter writing somewhat difficult.

I shall be too happy for G[oldwin] Smith to be incorporated in our work[2], if 'indeed it be a work, which I more than doubt'; and the more so, as he obviously thinks we are more given to talking than acting, which is partly true. We shall be a laughing-stock unless the book is brought out soon after Christmas. Will you write to Temple on the subject? I have hardly leisure. . . .

Vaughan gave his second lecture on Saturday. In point of style and comprehensiveness it was quite equal to the first. But I thought his unmetaphysical nature showed to some disadvantage. He seemed to expect to find in History simple ultimate laws, analogous to the Law of Gravitation in Physical Science. The instance he gave was the Bequeathal of Property as a simple ultimate fact of the social state. These 'ultimate facts,' while in the physical world they have a simple beauty, are in the world of history of a very meagre and dubious character. You will receive this criticism *cum grano*: it is almost a shame to criticize so beautiful a composition.

Have you seen a pamphlet by a man named Whiston, which seems to make out a very strong case against the cathedrals for breach of trust? It is very ably done, and, considering the provocation, not intemperately [3].

Walker [4] (who now appears to me in a new character as Patriarch of the Schools), and the φυσικοί, or rather Greswell, suborned by Big Ben [5], have been trying to stir up an opposition to the Modern Literature School. They think they have gained a School for Physical Science, and desire to make that com-

[1] Jowett was now examiner in the School of Literae Humaniores.
[2] On University Reform.
[3] Whiston was Head Master of Rochester School, and afterwards gained a lawsuit against the Trustees.
[4] R. Walker, Reader in Experimental Physics; Examiner in Mathematics, 1849.
[5] Dr. Symonds, Warden of Wadham.

pulsory. There is no likelihood of their plot succeeding. Walker will only endanger what he has already.

You have sometimes given me money for charitable purposes. You must stop me if I am importunate. I would not ask if I thought you had many other claims upon you. I am very desirous of raising a small sum to enable a poor man to emigrate, who was once a rich, well-to-do farmer. He had a turn for literature, which, I fear, did not agree with the farming. He is now old, about sixty, and told me that he felt he was beaten in life, and saw no help but 'resignation to the will of God.' I have assisted him several times during the last few years, but it is no use assisting him in this way; and I can hardly afford to give him and his wife the means of emigrating without help from others. He has a son in America who invites him to come out, but as the father is almost in the workhouse, this is impossible without help.

If you knew him you would be pleased with his manly, independent way. His name is James Sadler. He formerly had a farm in this county.

To the Same.

[1849.]

One word about Rugby. Amid the present dearth of candidates, I think Lake is inclined to stand. There are many pros and cons in the matter, certainly. . . . Still I doubt whether any one will be found who unites the same ability, experience, and force of character, or who would go to the work in an equal spirit. Lake has written to Babington to ask his advice: if that is favourable, I hope that he will stand. In his case the only doubt, I think, is health. Will you tell me what you think?

Many thanks for your munificent gift of £5. Mr. Sadler is, I believe, already on his voyage to America.

I began this letter at half-past nine. It is now half-past eleven. Vaughan has been here in the interval, in one of his contemplative, sentimental moods. I like to hear him talk better than anybody. He declared that Arnold 'played the devil' with the Latin Verses when he first went to Rugby.

Will you tell Bunsen that they do not suppose themselves to have acquired any new MS. of Clemens Alexandrinus at the Bodleian since Potter's edition, but think it would be worth while to try whether Potter used all the MSS. which they have. Bandinel offered to collate two or three passages for him by way of experiment.

To the Same.

At Mobier's. 11 Lansdown Crescent, Bath.
[*Nov.* 1849.]

The 'Sheepskin[1]' has devised a very good plan for the Modern History, which he has been propounding to various Masters and C[ommon] Rooms. The plan, as nearly as I can remember, is as follows:—

Necessary. One of two portions of English History, which is to be divided at the reign of Henry VII. The first of these portions to be accompanied by the part of Blackstone relating to the (Feudal) Laws of Real Property: the second by that part which treats of the Constitution.

For Honours. Both portions of English History, with the corresponding portions of Law.

But one of these portions may be commuted for a portion of some Foreign History, which is contemporary with the English History. In this latter case Civil Law or International Law must be taken up. And in any case for Honours the 'Blackstone' may be commuted for the 'Civil Law.' To-morrow the die is to be cast for Rugby: if Lake wins, we gain ; if he loses, we gain still by his remaining at Oxford. Shairp thinks that his enemies have been too active to make his success likely[2].

I spoke to the 'Sheepskin' respecting the 'Arnold Memorial,' urging the unwillingness of old bachelors to submit to an examination. He seemed partly to assent, but any impression which does not arise in his own mind of itself is washed away by the next tide. I think he would be very unwilling, however, to do anything that you disapproved of.

[1] H. H. Vaughan: see *Life*, vol. i. pp. 97, 123.
[2] E. M. Goulburn was elected.

To THE SAME.

[1845-?]

I think of writing to the 'Sheepskin' to persuade him to change the fashion of his garments.

I send the sermon, ὡς σὲ μᾶλλον ἂν ἔλοιμ' ἂν ἢ τοὺς πάντας Ἀργείους [1]. The church was quite empty: the four Heads of Houses present and the wooden benches seemed equally unimpressible: about six friends of mine *nantes in gurgite vasto* below, three or four Undergrads in the Gallery, and a Balliol scout.—V.C. civil.

I saw the vacancy at Alderley and conjectured it would be offered to the next of kin. Surely in any but a worldly point of view you must have done rightly. Are you serious in asking about a fit person? I know of no one but Lonsdale, in whom I have unbounded confidence, for so difficult a situation. I never met with any one who had so many gracious qualities, who retained with such a thorough knowledge of the world the native simplicity of the human heart. I think he would be an equal blessing to the parish of Alderley and its lord. To him, of course, it is of no great importance, and it is a dream to suppose that any patron would give away the living to a stranger. There are doubtless a dozen excellent young men whom Lord Alderley knows, and a thousand who can be highly recommended. I doubt whether there is one among them who has the peculiar qualifications of Lonsdale.

To MISS ELLIOT.

Oct. 27, 1860.

I do not know that you care to plunge into the abyss of Theology. But I shall always maintain that there is no abyss, and that, without relying on fables and fancies, any one who will may find their way through this world with sufficient knowledge to light them to another. . . .

Will you give my best thanks to the Dean for his letter? My lucubrations [2] must have come upon him at a very inconvenient time. I hope, if I may venture to say so, that he will

---

[1] Cf. Soph. *Phil.* 46. The quotation is not exact.
[2] *Life,* vol. i. p. 343.

not give up the Prolocutorship. There is a mystic influence in *position* which any one who intends to write on ecclesiastical matters is unwise to give up. . . .

To THE SAME, AT CANNES.

BALLIOL COLLEGE, OXFORD,
Dec. 4, 1860.

I write a line to thank you for your kind letter. It gave me great pleasure to hear from you, though I fear I shall only bore you in return by telling what can be of no manner of interest. I rather feel like the reformatory boy (your sister's friend), who said, 'it was not for the like of he to write to a young lady like her.'

I am glad you are enjoying a good climate ; let me enhance the pleasure by telling you that this has been so far one of the worst of English winters. For several days, I think I may say weeks, we have been dark and murky, too misty to rain much and too rainy to snow—the most disagreeable compound of damp and cold that the poor, weak lungs of consumptive patients can inhale. When the world, that is to say the upper ten thousand, becomes truly civilized, they will migrate in a body like swallows at the approach of an English winter.

Another Bishopric is vacant (Worcester): it produces a flutter among the caps and gowns and in clerical circles, but, as you told me, now raises no palpitation in your family. Yet I am half sorry for this *Nolo Episcopari.* I hope some one will be appointed who is not an Evangelical or H. C., and who is disinterested—not a sleek waiter on Providence creeping up the ladder of preferment.

I was greatly pleased to hear that your sister was better. It would indeed be a mistake to come home without seeing Italy at such an interesting time, and I hope you will plan a good tour and have many visions about it. Visions and dreams do no harm on such subjects when for some reason or other we are unable to carry them out. It is an old charge against me, that I scheme for others when I am not going to travel myself. . . . I do not know that I have any Oxford news to tell you of interest. We make the most of the Prince during his last fortnight. The Heads of Houses are not more energetic than usual. (What a ridiculous position that of a Head of a House is—a man with nothing to do, trying to be a Don—all of them ready to stand by their order as though the salvation of the country depended upon it—they are the ruin of the University for all useful purposes.) Your friend the V. C. [1] has been getting himself into great trouble by procuring an Act of Parliament during the Long Vacation without authority from the University.

Dr. Stanley has been most kindly and vigorously trying to get an endowment for the Greek Professorship, but hitherto has been 'dodged' by the inexhaustible resources of Dr. Pusey. Mr. Myers' book [2] is likely to be published with a short memoir and notice by Dr. Stanley. Mr. Müller is on the eve of his great contest, in which I wish him success, though I have never been able to settle whether he or Mr. Williams is likely to do most for the cause of Indian Missions. . . . About 1400 'wild curates' and others are expected in Oxford on Friday [3].

The Dean very kindly sent me a pamphlet about Convocation. I liked the pamphlet very much, and thought it quite made out its point against the Government. The point is important, as a matter of precedent, but I should have been very sorry if it had led him to resign.

Is Lord Brougham with you at Cannes? If he is, tell me of his sayings and doings when you write. Did you ever see enough of him to write 'A Lady's recollections'? I do not suppose that he often says remarkable things in themselves. But many common things that come from a person who has occupied his great position have a kind of originality, and he must be inexhaustible about events and great men who were his contemporaries. . . .

TO THE SAME.

[1861.]

I paid my annual visit to Tennyson last week. Shall I tell you about him? This year he has written nothing but a short piece called 'Boadicea,' in a very wild peculiar metre, with

---

[1] The Rev. F. Jeune, Master of Pembroke.

[2] *Catholic Thoughts.*

[3] For the election to the Professorship of Sanscrit. See *Life*, vol. i. p. 291.

long lines and innumerable short syllables. It is very fine, but too strange to be popular. He had been ill, and greatly suffering and depressed I fear. The more I see of him the more I respect his character, notwithstanding a superficial irritability and uneasiness about all things. I have a pleasure in repeating this about him, because I find he is so greatly mistaken by those who don't know him or only know him a little. No one is more honest, truthful, manly, or a warmer friend ; but he is as open as the day, and, like a child, tells to any chance comer what is passing in his mind. He sometimes talks of going on with 'King Arthur.' For my own part I hope he won't ; he has made as much of it as the subject admits. Twenty years ago he formed a scheme for an epic poem on ' King Arthur ' in ten books ; it is perhaps fortunate for himself that circumstances have prevented the completion of it. He dislikes Byron, but speaks very generously and warmly of Wordsworth. The subject on which I think he is most ready to converse—sometimes over a pipe—is (what do you think ?) a future state, of which he always talks with a passionate conviction. He is the shyest person I ever knew, feeling sympathy and needing it to a degree quite painful. Please not to repeat this to the vulgar, who can never be made to understand that great mental troubles necessarily accompany such powers as he possesses. I should not tell it to you if I did not think *you* would comprehend it.

To THE SAME.

April 1, 1861.

The Bishop of London [1] means kindly by me and Dr. Temple, but he is very weak, always under the influence of opposite or rather alternate impulses. He can't make up his mind to side with the educated few with whom he really agrees, against the many-headed mob of whom Lord Shaftesbury is the patron. He says privately, and is willing that it should be repeated publicly, that he has no fault to find with Dr. Temple's essay or mine: but no one could gather this from his signature to the Declaration [2] or from his speeches in Convocation calling upon us to disavow our companions in distress.

[1] A. C. Tait.   [2] *Life*, vol. i. p. 297.

To Miss Cobbe.

[1861.]

. . . I write a line to thank you for the little pamphlet you have sent me, which I read and like very much.

There is no end of good that you may do by writing in that simple and touching style upon social questions.

But do not go to war with Political Economy.

(1) Because the Political Economists are a powerful and dangerous class ;

(2) Because it is impossible for ladies and gentlemen to fill up the interstices of legislation if they run counter to the common motives of self-interest.

(3) (You won't agree to this.) Because Political Economists have really done more for the labouring classes by their advocacy of Free Trade, &c., than all the philanthropists put together.

I wish that it was possible as a matter of taste to get rid of all philanthropic expressions, 'missions,' &c., which are distasteful to the educated. But I suppose they are necessary for the collection of money, and no doubt as a matter of taste there is a good deal that might be corrected in the Political Economists. The light of the feelings never teaches the best way of dealing with the world *en masse*, and the daylight never finds the way to the heart either of man or beast.

You see I want to have all the humanities combined with Political Economy. Perhaps it may be replied that such a combination is not possible in human nature. Excuse my speculations [1].

To A. P. Stanley.

Royal Crescent, Whitby,
July or *August*, 1861 [2].

. . . I am heartily glad you are going to have a good holiday. It is well deserved. I wish I were your companion, and if I have not become too much of a bore shall try next year

[1] See Miss Cobbe's *Autobiography*, vol. i. p. 317.
[2] *Life*, vol. i. p. 340.

to have a journey with you. When you come back we shall have numerous interests and duties in common, to be pursued with new strength and not given up while life lasts.

I have no reason to complain, and great reason to be thankful (to use the ordinary phrase), that the way of life is so much clearer than it seemed three or four years ago. I believe that what we and others have done for University education is as nothing in comparison with what may be done in the course of the next ten years. It is certainly pleasant, and I think invigorating, to look forward to a long period of activity in the future.

. . . I won't repeat what I shall always feel for what you have done for me during the last two years. Farewell! Make yourself as happy as you can : it is the best preparation for new work.

To Miss Elliot.

WHITBY, *Aug.* 4, 1861.

. . . I am glad that you are going to Rome. (The words have not so alarming a sound as they had ten years ago.) You will probably see the election of a new Pope. What a subject of speculation the future of the Roman Catholic Church is! The greatest difficulty in reforming [it] is occasioned by the poverty and celibacy of the clergy. Still I think they might at once get a system of education which would raise the people above the clergy, and they should take the Clergy out of the Catholic Seminaries and send them, as in Germany, to the Universities. Then, perhaps, in the next generation the problem would begin to clear up, by change of ideas in the people and clergy themselves. Baron Ricasoli is said to be a kind of Protestant, or rather a believer in some very simple form of Christianity. He has not done anything yet to give proof of what he is able to do. I do not think the impression of him in England is very favourable. He does not seem to have the power of concealing his 'grim earnest' under easy pleasant manners like Cavour or Sir Robert Walpole. If a man can't do this, he wears himself out and bores others. Never be serious in life unless it is absolutely necessary, as, for example, at a funeral.

I read a charming little book (not published) which, if you have not seen, I wish I could send you. It is the Diary of the Dean of Westminster's [1] mother in the years 1799 and 1800. The book contains a good deal about the Dean of Bristol's father, whom Mrs. Trench saw at Dresden with Nelson and Lady Hamilton, 'Antony and Moll Cleopatra' as he used to call them. Nothing could be pleasanter than what is said of Mr. Elliot, or more unpleasant than what is said of Antony and his lady. I have seldom read anything so good as the sketches of life and character which are given by the authoress of the Diary, who must have been a person of great talent and sense.

So you are going to learn Italian! It is a most excellent resolution. Pray read Dante over and over again. I always feel ashamed that I am unable to do so, and have been often reminded by Tennyson that it is a real disgrace. What a hard thing it is to educate oneself in later life, when the memory is or seems to be like a sieve, and some pains are necessary to prevent going back—to say nothing of going forward. Still I believe there is a way, if one could find it out. I think writing is on the whole the best way (for mere reading is not a sufficient object), and in writing it seems to me that great things can be done by industry and judgement. I would not have a person wait until they are convinced they have a genius —for no one who has a genius begins by discovering it for themselves.

To THE SAME.

Oct. 10, 1861.

I am sorry to hear that the Dean is thinking of resignation of the Prolocutorship. Is it not a mistake? I have ventured to write and say that I think so [2]. As to the injustice of their proceedings, that can't be helped and ought not to be complained of. No ecclesiastical body or person should be required to con-fine themselves to rules of justice.

A day or two ago I was at Clifton. . . . I like staying

---

[1] R. C. Trench, afterwards Archbishop of Dublin. The *Memoir* of

Mrs. Trench was published in 1862.
[2] See *Life*, &c., vol. i. p. 355.

with Dr. Symonds: he is so wonderfully kind and attentive; though I have always the feeling that if I were to remain with him long I should be utterly spoiled, and become, in Dr. Johnson's language, 'a complete rascal.' He has a perfect genius for kindness. He certainly deserves to be called 'the beloved physician.'

To Miss Cobbe.

[1862.]

I shall certainly read your paper on Political Economy, &c.

Political Economy seems to me in this imperfect world to be Humanity on a large scale (though not the whole of Humanity). And I am always afraid of its being partially supplanted by Humanity on a small scale, which relieves one-sixth of the poor whom we see, and pauperizes the mind of five-sixths whom we don't see[1]. . . .

To Miss Elliot, at Rome.

Oxford, *February* 2, 1862.

. . . Doubtless it is a thousand times better to be enjoying pictures in Italy than presiding over that august body of nonentities, the lower House of Convocation. I am very glad that he[2] had nothing to do with the follies of last year. Only I sometimes wish that as people muse on these things 'the fire would kindle within them, and they would speak with their tongue.'

I hope that you and your sister enjoy Rome, and don't try to improve yourselves more than is absolutely necessary. I have never been there—nor further than Florence in Italy. I should greatly like to see 'the ghost of the dead Roman Empire sitting crowned upon the grave thereof.' (Did you ever hear that famous expression? Is it not grand?) Though the ghost of late years has grown very dim and meagre, I don't think he is destined to die yet: or rather, being dead already, his term of existence is not to be calculated. I sometimes wonder whether reformation or resistance to reformation would soonest bring him to an end. Upon the whole I rather approve

---

[1] See Miss Cobbe's *Autobiography*, vol. i. p. 352.
[2] Dean Elliot.

of everybody dying game, and making no sign of repentance. There is so much dust in the attempt to repair rotten houses. Suppose the case of an old gentleman with a house and garden and a field beyond. You try to persuade the old gentleman that he would be so much better off without the house and garden—in the open air or in a lodging—and instead of the field he should have a few pence a week allowed him. Would any old gentleman of moderate sense agree to this? Which things are an allegory.

Did you see my poor friend Mr. Clough at Florence? He was a very fine creature and would, I think, have been a great genius if circumstances had favoured—that is to say, if he had not been overworked. Yesterday I went to see his widow, and spent the day in looking over the remains which he left. There are very noble things among them; he was a real poet, and when his remains are published, will be acknowledged to have been so by the world. Carlyle has said of him that he was the most high-principled man he had ever known. And this was true; and yet in his opinions he was quite alone in the world, very heterodox, yet perfectly calm, and with a kind of faith in knowing nothing. I never saw anybody in the least like him. He is laid in the Swiss Cemetery at Florence.

I paid my Christmas visit to Tennyson as usual. He has had a bad illness, but the illness has left him better than I ever saw him, at least in mind. He has written a very beautiful dedication of the Idylls to the memory of the late Prince Consort, and he is busy with a new poem—a curious story (said to be true) of a fisherman who was supposed to be lost for years; meanwhile, his wife marries again, a former lover, who is a miller, and presses his service upon her in distress. Years pass away, and the fisherman returns and takes one look at his wife and children from the other side of the street and departs for ever. You can imagine what may be made of this.

You asked me whether I knew Mrs. Cameron in one of your letters. Indeed I do, and like her: she is a very honest, really kind, enthusiastic person: perhaps she has a tendency to make the house shake the moment that she enters, but in this dull world that is a very excusable fault. She is a sort of

T

hero-worshipper, and the hero is not Mr. Tennyson—he only occupies the second place—but Henry Taylor. . . .

I was very much interested with what you said about ――――. Some persons are put in such a position that it is necessary to abuse and victimize them. I am rather inclined to believe that he is one of them. No man can carry a fire about with him for thirty years who has not real genius, although probably he has with this some of the weaknesses of genius. I don't mean to say that it is wrong to abuse him, but there must be a higher judgement as well.

To A. P. STANLEY.

May, 1864[1].

I am rather doubtful about the Lord Chancellor's proposal of bringing in a bill to attach a canonry to the Greek Professorship, chiefly on the ground that he would be taking off the shoulders of the University a burden which they ought to bear, and would be willing to bear, in a year or two. Is this worth while?

The University has received from the Crown, and is still holding, firstly, a remission of the Degree fees; secondly, a large patent or privilege (i.e. as an exception from the Queen's Printers' patent) of printing Bibles, which produces an income of £10,000 a year or more. In return for these privileges the University says, 'The only professorships that we refuse to endow out of the income given us by the Crown are the Crown professorships.' I have always imagined that the University might receive an intimation from the Crown that the privilege would not be continued unless the Crown professorships were endowed. This is more agreeable to my sense of justice than the appropriation of canonries to their endowment.

To PROFESSOR LEWIS CAMPBELL.

Nov. 1864.

We have been very much pleased with Wallace[2]. There was unfortunately no exhibition vacant for him. He will,

---

[1] *Life*, vol. i. pp. 315, 316.
[2] Afterwards Whyte's Professor of Moral Philosophy.

however, obtain one in the middle of February, and is to have rooms at the beginning of next Term.

Would you kindly put him in the way of getting up composition, especially Greek and Latin verses? I have considered the matter, and think that he had better do this. With his powers it will not be difficult, and he must necessarily miss many minutiae of language if he does not, and also be at a considerable disadvantage . . . Will you select some passages of Greek and Latin for him to learn by heart, and endeavour to inspire him with an enthusiasm on the subject?

To the Same.

Dec. 1864.

. . . I think that your preaching to the students would be a very good thing. I hope no Jenny Geddes will throw a footstool at your head.

Where would you preach? I suppose in the College Chapel or Church. Is there any legal bar on the Presbyterian side? I don't think that there is anything inconsistent with your position as a clergyman of the Church of England . . . I should advise you to take extreme pains with the sermons—make them as clear as day.

To the Same.

[The following letters on a question of Greek criticism will interest none but scholars, but they are inserted as showing what Jowett thought in 1865 of an argument which has received more attention of late years than when it was published in 1867.]

Jan. 6, 1865.

. . . I think that you are quite right in supposing that the *Sophist* and *Politicus* represent Plato's second (? third) manner when the poetical or metaphysical conception of the ideas was beginning to pass into the logical or Aristotelian one : and that this, so far from being a reason for doubting, is a reason for accepting them. . . . I fear that I make but slow progress with my own work, being at present occupied with translating the *Republic*, which is a long task.

T 2

[1865 or 1866.]

. . . I think that your argument is perfectly valid, and of real value in reference to the *Politicus* and *Sophist.* If I understand rightly, you mean this :

Making a selection of the characteristic words in the *Timaeus, Critias* and the *Laws*, you attempt to estimate the proximity of the other dialogues to them by the number of words which you find common to the *Timaeus,* &c., and to them. The only doubts appear to be

(a) What are characteristic words? and how far (β) the words which you term characteristic, e.g. in the *Timaeus* and *Phaedrus*, arise from the peculiar character of the dialogues?

But after making these deductions, I think that enough remains to add greatly to the probability that the *Sophist* and *Politicus* are later than the *Republic*.

To LORD WESTBURY.

PRIVATE.   OXFORD, *July* 3, [1865].

MY LORD,

I have long wished to write and thank your Lordship for your great kindness and generosity in bringing forward the subject of the Greek Professorship in the House of Lords last year. May I venture to do so now ?

I have read what has happened in the papers of this morning with great sorrow. That will be a general feeling when people have had time to reflect. They will remember that the greatest social improvement of our time, the change in the law about divorce, was carried through the House of Commons by your Lordship ; they also know that there is more hope of real reform in the law from your Lordship than from any one else. As I am altogether a stranger to you, I will only venture to express a strong hope that you will not be induced by the recent attacks to retire from public life. That would be playing into the hands of your enemies. No man of ability was ever ruined except through his own weakness. A great man ought not to allow his last public appearance to be such as casts a slur upon his fame. I say this, because I feel certain that your Lordship, if not wanting to yourself, has a future in the reform of the law and in other ways, perhaps better and greater than the past.

Excuse the plainspokenness of good will, and
Believe me,
Your Lordship's obliged servant,
B. JOWETT.

To PROFESSOR LEWIS CAMPBELL.

Dec. 25, 1867.

A happy Christmas and New Year to you and yours.

. . . I am glad that you keep up the notion of taking part in a Commentary at some future time. I don't think that any one should have many things in hand at once. But I believe that a great deal may be done by looking forward for ten years and economizing and collecting stray thoughts. That is what makes a great life even for persons who are conscious that they have no remarkable powers (like myself).

Life is self-devotion: and I expect you to do better and better every year.

To THE SAME.

INGLEWOOD, TORQUAY, [*Dec.* 1869].

. . . We have made great progress with the Test Question [1].

I hope that Sophocles is progressing, also the Essay on the Translation of the N. T [2]. I think that you should work out the kind of change that is required in a new translation—not pedantic alterations of aorists, or an attempt at a spurious accuracy in altering language which is popular, but a real correction of great mistakes. 'The Idea of a New Translation.'

I think that your Essay might extend in length to sixty or eighty pages. It should be absolutely undoctrinal, and should contain the passages arranged under the heads of the controversies to which they relate, e.g., 1. Trinity; 2. Asceticism; 3. Calvinism; 4. Catholicism. There is the version of the four clergymen, and also a little book of Professor Scholefield's that

---

[1] See above, p. 18.   [2] See *Life*, &c., vol. i. p. 405.

I would advise you to get. There are, too, some publications of Professor Selwyn. Please to keep the project quiet for the present.

To R. B. D. MORIER.

[1870.]

(Excuse bad writing as I am in a railway carriage.)

I am very sorry that I cannot come to Darmstadt this Easter. I had always intended to pay you a visit when the four vols. of *Plato* were finished, and still hope to do so. Since my dear mother's death I am a good deal tied to Torquay. . . . I still think that there is something to be done in the way of making Christianity, whether under that or some other name, a reality. The daily life of people has been one thing, and there has been a mass of doctrines as well, with which they have muddled their minds. The simple love of truth and of God, and the desire to do good to man have hardly been tried as yet, and people would tell you that they cannot be tried. There is something in your transcendental fluid; in some form or other—religious, moral, or metaphysical—men must rise above their daily life. I always feel the danger of utilitarianism or materialism lowering the character of education and of life.

I am very glad that you are thinking of an 'opus.' You should choose a subject in which your German friends can help you, and which will be of some permanent value. My *Plato* is only a translation, but I have a satisfaction in feeling that it may influence the English and American world in the right direction long after I am gone.

I am afraid that the Irish Land Bill will do harm and not good; (1) by extending bad and uncertain customs; (2) by plunging the whole country in litigation; (3) by fixing rents in a court of law. I would have gone on a different tack: (1) customary leases; (2) great advantages to property let on lease; (3) compensation for improvements; (4) a small bonus to the evicted tenant: (5) loans for improvement, emigration, buying up of customs, &c. I think that people have an exaggerated fear of the Irish people and their American cousins.

The Government are going to bring in the Oxford Test Bill

immediately. I do not think that they are quite so flourishing as they appear. They are a good deal in the hands of their own extreme left, as is happily evident in regard to the Education Bill. Bright, as I hear with regret, is not likely to come back again. He was useless as an administrator (like putting Tennyson in office) but he was a good influence. . . .

To Mrs. Tennyson.

BALLIOL COLLEGE, *March* 10, 1871.

I have intended to write to you for a long time past and thank you for your kind note about Sir A. Grant which gave me great pleasure, and also to thank Alfred for his acknowledgement of my book. I hope that I shall live and do some other things : I am not satisfied at present.

I have long given up the expectation of seeing you and Alfred here, though there are few things which would give me greater pleasure. Are these really the worst times for Europe, or do all times seem to be the worst when our minds choose to be in opposition? I think that they are really very bad, when Europe has at least 400,000 of soldiers (or more) who by a necessity of their natures must go to war sooner or later, and there is less and less of a controlling opinion or balance of power. I would rather not go either to France or Germany for some years, the thought of them is painful.

Meanwhile there is considerable excitement about Purchas, Voysey and Kennet. I think that we shall have some great ecclesiastical change ; the present state of things is too great a farce to last much longer.

The dinner which they forced on me reluctant was very pleasant.

To R. B. D. Morier.

Jan. 16, 1873.

I went to stay with Lord Westbury last week (not with any such views as you might suppose). What an extraordinary man he is, gifted with the greatest powers of speech I have ever known. He is one of the kindest of men and one of the weakest, very sensitive and always wanting sympathy.

But this the world will never understand, nor should I mention it except to a person who understands human characters. A weak man of extraordinary abilities is always misrepresented, especially if he has, like Lord Westbury, uncommon courage and self-reliance. (Is not this partly the story of Louis Napoleon ?) I believe that if he had ever had a real friend in life, he might have been one of the greatest men of his time. But it is too late now, and mere routineers have got his position and may possibly make more of it. . . .

To A. P. STANLEY.

OXFORD, *Jan.* 19, 1873.

Did I surprise you by a telegram which I sent you yesterday ? I thought that you had better consider the matter. The way I came to be interested in Lord Lytton was this : Last Sunday I dined with him tête-à-tête at Mrs. Halliday's (Lady Augusta's old acquaintance, Miss Farquhar) ; he was full of life and energy and talked about Plato, oratory, spiritualism and various subjects without appearing unwell. He was very kind and drove me home afterwards. But on Tuesday I grieve to say that he was seized with an attack of the brain which from the first appears to have been fatal, and yesterday morning when I left Torquay he was dying. So a long literary life comes to an end. He was only sixty-eight years of age, and yet I think that his writings, *Pelham,* &c., go back beyond our memory. He was famous all over Europe before Dickens was known. He left on me a very pleasing impression of kindness and sincerity, perhaps of vanity, which he declared that it was hard even at sixty-eight ever to get rid of. You will not wonder at my being affected by this, for just this time last week I was sitting talking with him about the Emperor Napoleon and other matters.

He was writing a novel which was just finished, called *Kenelm Chillingley.*

My impression is that the public would think him deserving of a place in the Abbey.

I shall be at Fremantle's to-morrow.

To the Hon. Miss Bethell.

Grantown, Inverness-shire,
July 21, 1873.

Though I hardly ventured to entertain a hope after the telegram which you kindly sent me, I am deeply grieved by the news of this morning. I am afraid that you and Lady Westbury must be in great distress. To have lost a father who was so remarkable a man is not simply the ordinary loss of a near relative. I think myself with pain that I shall never again hear that eloquent voice or exchange words and thoughts with him. He seemed to have a good will to me, and I am sure that I had a great regard for him, and the highest admiration for his abilities. He was a man of genius, whom accident made a lawyer, and the only lawyer in our time who was a man of genius. Then he was so extremely kind and his conversation so instructive ; the precision of it taught a lesson to his hearers. I am very glad that I knew him, though, alas ! for so short a time. He is at rest now in the hands of God, where we soon shall be too, beyond the praises and censures of men.

I fear that I cannot say anything which will give you much comfort, nor do I write with that view. Grief must have its way, for weeks and months, perhaps for years. Still, I hope that you will not despair, but see what you can do to make a life for yourself and others and to keep things together in this new state of affairs. Sorrows almost always bring duties ; and this is perhaps the best of them. You know that you have the regard and sympathy of every one, and always have had them, if they are of any value. And I would not have you regret or reproach yourself about what you could not prevent or might have done. For I am sure that you always did what you could and what was right. . . .

Will you remember me to Lady Westbury? I am very sorry for her. She has been most devoted in attending on your father.

What a number of eminent men have died this year. The world will have no one to take care of it, if this goes on.

To A. P. STANLEY.

GRANTOWN, *July* 23, 1873.

Let me say two or three things of Lord Westbury, though
I do not know that they will be of any use in your sermon.

1. He was one of the kindest men I have ever known. To
see him to advantage you should see him at home in his own
family; nothing could be more amiable, or more in contrast
with his sardonic utterances in public.

2. It is a mistake to suppose that he was an irreligious or
irreverent sort of man (he fell very easily under the influence of women, and with all his great capacity he was
not a man of the world). But he was certainly not a sceptic
or an infidel. He told me that until he had to consider the
Essays and Reviews Judgement he had always accepted the
orthodox views of religion, but then he saw how untenable
they were. He had a dislike of Darwinism, against which he
would declaim with great eloquence; he had also a great dislike of priests and churches, but not of religion.

I think that he was an unhappy man—he never seemed to
enjoy anything—partly from the consciousness of the falseness
of things about him, and perhaps also from a consciousness of
the falseness of his own life. . . . He was very reserved and
self-controlled.

He was fond of talking about his father and his brother and
his struggles in early life. It is a mistake which I see in the
Scotsman to suppose that he had to creep at all. From the
first he was a very bold, courageous man, ready to beard Lord
Brougham or any other judge.

As a lawyer he was thoroughly liberal and sensible—always
inclining to common sense; he was, I believe, the first person
who talked of uniting law and equity, or rather of allowing
equitable principles to supersede law. He thought that the
Judicature Bill mingles them together pell-mell in a crude
fashion. The last time I saw him, three weeks ago, he drew
a ludicrous picture of the effects which would follow.

His political career was uniformly liberal and intelligible ;
he retained to the last a sort of half Radicalism. He was the
person who protected the earnings of married women and

'sanctified marriage by instituting the divorce court.' I am very sorry that he is gone, more than I can express, and more so because his life was partly *vie manquée.* He made a great impression on me ; I have the tones of his voice constantly ringing in my ears. I was very glad to see what Lord Selborne said of him.—He had faults, but he fell quite as much from his virtues : a great part of the opprobrium which has been heaped upon him arose out of the *Essays and Reviews* Judgement.

I am sorry about S. W.'s [1] death ; though I do not think him a public loss at all. And now what will happen to the Church ? Must things be worse before they are better ? Are we to have at a later stage *ultramontane* hatreds revived in England ?

I think that the Liberal party in the Church or rather among the laity have fought badly. They have fought with their hands tied behind their backs, not daring to say what they thought. This must fail. While the orthodox party have tried to make religion and morality inseparable from miracles and sacraments, they have never opposed any counter theory to this—they have never, in short, ventured to look matters in the face in the light of the nineteenth century. There is no more reason for believing in the immaculate conception of Christ than in the immaculate conception of the Virgin, or in either, than in the 'La Salette [2].' But perhaps I am writing what you will not care to read ; but I cannot help saying at times what I feel and know.

To the Same.

MUNICH, *Sept.* 23, 1873.

You are very good to write and ask about my health. I am much the same (thank you) as I was when I staid at

---

[1] S. Wilberforce, who was killed by a fall from his horse. Cp. *Life*, vol. ii. pp. 53, 54.

[2] For the appearance of the Virgin at La Salette on Sept. 19, 1846, cp. Murray's *Handbook to France*, 1884, Part ii, p. 229 ; and

Edinburgh Review, vol. cvi. p. 9 ff. La Salette is about sixty miles from Lyons in the diocese of Grenoble. On the anniversary of the apparition from fifty to sixty thousand persons assembled on the mountain.

your house, that is to say, not up to much intellectual work, but not otherwise unwell. I intend to work about half time during the coming year. It is a little discouraging to have so many things to do, and to find one's powers of doing them decrease. Still I hope that both our lives may go on 'broadening to the end.'

I was disappointed to find that you were not made Bishop of Winchester ; more for the sake of others than of yourself. People say that the most distinguished clergyman of the English Church should not have been passed over. I am not of the opinion of those who think that you can possibly have as much influence as a Dean as you would have as a Bishop, though you probably have a quieter life. You know my old theory, that the last years of life ought to be the best, and the most distinguished, and most useful. I still hold to this, though I am a little laid on the shelf at present, and I pray that it may be so both for you and me.

I return to England at the end of next week, being at present with Morier from whom I hear a great deal that is interesting about politics and the Old Catholics[1].

To R. R. W. LINGEN.

BALLIOL COLLEGE, *May* 31, [1874].

Many thanks for your kind and liberal gift to the New Hall. We have a good design, I think; and shall begin in the Summer, as soon as we can get the contracts settled.

Will you not come down here in Commemoration week, when the University turns into Vanity Fair ; or on Saturday, June 13 ? We might then have a good walk and talk about the New Hall, about Liberal Politics and other matters.

I hope that you are going to take a rest this year; or you will wear away sooner than you ought: at our age we ought to husband life. We have more in our power now than when we were young, if we do not lose health and spirits.

Your long letter was very acceptable to me (though I have not time to answer it at length) and reminds me of old days when we use to write to one another, about the years 1844 and

---

[1] See above, p. 72.

onwards. Since then I fear I have acquired a 'cacoëthes non scribendi,' but sometime in the long vacation I may, perhaps, retaliate upon you.

The Liberal party is at present in a most miserable condition—disunited, without leaders, and without principles [1]. For the last five years they have had sham leaders who have ruined them, and have now deserted them. There was ability enough for two or three ministries in the late ministry, but there was no consistency or looking forward into the future. They raised the hopes of the Dissenters about the Irish Church, and then betrayed them in the Education Bill. They exaggerated economy, which though important is not the first thing either in a household or a state. I cannot think that the Irish Church Bill was done in a right way—certainly not the Licensing Bill, and the dissolution least of all. There is nothing but the abolition of University Tests (which was done by Gladstone against his own convictions) which can be regarded from the Liberal point of view with unmixed satisfaction.

I agree quite that any Liberal Minister should set the Clubs and Society at defiance, and try to fight real causes and educate the people up to them. Some changes in the Education Bill, such as the enforcement of schoolboards everywhere, and easing the rates out of the consolidated fund to undenominational Schools, ought to be among the first battles fought. I perceive that I am more favourable to the Dissenters than you are. I cannot see why their having made mistakes in the matter of Education should subject them for ever to the control of the Established Church, which, if you put yourself in their position, is very oppressive.

I think that the Liberal party must shortly approach the question of an Established Church. It can hardly be allowed to go on as it is. If left to itself England will pass into the same state of division as France and Germany, and we shall require a Bismarck to set it right. My idea of reforming the Church would be to begin with the question of patronage,

[1] Gladstone resigned on Feb. 17, 1874. For the remainder of the year he took but little part in politics, and in the following January resigned his post as leader of the Opposition.

which is felt to be a great abuse, and is really so. I should not appoint by popular Election, but by delegates selected from a district or Archdeaconry. In the election of these delegates I think that all respectable inhabitants should have a share.

But about these and other notions which have come into my head of late, I should like to have a talk with you. Will you give my kind regards to Mrs. Lingen, and will she write me a line to say whether you can come here on June 13, or any day in the first half of the next (Commemoration) week?

To PROFESSOR LEWIS CAMPBELL.

FLORENCE, *Sept.* 14, [1874].

. . . It gives me unmixed pleasure to hear that you are getting on with Sophocles. If you can complete a Sophocles with a translation, an Aeschylus with a translation, and the edition of the Republic, you will have left your mark, and done as much as can be done in this sort of work. We have the battle of the Classics always to fight against the aesthetic and scientific tendencies of the age. I hope that we shall save Greek both in the English and Scotch Universities.

At present I am off work, and during the next year intend to work only three hours a day for seven months in the year. But I hope to get through nearly as much as I have done in a less drudging way: I mean to get all the assistance I can from others, and I would advise you to do the same.

To PROFESSOR EDWARD CAIRD [1].

BALLIOL COLLEGE, *Jan.* 5, 1875.

I have not heard of you for a long time, and should be much interested to know about Kant [2]: when will he appear? I sometimes think that we Platonists and Idealists are not half so industrious as those repulsive people who only 'believe what they can hold in their hands,' Bain, H. Spencer, &c., who are the very Tuppers of philosophy and yet have gained for themselves fame and name.

[1] Now Master of Balliol.
[2] Prof. Caird's work on the philosophy of Kant.

Green's is an important book, though it will not have many readers ; it presupposes more knowledge of Hume and Kant and Locke than is ordinarily possessed by students. Mr. Martineau was praising it to me highly the other day. I think that Green should now tell us what he thinks himself. For quite as much may be said on the ground of inconsistency against Kant and Hegel, as against Locke. And I don't quite like criticizing the great Englishman from our point of view instead of trying to catch his own.

I have tried to set Green to fight with the Philistines—Bain, H. Spencer, &c., and he seems well disposed. He takes a year of holiday (a Sabbatical fourth year which ought to exist in every College and University) next year, so that he will have time to make the attack.

I hear that your brother's sermon in the Abbey was a splendid success.

To R. B. D. Morier.

January 26, 1875.

Let me begin by dispelling an apprehension which may perhaps arise in your mind that you will be expected to answer this letter. Nothing of the sort. About the middle of next month I shall expect a letter from you, but till the Essay is finished don't trouble yourself to write.

I hope that you will take the utmost pains with it which you can in a short time. Since I wrote to you last I have invested five shillings in 'Macmillans' and read your articles. Shall I criticize them a little? They seem to me rather too fervid and not sufficiently connected ; and if I were criticizing one of the Essays you used to read to me in old times, I should say, 'not impersonal enough.' I quite agree with the general principles of them. Your writing has a considerable swing, but it is not a continuous swing from the beginning to the end of the article. I am delighted to hear that you have acquired regular habits of writing, for I am convinced that you may become a very distinguished writer; and in the present state of politics, when all men's minds are weak and impressible, this is the greatest power which a politician or diplomatist can exercise.

I have reluctantly come to the conclusion that I cannot go to Rome or out of England this Easter, though I have pleased myself with the dream of doing so for several months. Shall I tell you why? The Easter Vacation this year is only three weeks and one day, and five days would be taken in going to Rome and five in returning. I am obliged to take care of my health, and I do not think that it would be wise for me to undertake this. But I will come and see you at the beginning of the Long Vacation, when I believe that Plato will be finished, and I shall try to persuade you to come with me to Switzerland and the North of Italy.

Don't hurry your Essay[1]: take more time if necessary, and insist on putting it last in the book. If you like to send it to me I will return it without delay, and will read it carefully. Don't give us too much of antiquarianism. The German Land Tenures of to-day, not of two thousand years ago, are what concern us.

To THE SAME.

February 18, 1875.

Where is the promised answer to my letter? Though I admit that your letters which are written with your own hand are of more value than mine. Shall I have an after-dinner talk with you?

In the first place, what are you doing? Is the Essay finished, and would you like me to run my eye over it? I hope that you will take the utmost pains with it, and do not after the manner of the Germans, begin the Trojan war with the egg of Leda! You only want a little pruning and a little more sustained connexion to be a very eloquent and able writer. What a great thing it is to write a good paragraph—well constructed, and having the strength in the whole and not in any one phrase or sentence.

There is nothing upon which I have set my heart more than your success in life, and I have rather come to the conclusion that considering the chances and uncertainties of diplomatic appointments, and the uncertainty even if you were appointed to a great post of being able to do anything, this must be

---

[1] On the Prussian Land Laws; see *Life*, vol. i. p. 441 *n.*

accomplished chiefly by writing, which seems to me to be the most satisfactory, although the most laborious way of working. There are several subjects for which you have the materials, such as Land Tenure, Local Government, the state of European politics in the latter half of the nineteenth century, and the like. No one could sketch the characters of some persons who have figured in the latter as you could. It is well to have some work of that kind before you and to make preparation for it. I hope that you and I will never lose enthusiasm; I give up none of the plans of which I talked to you in the *Englischer Garten*, though I know that life will come to an end before I have completed them.

About politics I have not much to say; the Ministry, as a Tory young lady said to me the other day, 'seem to be getting on very nicely.' Nothing has passed in Parliament, according to Lord Bacon's joke, ' but ten days.' I think that they were quite right in making Lord Hartington leader. Forster is not to be depended upon ; he has the double-mindedness of Gladstone, and more than his ready sense and acuteness, without his genius and simplicity of character. He would have been always selling the Church to the Dissenters and the Dissenters to the Church. How completely Gladstone has ruined his party ! By his Irish University Bill, by his letter to the electors, by his quarrel with the Roman Catholics, by his making Fortescue and Cardwell peers, by his own withdrawal, though still hovering on the scene. Lord Granville, I am told, thinks that he will reappear.

His abdication is very different from Peel's. Everybody wanted to know what Peel thought, and everybody fears Gladstone's powers of speech.

To THE SAME.

March 30, 1875.

Thank you for your two long letters, which were very interesting to me. I am delighted that you have taken to writing, and think that you will succeed in it.

When we meet I should very much like to talk over with you the plan of your work, but in writing at a distance one is very liable to be misunderstood, and any criticism may do more harm than good. I always try to adapt what I say to the character which is best suited to the writer. But it is very difficult for him to see this, or for me to be sure that I am really advising him for the best. I am always of opinion that, whether in writing or in life, it is a great advantage to a man to add the qualities which he has to those in which he is wanting.

Do not attempt in politics to make bricks without straw, or imagine that you can call back the English political world of half a century ago. Is it not the beginning of politics to take things as they are, holding up ideals at a distance, but not confounding them with the possibilities of actual life? But I am afraid that I shall be clipping your wings if I take away from you any part of the enthusiasm which impels you to write. I quite agree with you in thinking that a book is worth a hundred articles.

I shall come and see you some time in the summer, either going or returning, about the end of June or the beginning of August. I shall try to get you to come with me on some Swiss or Tyrolese expedition; or perhaps to the Italian lakes. You must let me know what time will suit you best.

I have been hard at work for a long time now, finishing Plato. I rather regret that you read the *Republic* in the old edition, for the new will be a great deal better, and I cannot expect you to read it over again. The text is altered in several thousand places, and the Introductions amended and enlarged. I daresay that you may have observed that I have attacked a good many of my private enemies under the disguise of the Sophists, but can you expect me to attack yours too? Considering what the world is I have never felt much indignation with the English newspapers, not even with the *Times*, which seems to me to be much more respectably conducted than any other press, and to be rather above than below the tone of its readers. Did I ever tell you of a visit that I made once to old Mr. Waterton, the Yorkshire squire and naturalist? He was a great stuffer of birds and animals, and had a menagerie of hideous monsters, whom he had made to represent all his enemies; among them was a beast who was supposed to be the emblem of the *Times* newspaper. . . .

I most entirely agree in your notion of the effect of new discoveries in knowledge, although Plato was not so mad about mathematics as you suppose, because it was the only kind of knowledge worth speaking of which was known in his day. But I strongly think that we are suffering, and shall suffer for some time to come, until the world recovers its balance, from the ideas of physical science. There is a fellow named Herbert Spencer . . . who knows a little of physical science, and gives back to the scientific men their own notions in a more general form. Of course they worship him as a god, and instead of being thought an empty sciolist, he is regarded by them as the philosopher of the future. I hope that we shall some day put a spoke in his wheel at Oxford, but at present he is rather swaggering and triumphant.

Physical Science has fallen under the dominion of metaphysics, and out of the two is generated something worse than either, having the generality of the one and the positiveness of the other !

Why are you so exasperated against all ministers and ministries ? I am afraid that you will never get on if you do not assume a more Christian temper. I think as you get older that life is too short to allow a person to indulge all his aversions, and therefore I am disposed to be very charitable even to G. and F.,[1] whom I regard as having ruined the Liberal party. The present Ministry are considerably damaged, but I suppose that they will go on until Dizzy drops, and then we shall have a coalition, which will be the best thing. . . .

To the Same.

West Malvern, *April* 15, 1875.

I am glad that you have the fever of authorship upon you, and shall be very much interested to hear of your plans when we meet. . . .

I do not wonder at your rebelling against my doctrines of Christian charity. There is a great deal in your view of sincerity in love and hate, but still I feel that in this difficult world nothing can be done without great prudence and self-

---

[1] Gladstone and Forster.

restraint. These are not ignoble qualities when they are not used for our own advancement. I often catch myself saying things about persons which I would rather not have said afterwards, and I have an unpleasant feeling when I have to act with any one against whom I have spoken. I quite admit that people's conduct must be determined for the most part by their character.

I am at Malvern for a day, and have not read your paper with sufficient attention to do it justice; I will write to you about it in a few days when I have. You are quite right in supposing that Mill has his roots in Bentham, who was a far greater genius, though crabbed and unreadable. Dumont, a Frenchman of genius, arranged several of Bentham's works, especially his *Principles of Legislation*, and made them readable. You had better get the book.

I do not assail either Mill or Bentham indiscriminately. There was a self-devotion in Bentham and a dignity of character about Mill which has done a great deal for politics. We will have many talks about this in the *Englischer Garten* or in some pleasanter place.

I should like you to see the Hall, which is beginning to appear above ground. What pleases me more than this is that I have carried a large scheme for Scholarships and Exhibitions which will, I hope, keep us going for the next ten years at least.

To the Same.

BALLIOL COLLEGE, *October* 28, 1875.

I was very much grieved to get your letter to-day. You seem to be quite discouraged and cast down, and no wonder. A gastric catarrh and two attacks of gout are enough to pull any man down and take away from him his better mind.

Though I feel for you, I cannot quite take *au serieux* what you say under such depressing circumstances. 'Be cheerful, sir¹,' and look for better days. You have lost four, and may perhaps lose six, months of life, but you will be as well as ever again and as able to work some day.

I know that I have not suffered as much in my whole life

---

¹ Shakespeare, *Tempest*, iv. 1. 147.

as you have in the last six months, and therefore I have no right to moralize to you; but I am really anxious that you should keep up your spirits, because it is so important for your recovery. You fat fellows, like Falstaff, 'dwindle and pine away' the moment 'bad humours are run upon you.'

If you had not forsworn foreign politics, I should write to you about Russia. My friend Lord Ramsay, who has just come back from St. Petersburg, declares that nothing can exceed the hatred of Russia to Germany. He found it among the merchants at Nishni quite as strong as at the Court. The emperor alone stands out against war; but if this is true what is to become of Germany, what of Europe?

I wish that you would write me a few lines when you get a little better, for I am grieved about you.

To THE SAME.

OXFORD, *December* 12, 1875.

I wish that you would write me a few lines as soon as you receive this. I want to hear that you are in better health and spirits. I am not very soft-hearted, but you are one of five or six persons whose well- or ill-being really makes a difference to me.

I hope that you will find your way to England this spring. There is much going on or not going on which it is worth while to see nearer. I begin to think that there is not a statesman in England whom any one would trust in a time of war or crisis. Of the present Ministry, Sir S. Northcote appears to be most relied on; he has quickness and good sense, but he is not a man of any calibre or power. In case of war the ruin will be terrific, far worse than the Crimean War. The statesmen of to-day are of an inferior stamp to those who failed then. Perhaps their task is harder; as there is less power of commanding there is also less power of obeying.

The Gladstone Ministry have messed and muddled in a good many ways, but they did two important things: (1) they contributed to the pacification of Ireland; (2) they saved us (at the cost of eating a good deal of dirt) from a rupture with America. But oh that we could be governed for two years by Pitt or Peel ! . . .

—— talks as if he were going to shake off the dust of his feet and never see Oxford again. It is, perhaps, a pity that the Apostles were told to do this, for it has given some who are not Apostles an excuse for doing it (in spirit).

A few days ago the Crown Princess sent me her kindest regards. Will you give my duty to her when you write? I remember with pleasure that about twelve years ago, when I was rather down in the world, she came to see me in Oxford, and her visit was a great good and encouragement to me. The recollection of this leads me to speak to you of a plan which has sometimes occurred to me: you will be the best judge whether it would be practicable or desirable. If she would like her son and his tutor to come to Oxford for a time and learn English and make acquaintance with English people, I would gladly take them into my house. I could teach him some things, such as Political Economy, and talk to him about others. The young prince might come *sans cérémonie* for a short visit and see how it suited. . . .

I still think, my dear friend, that you will conquer that last and worst enemy, the gout, and find an opportunity for doing some great service to England or Europe. Don't you think it possible that Prussia, under the fear of an imminent war with Russia, which can hardly be deferred many years, may be induced to restore Lorraine to France? Germany, though at the top of Europe, is really in a most dangerous position. She ought to agree with one of her adversaries quickly. If she does not, there may be a sea of blood such as there has never been anything like in a former age.

I have read two political books worth reading lately, which I recommend you, *Cassandra*, by Mr. Greg, and Cairns' *Political Essays*.

To the Marquis of Lansdowne.

Ensleigh, Torquay, *Jan.* 2, [? 1876].

Goschen told me that Dizzy said to him after one of his speeches on University Reform, 'Though I don't agree with you, of course, I congratulate you on having a subject; it is such a good thing for a young man to have a subject.' Lord Shaftesbury is a striking example of what a great position a young politician may gain by fighting year after year an unpopular cause until he at last succeeds. I suppose that the same is true of Lord Russell fifty years ago in the matter of reform. . . .

I want to urge upon you that the real time for making a reputation and gaining a position in politics is when you are out of office[1]. Then you have independence and can act for yourself, and can make a carefully prepared speech. The difference between a man who has made a remarkable speech, whether in Parliament or out of it, is in politics enormous. To do it requires not natural eloquence, but a great deal of nerve, great industry, and familiar knowledge of a subject, and feeling about it. I do really believe that for a politician no pains can be too great about speaking. An important speech should be written out two or three times, and never spoken exactly as it was written. When once a person has gained the power of saying a few words in a natural manner to a large audience he can hardly write too much. (I remember reading this years ago in a MS. letter from Lord Brougham to Lord Macaulay, then just commencing as a speaker.)

Though a great many good causes have been fought and won, I do not think that there is any real difficulty in appropriating a subject. The originality of the politician consists in discovering them. There is no use in lamenting that this is not a time in which parties are clearly divided, and in which we can struggle for distinct principles. You yourself naturally have the army and the defences of the country. Then again there is the extension of education. Is it possible to connect this with the military questions? If you begin with drill in elementary schools and never lose sight of the young soldier afterwards (attached to you at a very small cost) will not the difficulty of recruiting disappear?

Then again there is another class of questions, the improvement of the Poor Law, the dwellings of the poor, local government, sanitary improvement, gas, water, &c., about which a large proprietor is expected to take a part, because he has influence and the best means of knowing about them. In legal reforms a layman can only lend a helping hand, e. g. in

---

[1] Lord Lansdowne had been Under-Secretary for War, 1872-4.

such a question as the registration of land, but lawyers without the help of laymen will never do anything. Are there not also questions about the House of Lords which have to be considered ? e. g. its mode of conducting business. At present the cry of all lawyers is that 'Acts of Parliament are so badly drawn.' It has sometimes occurred to me that the House of Lords, which generally takes Bills in their last stage, might correct this. To do so requires more time, but this should be a part of the Reform. Bills which have passed the House of Commons in one Session should be brought into the House of Lords at the beginning of the next, at any time within the year, the Long Vacation being like any other Vacation. A legal report should then be read upon them. The management of business in Parliament is becoming very difficult, and any improvement in it would be a great national benefit. This is more possible, I should think, in the House of Lords than in the House of Commons.

Every man should criticize his own mind and powers, and find out where his strength lies, what he can do himself and what he must get done by others. Indeed, the more we can disappear, and do without getting the credit of doing, the better, for it diminishes jealousy. Any one has accomplished a great deal who can induce four or five able men naturally to act together. Your house may be most useful in bringing together and keeping together a party. The more visitors you have the more you know the world, and the more people have a good will to you. It is a great exertion to be very hospitable, but you can also have times of quiet and retirement. You may reconcile enmities by making persons dine together, ' For everybody is a very good sort of fellow when you know him.' One of the best things that can be done in this world is to introduce literary men to statesmen, and clever struggling young men to persons of rank and position. The Whig party fifty years ago used to pick up young men of ability like Horner, Henry Taylor, C. Austin, Thirlwall, and others. And I am afraid that in these days you must not wholly decline the acquaintance of ' gentlemen of the press ' if you mean to be a politician. Society in England is a great deal too narrow and exclusive, and tends to become more so. To make it wider in a good sense requires a great deal of tact and great personal qualities. Yet any one who attempts it and who does not move entirely in the old conventional ruts of fashion and of courtiers, or retire into a select circle, will be abundantly rewarded in the variety of his intellectual interests and his real sympathy with many different persons and classes.

I have been running on as if you were an Undergraduate still, perhaps in foolish hope that something which I say will be of use to you. I know also that a person of a retiring character does not like to plan out his own performance in the future. But you must do so quietly if you mean to succeed, and to succeed in the higher sense is to live the best of lives and to confer the greatest blessings on others.

To R. B. D. MORIER.

Address, OXFORD, *January* 3, 1876.

I agree with you more than I used to do (and with Miss ——, who is always preaching to me from the same text) about the weak or superficial or haphazard or fitful way in which this country is governed. We are certainly much degenerated since the days of Pitt and Peel, or even of Lord Palmerston or Melbourne. But I do insist as strongly as ever that we must make the best of persons and of circumstances, and put them together and influence them as far as we can. Are we sure that we could do better, and do we make sufficient allowance for the difficulties of popular government? ἐγένετο λόγῳ μὲν δημοκρατία ἔργῳ δ' ὑπὸ τοῦ πρώτου ἀνδρὸς ἀρχή. It is difficult, but not impossible, to find these natural rulers of a democracy. In England there is less difficulty, or ought to be, because we are only half a democracy. I marvel at the ancient democracies in which judges, senators, presidents of the Assembly were elected by lot.

I am glad that you approve of my scheme of inviting the young Prince of Prussia and his tutor to pay me a visit. I shall be glad if you will write and propose it to the Crown Princess. He might come as a visitor for a few weeks to learn English and make acquaintances here; if he stayed longer, and the Princess is willing, he might become a member of the College. You know the sort of people who visit me at Oxford, and what I can do for him and what I can't. I shall be much pleased if I can be of any use to the Prince and Princess, and if they decline I do not at all mind. I have not mentioned the matter to any one but you.

To THE SAME.

February 15, 1876.

I am delighted to hear that you have at last got the preferment which you deserved [1]. Nothing of that sort which could have happened to any friend would have pleased me so much. I only regret that you should be taken away from Germany, but shall look upon this as a short interval of repose, and shall expect you soon to go to St. Petersburg or Vienna in a higher position.

To THE HON. MRS. PARKER [2].

Oxford, May 9, 1876.

I was very glad to hear from you again. Your letter reminds me of what are fast becoming old times, when I used to visit you at Hurton House and was received with so much kindness by your father; and he used to come and see me at Oxford and delight us all by his wonderful powers of conversation.

Like many other things in life, that is with the past now; and I fear as one gets older one must be content to lose many friends as well as some other good things, though not without compensation. I have been unwell for the last six weeks (as you kindly ask about me), though now I seem to be pretty well again. I no longer regard the east wind as a friend as I used to do. The College seems to prosper (we are about to open a New Hall), and I go on writing as I used to do and intend to do as long as I live.

Have you read Lord Macaulay's life or Godwin's life—both of them, though different, very charming in their way? I used to know Lord Macaulay and the sisters and nephews and nieces, who make so great a figure in the book. (That is with

---

[1] The appointment at Lisbon.

[2] Daughter of Lord Westbury; see letter of July 21, 1873.

the past too.) Lord Albemarle's papers and Lord Shelburne's Memoirs are also very interesting; so that we have been rich in biographies lately.

People who did not know him had no idea how Lord Macaulay was absorbed in his family. The life is instructive too as well as interesting, for it is the picture of a man who had a noble enthusiasm for literature and was 'devouring' books all day long.

It would give me great pleasure to see you if you are in the neighbourhood of Oxford.

TO PROFESSOR LEWIS CAMPBELL.

Dec. 29, 1876.

. . . You are quite right not to come to the banquet—an exhausting journey and without a sufficient object. I look forward to it with interest but with some anxiety. You will not forget us on the 16th. I read through the Archbishop of Canterbury's charge yesterday. A very weak and, I think, foolish production, of which the effect will last for six months at the utmost. He assumes a certain air of moderation, but he calls everybody who differs from him scoffers and unbelievers. He inclines more than formerly to the High Church, and wants to make a league of all Christians against unbelievers on the basis of the supernatural. I respect him for his hard work and earnestness, but I feel almost a contempt for him when I read his writings.

This will probably reach you on the New Year. May all good attend you. And may both [of] us prosper in our work during the next year; which seems to me to be the chief thing worth living for.

TO R. B. D. MORIER.

Jan. 27, 1877.

. . . I am pleased that you take an interest about Thucydides. It is an endless work, much more difficult than Plato. Yet the conviction always grows upon me that it is worth doing. As Lord Macaulay says, it is the greatest of histories, and is yet absolutely unknown to all who cannot read the Greek—and to most of those who can. To translate him seems to me the best thing which I can do for the History of Greece, because all other histories are reflections and makes up, and it is certainly a κτῆμα for the world to put them in possession (if I can really do this) of one of the greatest works of antiquity. There will be notes on the doubtful passages. But the classics have been edited and re-edited again and again, and although many authors have not yet been well edited, there is not much new to be gathered in this field. I have also translated the *Politics*. This is my contribution to the knowledge of Greek literature.

I have gossiped to you as to an old friend about myself, I wish that you would gossip to me about yourself. Are you writing anything? You are mistaken in supposing that I should not take an interest in it: 'I can think whereupon you say this,' e.g. when we parted at the Langham Hotel. I am always anxious in your writing that you should not be antiquarian or abstract. Any book on self-government in England must be based on a real knowledge and study of the country. One may lament the diminution of self-government, but what are the elements out of which you propose to restore it? This seems to me the first question. And if it is not carefully considered, there will only be paper self-government like paper constitutions. A great part of the centralization of the present day arises out of the necessity of correcting abuses, e. g. in the Poor Law or in Education. Local government, Vestries, &c., constantly in England mean only local jobbing. Another reason why there must be centralization is for the sake of uniformity. Also local government was more natural and necessary when communication between different parts of the country was difficult. I am afraid too that the hard-worked money-making Englishman is not good at his public duties, because he has not time for them. We may deplore this. But is it quite clear that a great physician or lawyer had better be attending meetings of vestries or corporations?

I say this (rather curtly) not to discourage you from writing your book, but to urge you to look upon this subject from different sides, and especially to ask yourself—What is the possible or desirable amount of self-government, given the character and occupations of people in England? There is no abstract truth about self-government. One nation is fit for it, another not, one nation has the elements for it, another not, and in each case we must make the best combination which we can of the central and the local.

Get a book which I have just been reading, Adams's *History of Japan, during the last fifteen years.* It is a marvellous story, seeming to reverse many generalizations about human nature. Now a nation has passed from the extreme of feudalism to the extreme of liberty, equality, and fraternity, and from the extreme of fanaticism to a very reasonable degree of toleration. Ten years ago when a noble passed on the highway the peasants knelt down and did obeisance; now the noble, the two-sworded man, and the peasant, serve indifferently as officers or privates. The Mikado, whom ten years ago no European and a very few Japanese had ever seen, goes inspecting schools. It is very important to the Japanese that they should continue to believe that the Mikado is a sort of god. But it is hard to see how a god can be a school-inspector.

(While I am writing, Sunday night, there is thunder—very uncanny at this time of year.)

Give my most kind regards to your wife and children. There is a house in Oxford which will be too happy to receive them for as long as they like whenever they come to England. I cannot ask you to answer this letter within forty-eight hours, for I have taken six weeks to answer yours. But I shall be greatly pleased to hear from you again. Of course you study the Eastern question daily. You may have a nearer interest in it some day.

To Professor Lewis Campbell.

OXFORD, *July* 14, 1878.

The sermon which I preached in the Abbey is not published. I have never published any sermons, because I have never had time to revise them. And if the time ever comes, I believe that the world will have got past them. For I observe that sermons, although they are supposed to speak of eternal truths, have of all literary productions the shortest life.

To Dr. Edwin A. Abbott.

OXFORD, *June* 2, 1879.

I have read two-thirds of your article[1] and think it admirable. It will make an era in English theology. You seem to think that I can be of some use in criticizing it. I will if I can, but it will require a good deal of thought to offer any real criticism. How soon must it be returned in a final shape to the editor?

If you and Mrs. Abbott could come down here for a day or two in this holiday week I would put aside other things, and we might go over it together. Any day this week up to Saturday will suit me. Or, if more convenient, I will send you a few pages day by day with annotations.

My knowledge about these matters is half forgotten and rather old fashioned.

Points which strike me on a first reading are here and there (1) a want of consistency in the language, in some places giving needless offence and again making more concessions to received opinions than are necessary; (2) too much attempt to give motives and reasons, where perhaps there are no reasons, or they are unknown or uncertain—people are apt to mix up the discrepancy which is certain, with the account or explanation of it which is conjectural. In all criticism of ancient writings it seems to me that we have too many attempts at construction—Niebuhr on the brain: (3) I should not be disposed to take the views of Lightfoot or Sanday without a searching examination, because I think that, unconsciously to themselves, their use of the facts is limited by preconceived conclusions. (There is not much of this.)

You must expect to be very much attacked, and you want the article to be read by the greatest number of readers possible. Therefore I would admit nothing doubtful, and I would make it in form as palatable as it can be without sacrificing the truth.

---

[1] The article *Gospels* in the *Encycl. Brit.* ed. ix.

To R. B. D. MORIER.

OXFORD, *Nov.* 11, 1880.

I send one line to ask how you are, not having heard of you or yours since we parted. I hope that you have gained your point with the Portuguese Government, and that when that is accomplished you will be carried off to some important sphere.

We in England have a dismal look-out in politics. The world seems to be cracking in several directions: the East hastening towards anarchy and misery, and Europe at any time liable to sink into a great war which is perdition. The Irish question has been allowed to reach such a height that it cannot be solved without a good deal, probably, of bloodshed. The Radical leaders are pushing on the party in a direction which they do not intend to pursue themselves, but will not be able to restrain. We have only the beginnings of democracy as yet; and democracy in an old country is very different from democracy in a new one which has boundless land. All this might be met by (1) force of personal character if the Whigs had any force; (2) by a move for education if there were any considerable interest about it. To me it seems that the political world is going down hill, or is it only—for I must fairly put the other alternative—that I am getting old?

I rather hope that you won't deprive your boy of the advantages of going to Eton. I know your fear of public schools, but the dangers may be averted with care. On the other hand, you may be taking from him a whole piece of life which cannot be restored, a recollection which would have been always delightful, the power of making friends for himself and of forming his own character. If you are at Lisbon or Constantinople he can come to me during his vacations; I shall be very glad to look after him for you.

I had a delightful visit to Lady Airlie this year. She talked really eloquently about many things, especially of the use to be made of the later part of life, when one's early interests begin to fade away. She has gained a higher idea of things since her illness. At her house I saw Captain Hozier, who had been looking up the French and German armies. He says that the improvement of the French army is enormous, and that they will soon be a match for the Germans. Some well-informed persons, like yourself, tell me that the French do not want to fight, and that the passion of money-making has taken possession of them ; others say the opposite, and I own it is difficult to me to imagine how a vain people like the French can sit down for ever under a defeat. I think that our interests in England are with Germany and our feelings with France.

Will you write me a few lines when you are at leisure? With love to your wife and children.

To THE SAME.

WEST MALVERN, *Jan.*, 1881.

I think that I will write a line or two while yours is fresh in my mind. And first let me thank you for your kind thought about my health. I will promise you that if I have any return of the bronchial cough I will go southwards. For the present an excellent doctor in London seems to have cured me, and I have had no touch of it for about eight months.

Do not rave at the world so much ; it is in a bad state—worse, I think, than formerly—England and Ireland, France and Germany, Germany and Russia, the whole East in considerable danger of exploding. But, as you know, to take the world and the leading men in it as they are is the beginning of my philosophy. I have no doubt that you know many scandals and weaknesses of which I am ignorant. Still, are not men to be judged upon the whole and in the long run by their public sayings and doings? No one has less sympathy with Gladstone than I have ; I think that he is getting into a state, when, as Goldwin Smith used to say, 'while his powers of speech are enormously increased, his reasoning powers and self-control will diminish in an inverse ratio.' (This is not a good prospect for the country.) But, at the same time, he has immense power and popularity : 'whoever falls upon him will be broken, but upon whomsoever he falls he will grind him to powder.'

I was delighted to read Lord Kimberley's letter and to hear of Lord Granville's offer to you. I wait anxiously to hear who is appointed to Constantinople. They are liable to think: (1) that you are not manageable enough; (2) that you have never been in the East. And there is much to be said against going there on the ground that you will not be supported, and also that the Sultan, like George III, is a madman. Still, it is a great thing to have a hand in the future of the Eastern world.

You do not tell me half enough about yourself. I want to know when the Portuguese affair will be settled.

As you say, you and I are within a 'measurable distance' of the end. But remember that you must take credit for eight or nine years more than I can: I am quite determined under all circumstances to hope in this life and in another, and to work to the last day of my life in some fashion or other. The ideals of youth (though they had an admixture of folly and sentimentalism) were the best part of either of us, and we must not lose them when we are beginning to have the power of realizing them. Your constant appreciation of me (though undeserved) has been an important element in my work and has taught me many things. Two and thirty years ago I went with you to Scotland, and every year since I have had young fellows with me, and though some persons think that I waste my time in this way, it seems to me the best and most successful part of my life. The prosperity of the College has been bound up with it more than with anything else. It is the best of my recollections that I have done good by it, and I do not think that I have done anybody much harm. (You see how pleasant it is to talk about oneself.) The Thucydides still hangs upon my hands—the third volume containing the Essays—and I have no proper leisure to devote to it. It will be finished in the course of the year.

I have urged you before, and urge you again, to write down recollections of your own time: of the persons whom you have known, and of events, such as the Franco-German war. It is really not a difficult thing to do, and the work would be of great interest. Something of an 'autobiography.' You have much more literary talent than you suppose, because you have never cultivated it. And writing even more than speaking is a most valuable auxiliary to a statesman or diplomatist. . . .

You must be tired of politics, therefore I shall not enter upon them. Write to me when you feel disposed, for I am always pleased to have a letter from you.

To THE SAME.

OXFORD, 1881.

I should like to hear from yourself about your prospects : you and I are such bad correspondents that I must not quarrel with you about that. Politics are in rather a gloomy state. The Irish nuisance is abating, and the Irish members have nearly succeeded in convincing everybody but themselves that they must be put down, and that for the present at least Ireland must be governed by the strong hand. Nothing but the land league and the Parliamentary nuisance would have persuaded the left wing of the Liberals of this. So that though there has been great evil, I am inclined to think that the 'giving them rope' has been the best policy in the long run. Before six months ago people like Lord Derby were beginning to think that Home Rule must come. Now Home Rule means either the perpetual application of the curb by England or an Americo-Gallican republic. Perhaps I should rather say that the 'extension of rope' principle has had considerable advantages, but it is hard to estimate the counter-balancing disadvantages in the demoralization of the Irish people. The hope is that the Irish, like other Celtic people, easily forget impressions which have taken a great hold upon them.

The Transvaal is an ugly business, and will look still uglier if the Dutch at the Cape are inspired with a sympathy for their Boer cousins. I saw Sir Frederick Roberts here the other day—a keen practical sort of man. Then there is Candahar, which in accordance with prevailing opinion—peace party and breeches pockets—is going to be given up. But no one seems to consider what will become of those who have stood by the English in the struggle.

To J. A. Symonds.

OXFORD, *Sept.* 12, 1882.

I write a few lines, not that I have anything to say, but chiefly to tell you that I had a very pleasant and prosperous journey home, and that I have not forgotten Davos.

I should like to hear from you when you have spare time. Suppose you write to me when you get into your new house, which should be a day of festivity with you. It must be very tiresome to live in an hotel.

The Italian history will always interest me. I think it most fortunate to have such a work in prospect; and no Englishman probably has ever been so well qualified to under-take it by previous study as yourself. It is the flower and blossom of Modern History, as Greece is of ancient, and it is through Italy that Greece has been communicated to us. It is all alive with great ideas and great men. To you who know it so well, the fair country and beautiful cities will always be present as a sort of background. The physical features and the elements of race will be disposed of in the introductory chapters. The true interest of history begins with remarkable men and their actions. They may have had physical antecedents, but these cannot be traced : nor is history to be confounded with the philosophy of history. The ideas or categories under which history may be finally summed up by Herder, or Hegel, or Comte, are quite distinct from the motives which animated great changes.

What is the difference between a chronicle and a history? Is it not this? that a chronicle is a record of facts ; a history blends facts and ideas.

One thing to be done in writing a history is to form a distinct estimate of the value of each authority (not to patch one quality of evidence with another). A second thing is to calculate the proportion of the work and the relative import-ance of one part to another.

It is rather presumptuous in me to write down these commonplaces, which will have occurred to you before they would to me. Please to regard them only as showing that

I take a great interest in your work, and that I hope to live to see the completion of it.

You will have to write under rather hard conditions, by scraps and not more than an hour or two at a time. But scraps, if they are well arranged, begin to form a great collection in months and years. I think that you know the difference between happy and voluntary labour, and the labour which oppresses and coerces the brain. And keep the mind at rest : we must leave the issues of life or death in the hands of God, and be of good cheer.

With best regards to your wife, and love to the children.

To Professor Lewis Campbell.

March 26, 1883.

. . . I have been looking lately at Conington's *Choephoroe* and *Agamemnon.* He appears to me a much greater scholar than I used to think him. But I never liked him, and therefore never saw the good side of him. With how many persons has this been the case ?

. . . I hardly like to speak of the losses which we have had during the last two years. Stanley, Tait, Green, H. Pearson, and now Henry Smith and Toynbee. They were all my dear friends, some better known than others ; and they were all amongst the most remarkable men in this country. They can never be replaced. Henry Smith seems now to be recognized as the greatest English mathematician of the century ; I did not know this during his life-time, and used to think him wanting in originality because his mind was absorbed in the mathematical world. Toynbee also was gaining for himself a great name at Oxford and elsewhere. He was only thirty when he died. I also deeply regret the death of the Master of the Rolls, though he was only a common acquaintance. He was the greatest lawyer living, and very public-spirited. M. Knight seems well and is always improving. He and his sister make life easier to me, he in my writing, and his sister in housekeeping and matters of business.

About translation I think as I always did—that we should aim at the translation reading as original writing : English first (in one sense) and Greek afterwards. The Cambridge

translations, such as Davies and Vaughan, show that they know how the Greek should be taken, but according to my view they are full of mistakes, because they fail to express it.
. . . Symonds was very much depressed when I left him last year. But he is now very much better and greatly pleased with his new house. He is always writing. His is one of the most fertile and fruitful brains which I have ever known. I still hope that he may do considerable work.

To SIR A. GRANT.

BALLIOL COLLEGE, *Dec.* 23, 1883.

I write to thank you for the two volumes[1] which came yesterday. I have read them nearly all through, not without some injury to the eyes, and I staid up into the small hours of the morning : I have no doubt that as they have interested me they will interest others, and that your book will have a large sale. You seem to have managed very skilfully not to give offence. I think that everybody will be grateful for the work, and that it will be a worthy crown to the ' Tercentenary '. . . .
This Vice-Chancellor employment is very interesting to me, and gives an opportunity of doing many things which could not be done otherwise. I am afraid that it defers the *Politics*, to which I have done nothing during the last three or four months. Now you have the *History of the University* off your hands I hope you will not forget Aristotle and Philosophy. It is no exaggeration to say that your book on the Ethics has done more for the study of Aristotle in England than any other book. And you have still many years of life before you, and in some senses the most intellectual years of life, in which our thoughts, if we can only retain energy, are most valuable. With best regards to Lady Grant.

To L. DYER.

BALLIOL COLLEGE, *July* 14, 1884.

I have to thank you for two books which you have kindly sent me—one, *A Day at Athens with Socrates*, which I think you said was by a lady. I am very glad that a lady takes an interest

---

[1] Grant's *History of the University of Edinburgh*.

in such subjects. The *Odyssey* is a more important book[1]. Your friend is perhaps the hundredth translator of Homer, and probably there will be a hundred more. The fascination of the original is somehow inexhaustible—I feel it myself, and could gladly spend the rest of my life in trying Homeric experiments. But I have determined to do no more translations.

Your friend's work seems to me very good in parts : I have read one or two books with interest, and am not surprised that an audience was willing to listen to him. The great difficulty in translation is to get the firm sort of logic which keeps the whole page and indeed the whole book consistent with itself. This is far more important than fine or poetical expressions for which schoolboys seek.

I hope that you are getting on well at Harvard : I often hear of the affection with which you speak of Oxford and of Balliol. Thank you for it. You had great success as an undergraduate at Balliol, and I hope you will have still greater success as a Tutor and Professor at Harvard : I suspect that the American undergraduate is more difficult to manage (like the Scotch student) because he resents any attack on his independence, as he thinks it. Good lectures, good teaching are valuable to all students. . . . I am sure that you will and can succeed in the long run. But at every age, and perhaps, every two or three years, one should review one's own doings and manner of doing—if life is not to be a failure. You have got into one of the best corners of the world, and you should do the utmost to fit yourself for the post.

We had a great Balliol gathering to meet the new Speaker of the House of Commons a fortnight ago (an old member of the College), I wish that you could have been there.

I shall look forward to seeing you in England in the course of the next year or two.

To Sir R. B. D. Morier[2].

July 28, 1884.

I dare say that you remember about twelve or thirteen years ago a wish expressed by your dear sister to give £100 a year

---

[1] Professor Palmer's *Translation of the Odyssey.*   [2] Morier was gazetted K.C.B. in 1882.

(afterwards reduced to £70) for the benefit of poor students at Oxford. At your suggestion she entrusted the administration of it to me, and I used to send her an annual account. These accounts will probably be found among her papers. She gave the money partly with the view of carrying out some practice of her husband's, who devoted a portion of his wealth in a similar manner.

The money has been a great help to me and done real good . . .

To C. P. Ilbert.

July 29, 1884.

I agree with you that one of the greatest mistakes is sending out Gordon. It seems to me that England should make some considerable sacrifices about Egypt, and so claim a justifiable interest in the country ; it would be worth while for her own sake (commerce, &c.), and I think that we should try to alleviate the lot of semi-civilized countries, when we are naturally brought into contact with them.

To Mrs. Marshall.

Dec. 14, 1884.

I am like you pleased, but sorry at your leaving Oxford[1]. . . .

I think that you and he have taken for your own one of the most interesting subjects of human knowledge and of the greatest practical importance, and that you will have the best opportunity of teaching it. I should like to give him one piece of advice (though I have no business to give it, nor do I expect him to take it), which is not to overlay his *opus magnum* with mathematical forms or symbols : or to imagine that in such subjects these can be real instruments of discovery (however natural they may be to his own mind as a mathematician). I was very glad to hear that they were to be relegated to the appendix.

To Professor Marshall.

West Malvern, *Dec.* 25, 1884.

I write to thank you for your kind letter. It has been a great pleasure and happiness to me to have known you and

[1] On the appointment of Prof. Marshall to the chair of Political Economy at Cambridge.

Mrs. Marshall. Thank you again and again for your never-failing affection to me and for your attachment to the College. We shall greatly miss you at Oxford. The undergraduates say to me, 'Who will teach Political Economy to us now?' I have no doubt that there is an excellent field for teaching it, both at Oxford and Cambridge, partly because it is 'in the air' now, and also because it enters so largely into various University examinations. I think you are to be congratulated on the subject of your professorship, both on this account, and also because I believe that an immense deal may really be effected by it for the good of all classes. We shall be able by the help of Political Economy to look communist movements in the face, to predict them a few days or weeks beforehand, and to make the best use of the interval. . . .

Will you be surprised at my attacking you about symbols? (rather unfair just when you are leaving us and in a letter to your wife). I seem to see that various persons, such as De Morgan and Boole, have tried to apply mathematics to subjects which did not admit of their use and have rather deluded themselves and others. (Henry Smith had this feeling about such attempts.) Now I do not object to their application to Political Economy-provided they are not regarded as a new method of discovery, but only as a mode of expressing a few truths or facts which is convenient or natural to the few whose minds easily adopt such symbols. Political Economy is human and concrete, and should always be set forth in the best literary form: the language of symbols may be relegated to notes and appendices.

I have worried you enough about this matter, in which I have always fancied, perhaps erroneously, there might be a danger to your *opus magnum*. . . .

To MRS. MARSHALL.

BALLIOL COLLEGE, *Feb.* 22, 1885.

I have delayed longer than I intended answering your very kind letter, as I am afraid that busy people sometimes do with friends, because they know that they will not be offended. Will you forgive me, and let me thank you most heartily for your present of a charming reading table and some knitted work.

I am glad to hear that you are happily settled at Cambridge, and am not sorry to hear that you have left a part of your heart behind you at Oxford. The friendship of you and your husband has been a great blessing and good to me. And not to me only; for your departure is considered a general loss both to the political economy and the society of the place. . . .

You and Mr. Marshall must come and see me next Term. There is nothing that I like better than introducing my friends to one another. And I sometimes feel that nobody has better friends than I have. That is my experience of life. Excuse this piece of egotism.

Oxford is going to admit ladies to the Musical Degree : and we are fighting over the examinations which it is desired to specialize by all the faculties, whether with due regard to the interests of general education I am doubtful : we are also about to have a Medical School, which Dr. Acland, who has hitherto prevented it, is obliged to swallow, not without many wry faces. I must likewise tell you, what may perhaps have a faint interest for your husband, that the College, having the ' singular privilege of electing its own Visitor,' yesterday elected the Lord Justice Bowen to that office (an old Fellow of the College).

Thank you for the paper containing the account of the conference. I have always thought that the Economists carried *laisses faire* to an extreme, and that the Government ought to do for us what it can do and we can't. But now the pendulum is swinging too far in the opposite direction, and hopes are being roused which, after causing a great deal of disturbance, must end in disappointment. We want to have the question of *laisses faire* versus Government interference more illustrated by facts—of course the question is very different in different countries.

I have been reading three biographies, all of them well done and very interesting, George Eliot, R. W. Emerson, and the Count Pasolini [1], the latter I had not heard of before. He seems to have been one of the best sort of Italians.

---

[1] Count Giuseppe Pasolini (1815-1876), President of the Senate of Italy.

If you are disposed to run over to Oxford for a day or two at any time, it would give me great pleasure to see you.

To LADY TENNYSON.

BOAR'S HILL, NEAR ABINGDON,
July 6, 1885.

I recognize your handwriting on a little packet which you have kindly sent me containing *Country Conversations*[1]. It is an odd little book, which I value, because it is not published—interesting in a way, but sad, if it truly represents the thoughts and feelings of English farmers and labourers.

I hope 'Laotsee[2]' has prospered. I shall consider myself fortunate if I have succeeded in finding a subject for Alfred. The old Philosopher must have been a wonderful being, who got further away from the world and its ideas than anybody else ever did.

I am staying at a house about four miles from Oxford, where I intend to remain during the greater part of the summer, working at Aristotle's *Politics*. Hallam very kindly asks me to come and see you. I wish that I could, but I fear that I must put off my visit until the book is finished.

Will you give my love to him, and also my best remembrances to Lord Tennyson?

To PROFESSOR MARSHALL.

OXFORD, *Jan.* 5, 1886.

. . . At Oxford, as you know, we follow the Cambridge lead, sometimes with uncertain steps. At Cambridge, I see that you have made a very important change lately, by admitting affiliated students to a Degree after two years' residence. I have always been in favour of this change myself, but the University is against it, having almost a superstition in favour ·of residence. But I do not quite see how to stop at the limit which Cambridge has chosen. Must not everybody (say over nineteen or twenty, to keep out schoolboys) be allowed to start

---

[1] By Miss Tollet.
[2] It seems that Jowett had sug- gested the subject of the 'Ancient Sage' to Tennyson.

from the commencement of his second year if he offers a higher standard of attainment ?

Will you tell me what is thought at Cambridge about this question, and what is the exact change made ? Also will you kindly send me any papers which bear upon it ? Such a change as I spoke of above, to which the Cambridge move seems to lead, may have a very great effect on the future of both Universities.

To J. FFOLLIOTT.

OXFORD, *April* 18, 1886.

I should like to hear from you ; I want to assure you that Englishmen do not forget their Irish friends at this time. I am afraid that you must be feeling great trouble and anxiety. Other troubles pass away, but this is continuous, and involves country as well as fortune.

We have now got the whole of Gladstone's measure before us. I do not suppose that it will be soon carried, but we must remember that Gladstone, the great demagogue, is supported by universal suffrage, and that a considerable portion of the electors wish to make a sort of revolution in England like that which he is making in Ireland. I cannot bear to think that the loyal people in Ireland are to be surrendered to the disloyal, and that a great constitutional change is to be effected by crime and by disorder in the House of Commons. The Home Rule Bill is a terrible evil, especially as it will certainly be followed by the transfer of the Police into the hands of the Home Rulers and their Parliament. But I think it would be worse without the Land Bill ; I think also that the Irish members should not be wholly excluded from the House of Commons, but retained there in proportion to the taxation paid by Ireland (say thirty-five or forty), with a minority vote. Otherwise there would be no link between the two countries, for the checks and vetos will come to nothing. I should hardly think that the Land Bill, which I have this moment seen, will pass, or that, if it does, it will be possible to collect the rents for landlords, who will generally be absentees ; or that, if the new rent to the state is not paid, the English tax-payer will supply the deficiency. About the passing of such a Bill it is difficult to be confident, for it may be passed in ignorance of its consequences, from a general impulse towards Gladstone and liberality. Then there is the House of Lords, which will hardly pass either Bill without a great struggle, probably lasting a year or two, and ending in the destruction or transformation of the House of Lords itself. What interminable disorder and confusion.

So we in England make political reflections, and are uneasy and annoyed. But you are the real sufferers in reputation too as well as in property. Many persons who all their lives have been trying to do good to Ireland and to their tenantry are classed by Gladstone with the unfeeling landlords. This is very bitter, one of those trials which it requires the greatest courage and patience to meet. We have not yet got to civil war, that would be more bearable ; meanwhile, more than the virtues which are needed in war are required of you in peace. I daresay you will not be wanting to yourselves. The saddest thing of all is that the Irish people will probably be worse off than ever. And no man will be pacified when he has the wolf in his belly.

If you come over to England I shall expect a visit from you.

To C. S. ROUNDELL.

OXFORD, *Oct.* 14, 1886.

It is very kind of you to write to me : I value the sympathy of friends far more than the praises of newspapers.

I think that the V.-Chancellorship has been upon the whole successful, though not so successful as some persons kindly imagine. . . .

A good many years have passed since the days of the Greek Professorship. I have a vivid recollection of the kindness and support which I received from you and others in those troubled times.

I hope that you do not give in to the fallacy of getting old. I always think that the later years of life are the most useful and important.

To Sir R. B. D. Morier.

WEST MALVERN, *July* 1, 1887.

You were so very kind about my health that you will not think me egotistical if I write to tell you that I am a great deal better. The vertigo has almost disappeared, and though I am weaker than I used to be, I see no reason why I should not quite regain my health in a month's time. Meanwhile I work very leisurely and never so as to tire myself. Gull[1] thinks this is better than giving up work altogether.

I should like to hear about you, who must be oppressed by many cares about very important matters. Is the British motto to be, 'Being weak, seem so'? or would this frank confession take from us the little strength that we have? I suppose that we shall let our foreign policy drift and creep out of Egypt in the next three years. I am afraid that public opinion will not allow us under any circumstances to go to war, and on the other hand will never plainly say so. That seems to be the position which diplomacy has to acknowledge, and it is only by great dexterity and personal influence and character that peace with honour can be extracted from it.

Politics here go on fairly well, as far as the discrediting of Gladstone may be regarded as a success. But neither party seem to have any clear idea what alterations are to be made in the government of Ireland in the future—provincial parliaments, I suppose, with a reduction of the Irish members in the House of Commons, and a tight hold on the police.

To Mrs. Ilbert.

WEST MALVERN, *July* 25, 1887.

I have been trying the experiment for more than a week of living alone. Do you know it answers very well, and for an invalid is generally best.

Tuesday (to-morrow) week I go to the Deanery, Westminster, to talk about Stanley's life, and then to the Engadine about Thursday.

[1] Sir W. Gull.

July 28, 1887.

There are new experiences of oneself and of the world which come upon one in illness quite worth having, for they improve and enrich the character. And don't see things through the spectacles of illness, but keep the mind, although a little clouded by pain and headache, in the sunlight. Patience and the determination to get well is the temper of mind for illness. And yet restlessness and pain will often overpower all the motives which philosophy or religion suggest to us.

I get better here, but on condition of doing nothing.

To Lady Sherbrooke.

Colwood, Hayward's Heath,
Jan. 4, 1888.

I write to thank you for your most kind letter, which gave me great pleasure. I am delighted to hear that Lord Sherbrooke has some prospect of recovering his sight.

It always interests me to see the care that you take of him. You have made life happy for him under circumstances of sadness and depression. All his friends recognize this, and are deeply grateful to you. I wish I could believe that I live to make other people happy, as you do. Your words remind me that I ought to do so.

I am sorry to be obliged to decline your kind invitation to Torquay, a place which has to me many associations, for my mother and sister lived there for twenty years. But I have to return to Oxford to-morrow week, and my Vacation is filled up.

Tell Lord Sherbrooke that I am editing and partly rewriting a third edition of *Plato*. It has sold six or seven thousand copies. He used greatly to encourage me about the first edition.

I am really a great deal better : only, perhaps, rather more precarious in health than I used to be.

To Sir R. B. D. Morier.

Balliol College, *May* 11, 1888.

I am rather sorry that the Toynbee Hall plan has fallen through. The influence of the place and of Rogers and

Gardiner would have been good for Victor[1]. As you say, London is dangerous. I asked Victor to come and see me, but he was not able to come.

I shall be very glad if I can do anything more. I don't know when old friends can be of any good to one another if not in the difficulties of life.

Mat. Arnold is a great loss to me[2]. He was one of my firmest and dearest and best friends. Every year I had a higher opinion of him. No one ever united so much kindness and light-heartedness with so much strength. He was the most sensible man of genius whom I have ever known and the most free from personality, and his mind was very far from being exhausted.

He came down here and spent a quiet day with me about two months ago. He came to see his sister-in-law[3], who was near her end. She was a lady in whom I took a great deal of interest, because she had fought such a hard battle in life. I went to see her a few days afterwards. Now they are both at rest.

Things look to me better, both at home and abroad, than formerly. At any rate, those who say this time three months or six months or twelve months there will be war do not allow for possible hindrances, shrinkings, new combinations, &c. Is there any chance for the Emperor, not of recovery but of protracted life? I do not believe in miracles, but I believe in extraordinary powers or circumstances, great resolution, a great position having a marvellous effect on the body. Whether you are buried in St. Petersburg or come to London, you may have the satisfaction of thinking that you have one of the most important posts in Europe, and that unknown to the world the most important results may be accomplished by you. 'Peace or war,' that is the great question of all, to be thought of night and day, and in every conversation with another person, as a sort of regulating or controlling force to all that one says or does. It is hard to acquire the magnanimity towards opponents, the impartiality, the impersonality which great opportunities require.

I am not 'poking' this at you. But for both of us I feel intensely the responsibilities of the last stage of active life.

---

[1] Morier's son, who died in Africa, in 1892.

[2] Died, April 15, 1888.

[3] Mrs. T. Arnold.

To THE HON. MRS. PARKER.

OXFORD, *Dec.* 7, 1888.

I write to thank you for your kind present[1] which I value greatly, and like to have my name written in it by you. I have read it nearly all through with great interest; it reminds me of what are becoming old times. I think that the book is very fairly and discriminatingly written, and that it will tend to raise your father's memory in the opinion of the public. There is no reason at all to be disappointed with the result. It is a good biography and has the characteristic of biography which Carlyle so greatly valued, it tells the truth. I think your father would not have been displeased at the account which Mr. Nash gives of him.

I find that I have been unintentionally guilty of a deception. When the second copy came my housekeeper, Miss Knight, told me that I had already got the first, and that I had never noticed it. I shall venture to deposit the additional copy in the College library.

Will you accept of a new edition of an old book which I have just brought out[2]? I hardly expect you to read it, though you may find some things in it of interest to you.

I always remember with great pleasure your father's kindness and friendship for me. He was so pleasant and his conversation was so instructive. I never knew any one like him in lucidity of mind.

I hope that you will let me know whenever you come to Oxford. With kind regards.

To SIR R. B. D. MORIER.

Jan. 7, 1889.

I have read with the greatest interest your letter. I fear that you will lay yourself open if you get excited. You must remember that you have very wily people to deal with, who have no spark of generosity, who are watching for the trip of a word and want to ruin you.

I hope that you will not make it a personal quarrel with

---

[1] Nash's *Life of Lord Westbury.*
[2] The translation of the *Republic* of Plato.

Herbert Bismarck—a duel, &c., of which I have heard you speak. It would be ridiculous and may be sad, if you or he or both were wounded or not wounded, and English feeling would strongly condemn you.

May I say to you a thing which it rather pains me to say because it may pain you to hear it? The weak point of your diplomatic life has been that you have got the reputation of making things uncomfortable. Ministers don't think about your high aims or character, but only that a person who makes himself unpleasant to them is very likely to make himself unpleasant to people elsewhere. Bismarck very probably collects these things or the false reports of them against you, and, adding pressure of another sort, may induce Lord Salisbury to think that he had better get rid of you with an offer of Rome or Washington. I must add also that the sinister reputation of which I spoke has very much diminished in the last two years. These are not the times of Lord Palmerston or even of Lord Aberdeen.

Do not be vexed with me or think me half-hearted. I write this because I believe it to be true and from affection towards you.

I hope that you have before this had a joyful meeting with Victor. Give my love to him. When he comes to England I hope that he will come and see me.

To THE SAME.

OXFORD, *May* 13, 1889.

I write to say that I shall be in Oxford from July 2 to Aug. 10, and shall be delighted to see you. But why does Sir John Falstaff 'set himself down in the ranks of age,' when 'the truth is that he is only old in wisdom and experience?' But perhaps he will say that he hates such a stale jest. Then let it 'smack to him of the saltness of his youth.'

To THE SAME.

BALLIOL COLLEGE, *Oct.* 1, 1889.

I began an answer to your kind letter more than a week ago—that was more than a week too late. Thank you very much for your liberal contribution. I have raised about

B b

£3,000, and hope to raise about £2,000 more[1].   To accomplish
this for Balliol gives me great pleasure and satisfaction.   And
it gives me great pleasure to have a friend at a distance who
sympathizes in my projects.

We have had some long talks, but I never seem to have had
enough talk with you, as Johnson said he never remembered
to have had as much fruit to eat as he wished.   And you must
not think that I do not appreciate your Excellency, because
I, a poor ignoramus, prone to doubt, sometimes set up my
poor opinion against yours.   It seems to me, that if I can ever
be of use to you at all, which I doubt, it is only by telling you
occasionally what I think.

You and I are agreed that you should wind up your life by
writing.   You might write a book in the form of Reminiscences
such as has never been written, the foreign history of England
since you entered the Diplomatic Service, sketches of character,
royal persons, reflections from the inside upon great events, &c.
I am sure that you could write well, for you have a great deal
of imagination and power of language, but you have never had
sufficient practice.   The last ten years of life spent in this way
may perhaps be the happiest of all, for which you should be
making preparations now, and should look forward to as to the
final rest.

To the Marquis of Lansdowne.

Hurstbourne Park, Whitchurch, Hants,
Oct. 6, 1889.

The great event of the last two months has been the London
strike, which will, I fear, give the working class generally
a greater sense of their strength, if they are unanimous, than
they ever had before.   If we are to have democracy, we seem
to want the restraints by which it is held in check in America.
One of these should be a reform, and so a strengthening, of
the House of Lords.   There it appears to me that our friend
Rosebery is right, but that his Federation is a mere name.
He does not seem to see that there must be some proportion
between the members of a Federation.

[1] See *Life,* vol. ii. p. 345.

I hardly think that any compromise is possible between the Unionists and Home Rulers. For there is no measure of self-government which Unionists can grant, which will not strengthen the Home Rulers. Therefore we shall probably go on as we are with some change of persons until the next General Election, getting rid of the Irish question until nothing of importance will be left for an Irish Parliament. The only chance to the contrary is that some of the more radical members of the Unionist party may press forward Irish Local Government.

I have always the feeling in writing to you about Home Politics that you have much better means of information respecting them than I have. Nevertheless it interests me to write about them and perhaps does you no harm.

To MRS. DYER.

WEST MALVERN, *Jan.* 12, 1890.

I write to thank you for your very kind letter, and for the book which you have sent me[1]. It is a delightful present : just what I should have liked and perhaps might not have got for myself. I have been reading it all day and for several days. It is curious to think that there should have been such a gifted person as Edward Fitzgerald until lately living among us and almost unknown.

I hope that the lectures on Greek Art have been successful. I should like to hear about them. I want to tell you how greatly I know and love your husband, and how much respected he was in Oxford. I used to think that he did great good in the College. He was the friend of every one, and made them friends of one another : if you should ever settle among us you will have a warm welcome ; and will find enough to employ you.

I look back also with great pleasure to the career of four other Americans in Oxford, Parker, Richardson, poor Brearley, and Pearsall Smith, the only ones as far as I remember whom we ever had. I wish that there were more of them.

I am accused of telling every one to keep diaries. Do you

---

[1] The letters of Ed. Fitzgerald, recently published by Macmillan.

keep one? They seem to me to be a great help and interest in life. I would make a good collection of photographs an adjunct to the diary; so that one may live the journey over again after one has got home.

Will you give my most kind regards and love to your husband, and many thanks for the pains which he took about Lady W—— for me? The subscription gets on capitally; we had also, as he will have seen, a great success in the University Scholarships this year. So that I see no reason to fear that the College is in any way going down. I am at West Malvern plodding at the translation of Plato, which is a lifelong work. However, I like it, and do not lose interest in it.

You and Louis must come and pay me a longer visit when you return to England.

To Mrs. Sellar.

BALLIOL COLLEGE, *Oct.* 17, 1890.

Willy[1] is at rest, and you are alone, and are beginning to think about the future. It is a great and lifelong sorrow, but I know that you will not exaggerate it : it has to be borne like the other great crises of life. It must be very painful to think of for a long time to come, and there is a lesson which sad events carry with them not to be lost. The thought that our beloved ones are with God, and that the recollection of them may help us to serve him better, is a real consolation. One love has departed for the present : it may diffuse itself over many who still survive. . . .

To the Same.

BALLIOL COLLEGE, *Dec.* 22, 1890.

I have not heard of you for a long time, and should like to hear how you are and how Edmund is getting on. I am afraid it must have pressed very heavily upon you to have the second trial[2] so soon after the first.

I have often thought of you and Willy[1] during the last month. I feel that there is a vacant place among my friends

---

[1] Professor Sellar. See *Life*, vol. ii. p. 354.
[2] The illness of Edmund, Professor Sellar's youngest son.

which can never be supplied. He was so simple and selfless and disinterested, and when I read his book I feel that he had a great deal of genius. The world of his friends had a great love for him which will last while they live. . . .

How is my friend Willy [1] getting on? I am always interested to hear about him. I rather wish he could fit himself for some higher course in the medical profession than as a surgeon.

To Sir R. B. D. Morier.

BALLIOL COLLEGE, OXFORD,
Nov. 26, 1891.

Will you be able to come and see me again before you return to St. Petersburg? It would give me great pleasure to see you once more. I think that I am getting better, but very slowly. I feel again and again every day, and every hour in the day, that I cannot be too grateful for the affection of my old friends, of whom I count you one of the chiefest and best, and one of the most important to the *salus reipublicae.*

You will have been affected by Lord Lytton's death. It may possibly transfer you to Rome or Paris, to Paris or Rome. The last order seems to me to be the best for a man who makes it his duty to devote life to the maintenance of the peace of Europe—the highest diplomatic duty which can be conceived.

Rosebery has written an excellent book on the life of Pitt— quite admirable.

To the Same.

Dec. 16, 1891.

I hardly know whether to be glad or sorry at the news which I see in this morning's paper of your transfer to Rome, and I dare say that your own feeling will be of the same mixed kind. You have done a great work at St. Petersburg, and I hope that some one will be found to understand and continue it. On the other hand, as long as you live you will probably have a great influence with either Ministry on the Eastern world of Europe. But the chief reason for the change is the necessity of health. I do not think you could have stood two

---

[1] Professor Sellar's son.

or three more winters in Russia. And I hope that being released from this danger you will not do less, but more, for peace and for Europe than you have done at St. Petersburg. Now is the time for writing and correspondence and for gathering up the experience of life. (I believe greatly in the influence of political correspondence, half published, half private.) And I believe also, as you know, in the later years of life as the best and wisest and most useful.

I have not time to write any more as I am keeping all the Undergraduates waiting for Collections, but I did not want to miss a post. Many thanks for the little note. I think that we may do something for one another in the last years of life. I am sure you can for me, and that we may be more united than we have been.

To Mrs. Ward.

Balliol College, *Jan.* 24, 1892.

I have read nearly the whole of your book[1]. I agree with you that it is better than *Robert Elsmere*, and better I think than any novel since George Eliot. It is an extraordinarily pathetic and interesting tale about middle-class life, which is full of beautiful description of places, and contains a number of characters which produce a very vivid and distinct impression with a touch of heredity which gives credibility to the book. It is a picture of manners like Miss Austen, but in a different class, and like her without much ethical purpose. It is very natural, the events happen just as they would have happened in actual life. I do not object that there is no love-making in the book, and no virtue rewarded or crime punished. I see that there are a few pages about German criticism and a few contrasts of character arising out of the present phase of religion, but this does not at all mar the originality of the work; it is not at all a duplicate of *R. E.*

The children appear to me quite admirable, as true to life as the children of Murillo or Vandyke or Reynolds are in painting. The poor miserable Louise is such a sketch as Victor Hugo might have drawn.

I foresee that you may have a great future as a novelist, not

---

[1] *David Grieve.*

exactly by always keeping in these lines, but by always improving and thinking how you may picture the mind of the time,
and especially of the middle classes, getting rid of lords and
ladies so as to do great good. Dickens did great good in his
way by introducing the middle class to the higher. At the
same time the ablest would fail if it were apparent in the
work. It is one of the most subtle and delicate questions to
be thought about, but not to be spoken of, how classes can be
made to understand and respect one another.

To Sir R. B. D. Morier.

BALLIOL COLLEGE, *Jan.* 26, 1892.

I was just going to write to you when I received your letter.
I am delighted to hear that you remain at St. Petersburg. It
was clearly the right thing to do and a brave thing to do.
I did not say so when I wrote because I thought that the
change to Rome was a *fait accompli.* And now, my dear boy,
for the sake of England, for the sake of Russia, and for the
sake of peace, take care of your health and run no risk. Like
the general of an army you must preserve your life, or we shall
say that you ought to have gone to Rome. But I do not really
mean this, for in my opinion it is better to die at one's post.

The condition of Russia seems to be very miserable. Do
you see any way of gradual improvement? Or are there
impossibilities in the nature of things? To grant strict justice
and toleration, not to Nihilists but to the Russian people in
general, seems not an impossible thing even under a despotism.
Cannot the Emperor be turned into what Plato calls a virtuous
tyrant? I sometimes fancy you doing for the Russians, what
Sir James Hudson did for the Italians. I believe that the
Ambassador of a foreign nation may sometimes do for a people
what they cannot do for themselves, because he sees the situation more clearly and he is trusted by the monarch when his
own ministers are not—only as in so many other good things
which have to be done he must not be found out doing them—
or at any rate as in all difficult enterprises he must conciliate
everybody and everything.

I read an article to-day in the *Contemporary Review* about the persecution of the Stundists—they are probably exaggerated, but also in reality very dreadful. They are simple pious folk, and the Greek church is their enemy. Turgenieff used to talk to me about them. They are so called, I believe, from an old Lutheran book of devotion.

Turgenieff also told me that he believed there were 27,000 or 28,000 exiles of Siberia—they included some of the best people in the country. But he could not advise their coming back or being pardoned. He thought it would be too dangerous.

I am getting well, much better than when you saw me. Now my life has been spared I am passionately anxious to make a good use of the time that remains. The years increase in interest to me. One of my hopes is that I shall live to see you doing something great in European politics. And my hope rests on this, that I see no one or hardly any one who appears to me to combine the same originality, knowledge, and earnestness which you possess.

Take care of your health and do not forget to keep and put together your journal, with descriptions of persons, like Boswell.

To LADY ARTHUR RUSSELL.

BALLIOL COLLEGE, *June* 17, 1892.

Let me thank you for your beautiful gift of flowers. I have enjoyed them greatly, and being alone had them all to myself. Like other good things they quickly fade.

Did you ever read Burns' poem 'The Posy,' ' O love will venture in where it daurna weel be seen '—the most beautiful and fanciful poem about flowers, as it seems to me, which was ever written?

I hope that you are beginning to enjoy the summer and the beauties of nature in your beautiful county. They are very soothing in a time of sorrow. No one can do much to minister to the troubles of others, but the mind can do a great deal to minister to itself. There is a quiet happiness in thinking of those who are gone, and in living for others : perhaps sometimes in finding out new ways of doing good which, when the world occupied more of our thoughts, we should not have discovered. . . .

Shall I recommend you, or did I recommend you, a book to read—the happy life of Marianne North, a lady whom I knew, the flower painter?

I shall be very glad to hear that you are happy and at peace, and have found a new way of life. Will you come and take up your lodging here sometimes when you want to see your son? . . .

To A. PONSONBY.

BALLIOL COLLEGE, *Sept.* 28, 1892.

It gave me great pleasure to get your letter. I think it a promising sign that you are rather dissatisfied with yourself. It often happens in youth that we have a vague feeling of an ideal which we are longing to satisfy, but it seems to be out of reach and beyond us. Perhaps the longing will never be appeased, but it does us good if all our lives we are approaching nearer to it. You seem to me to form a very fair notion of your own deficiencies. As you say, you need concentration, and more knowledge and thought about serious and important matters. In short, you have to read for the Foreign Office in the most sensible manner that you can. It is true that you have some weak points, but you have also some very strong ones, and these too require to be cultivated.

Shall I make one suggestion to you? Read biographies of great men—statesmen, soldiers, philosophers, saints. There is no kind of reading more interesting, or which has a greater influence on character. It is one of the principal means by which a man may educate himself.

I suppose that you gossip all day long with the Pastor and his family. There is a great simplicity and goodness among people of that class in Germany. They are poor, but also educated. I fear that they must be rather puzzled about the state of religion which exists in Germany, and indeed in the world at present.

Yet though I say this, I do not at all regard these sort of difficulties as insurmountable. They are really artificial. To the poor they have no existence, and to the best people :— They become less every year, because we are beginning to recognize that religion is the fulfilling of the two great commandments, or at a higher stage the taking up the Cross and following Christ, and consists not in Ceremonies and Miracles or in any past facts, but in a Christian life. If any man has his mind fixed on justice, truth, holiness, doing good, he has religion enough. I believe that in the future religion will occupy the minds of men much more than it has in the past, and that it will be much simpler.

I am glad to hear that you are taking in earnest to Political Economy, whether this is valued or not at the Foreign Office. I am sure that nothing is more useful in the Diplomatic Service. A Diplomatist ought to study the economic condition of all the countries of Europe. He can study most of them on the spot, and under the best conditions of knowledge. If he has the power of writing, he cannot do better than write about them either in Reviews or Newspapers, or with his name. You see that I do not regard his profession as devoted entirely to gaiety and dancing.

Come and see me when you return to England. Perhaps we may do some more political economy together, or try our hand at some other kind of writing. I shall always be glad to see you, if you are disposed to take a few days' rest at Oxford.

 To Lady Tennyson.

BALLIOL COLLEGE, *Oct.* 5, 1892.

I am grieved to hear that life is slowly passing away: no one at this hour has a greater sorrow than yours—to lose the partner of your life, who was also the most distinguished man of his age. And no one has a greater consolation in the remembrance of the happy unclouded past, and in the unshaken faith that you are rendering him up to God.

It is better that you should survive him, and not have been taken first. For he could not have borne to live without you, and would not have known how to do so. He said a few words to me about a fortnight since, which meant 'that there was no one like you.' And your family and friends look forward to having you for a few years longer. We love you, and the world would be different to us if you were no longer here. You must help to arrange Hallam's life for him, and urge him to press forward, and not to be discouraged because, having higher duties to perform, he begins later in the race. And also to help to bring up his and Lionel's children. There is a friend to whom you have been wonderfully kind for thirty-five years, and have shown him never failing sympathy, and not grown tired of him during all this long time—he too hopes that he may be able to say or do something which will soothe your life by reminding you of days long past.

I bought the single volume edition of the poems to-day, and began to read them through again. Will you do the same, beginning with *In Memoriam*? What a volume of them there is! And how astonishingly good! To me and others they made epochs in our own life of the time at which we first read them. They never did us any harm but the greatest good. They opened our minds in the best manner to the new ideas of the nineteenth century.

There is no one who seems to me to have a stronger faith or a more real love of God than you have, and I know that they will not fail you at the time when you most need them. I believe that it is a duty to live as long as we can, and, feeling how imperfect our efforts have been, to try to fill up to the last what is wanting.

May God give you peace and rest. How can I thank you enough for all your ancient kindness to me?

To Sir R. B. D. Morier.

BALLIOL COLLEGE, *Oct.* 6, 1892.

I should greatly like to hear how you are, and something of what you are doing if you can spare a few minutes to write.

A fortnight ago to-morrow morning I took leave of Tennyson. Neither of us had any idea that we should meet no more. He was unwell and suffering, but his mind was perfectly clear, and from time to time during my stay there he was making small corrections of his poems. He had another volume just coming out as good as anything which he has written. He was the last great writer of the nineteenth century, and leaves the world of letters in darkness.

For the last thirty-five or forty years he and his wife have been the kindest of friends to me. She was a kind of saint, whom it was a privilege to know, full of affection and gentleness and sense. She was also a very good critic of his poetry, to whom he was very ready to appeal. Life seems to get poorer as we get older : there are so few remaining who knew us when we were young.

I have had another great trouble within the last six weeks, the death of Nettleship in an attempt to ascend Mont Blanc. He was one of the props of the College who can hardly be replaced. There is a great feeling about his death.

You too have had a terrible sorrow, never to be altogether healed in this world[1]. I think that sorrow should produce some good fruit in us, even though we are getting old and beginning to fall out of life. And I fear that we are both rather tending to some kind of agnosticism. Tell me, old friend—it is a question that I ask myself—do I feel more desire to do good to others, more love of truth, more interest in important truths than formerly ? Do I get better as I get older, or only keep on the accustomed tenor of my way ? I think that sorrow should in some way be turned to good.

Two small matters.

1. A copy of Plato came back to me yesterday, intended for you, but addressed by the Press 'Sir R. Morris, Rickmansworth'; I will keep it for you until you come to England.

2. The picture[2] gives great pleasure and satisfaction. A thousand thanks for so valuable a gift. I will attend exactly to your wishes ; at present it is hanging in the Common Room, but will be placed in the new Hall as a gift from me, when a rearrangement of the pictures takes place.

To Professor Jebb.

August 17, 1893.

What I should have to say at the Conference[3] will be very tentative. You cannot insert a piece into a scheme when you have not the scheme before you. I should have liked to talk over the subject very much. I think that I should be disposed to speak (1) against grading schools. They must vary with

---

[1] The death of his son Victor.
[2] A portrait of Sir Robert Morier by Lembach.
[3] Held at Oxford, on Secondary Education, Oct. 10, 1893; see *Life*, vol. ii. p. 424.

the circumstances of the locality and of the pupils. (2) I should suggest *abiturienten* examinations, giving the right of admission to the Universities. (3) I should allow all students who had passed this examination to be candidates without residence and without restriction of age for any University examination with or without honours, or for a part of any University examination. Does this take away your breath?

To THE SAME.

Sept. 18, 1893.

(1) I should like to have all the schools collected together by a common *abiturienten* examination, as in the joint board. (2) I should like them all to pass an examination without residence, to obtain some privileges which residence confers, such as ad· mission to the libraries under certain restrictions, and University distinctions and certificates of proficiency in any branch of knowledge, which the University professes to teach, without limitation of age and without residence. The last point they have at Oxford already. I [would] also propose to allow them to try without distinction of age for any prizes, prose or verse, if they had passed the original *abiturienten* examination; and if they had shown any considerable merit, that they should receive sums of money which might enable them to carry on their enquiries. (3) [These proposals] to apply equally to all branches of knowledge, classics, mathematics, the various branches of physics and physiology, history, theology, &c. I want to see whether there is as much or more intelligence among the many as amongst the few. 'The old order is changing, giving place to new.' The new is coming. Let us see whether there is room for both.

To SIR CHARLES TREVELYAN [1].

BALLIOL COLLEGE, 1862.

I suppose that the report which I see in the newspapers of your going as Finance Minister to Calcutta is true.

I write a line (not exactly to congratulate you, but) to

---

[1] This and the following letter were, owing to an oversight, omitted in their proper place according to their dates.

express the pleasure which I feel at your abilities being once more employed in the public service. I believe that your appointment will be the source of real and great good to India. And there is an opportunity, such, perhaps, as there never was before, for drawing out the resources of the country. I have a sort of confidence that instead of tying your arms behind you with strips of red tape you will leave nothing undone that can be done, and that your knowledge of the country will enable you to do many things that a novice from England could not have ventured upon. I wish very much the health of Europeans in India could be taken up by some powerful hand. That is a subject on which I always have a very strong feeling. The waste of life, which is, perhaps, best put as the waste of money, and the increasing unwillingness of Europeans to go to India, now that the people who have been fed on curry from their infancy are come to an end, is becoming a very serious matter. I cannot help fancying that the waste of life is quite preventible, if the Government could be roused to make the effort [1].

I should like to see you again before you go. It would be useless to ask you and Lady Trevelyan to come down here for a Sunday to see Stanley and me (will you?). But if not, I will try and call on you.

To LADY DALHOUSIE.

BALLIOL COLLEGE, *Nov. 27*, 1887.

I hardly know whether to write to you or not to write to you at this time when such an overwhelming calamity has fallen upon you.

Your dear son [2] was one of my best and kindest friends. He was a noble fellow, full of kindness and generosity towards every one. I valued greatly his stay at Balliol for the sake of his influence over the undergraduates, and I think that he himself regarded the time which he spent with us as one of the happiest periods of his life. Wherever he was, he was always trying to do good and to make others happy.

---

[1] Jowett had lost two brothers in India; see *Life*, vol. i. pp. 144, 252.
[2] See *Life*, vol. ii. pp. 67, 353.

And now after a year or two of suffering he is at rest. 'The spirits of the righteous are in the hands of God, and there shall no evil touch them.' It is sad that he should be taken at all, but not so sad that he should be taken now. For had his life been protracted, it would probably have been misery.

You will very likely be wishing to depart and be with him. But you will also remember that your life is more needed than ever now : and that there is nothing that he would have more desired than that his children should have the benefit of your care. You will not shrink in a certain sense from beginning life over again for their sakes.

He was absolutely devoted to you, and has often talked to me about you and your never-failing attachment to him, shown in so many ways. . . ,

VI. NOTES AND SAYINGS

The Creeds.

THE creeds have been repeated simultaneously by many millions, and some thousand times by each individual in his own lifetime. Does this make them more true? At any rate it enormously increases their effect on our minds. (1873.)

Orthodox commentators.

They substitute learning for thought, details for general principles.

They seldom inquire into the real probability of [Bible] miracles, or the evidence of others, e. g. ecclesiastical or modern miracles, or of similar phenomena, or into the meaning of miracles.

They seldom inquire into the nature of the documents, or compare similar documents, or in general compare Christianity with other religions.

They presuppose the doctrines of Christianity as already accepted, without either defining or proving them.

They praise those heterodox writers out of whom they extract admissions favourable to their own views.

They assume a history to be true which cannot be disproven, and to be genuine when no motive can be assigned for a forgery.

When the writing examined is graphic or detailed, that is to say when, like one of Defoe's novels, it makes an appeal to the imagination, they declare it to be historical.

Though changing their points of view they never, or very rarely, bring forward the mistakes committed on their own side.

They do not distinguish degrees of evidence, or attempt to estimate at all the nature of what is called internal evidence.

They do not consider the tendency to error and to innocent, as well as designed, illusion in all early literature and in all religion especially when organized. (1874.)

Old age.

Can a man write when he begins to be old?

1. Rousseau is said to have written for eleven years, from fifty-three to sixty-four; Cowper began to write poetry at fifty; Hobbes wrote the greater part of his philosophy after he was fifty-nine.

2. An old man writes out of the fullness of his experience, and therefore with the more effect.

3. He should write slowly and with the mechanical helps of secretaries, younger scholars, &c.—do nothing himself which can be done by others.

4. Having less superfluous energy he must concentrate himself more, and not let his mind wander over a variety of subjects. This is the remedy for some want of memory. At the time when the texture of the mind is beginning to give way, it becomes overloaded, like the digestion. The ways of age should be simpler, slower, and more occupied with a few subjects. The time is short, and passes more rapidly, and any work takes longer time than in youth.

5. He may not remember details, but he can judge from his previous knowledge; he knows where error lies.

6. He can put the crown on the work of others.

7. He must be young as well as old, full of hope though a little tired at times. (1874.)

Life.

If life is to be of any value it must be disinterested. (1874.)

Prayer.

Can there be prayer if the personality of God is no longer believed? I think so; prayer may be conceived as (1) communion with God; (2) recognition of the highest truth within us; (3) intense resignation to law, i. e. to the will of God; (4) intense aspiration within the limits of our own powers. (1874.)

Change of character.

People say : ' You cannot change the basis of character.' But you may combine opposites to almost any extent : and it is the combination of opposites which makes greatness. The art is to add age to youth and youth to age, to be all you ever were, and to add on something more (as far as physical strength will allow). Distinctly to recognize : ' I have a certain character ; I will add to that new qualities.' (1874.)

The working classes.

1. The working classes, if moral and educated, would be far more dangerous to the existing order of society because more capable of combination. They will never rise as one man till they are led by one man, who (like O'Connell and the Irish) embodies all their wants and feelings. (1874.)

2. An element in foreign politics not sufficiently considered is that the lower classes throughout Europe have now more sympathy, or will soon have, with one another, than any of them have with the upper classes of their own country. (1874.)

3. The working classes should be taught to demand a free education—free and compulsory. (1874.)

Liturgy.

1. The true idea of a liturgy is that it should sympathize with the higher mind or intelligence of the church or congregation, in which each individual is also raised by communion with his fellow-men :—Man rising to God in company with his fellow-men. (1874.)

2. Can anybody suppose that the chance collection of 300 years ago can be suited to us in the nineteenth century ? (1874.)

3. Ought not a recognition of the laws of nature to form a part of the services of the nineteenth century ? (1874.)

Religious revivals.

1. They seem to have a constantly diminishing influence ; the revival of the eighteenth century, Wesleyan and Evangelical, is a comparatively feeble imitation of the great Puritan

and Reformation movement; the revivals of the latter half of
the nineteenth century are a still feebler imitation of the
eighteenth.

2. They are half physical, half spiritual, the passions taking
the form of religion. If the physical enthusiasm could be
turned at once into the path of duty : 'Cease to drink, gamble,'
&c., they might be productive of the greatest good.

3. The decline of them is to be regretted; it shows that
religion is going out of the world; and with it some of the
highest elements of human nature.

4. In the present day there is not much to be done in getting
rid of superstition; everything to be done in the revival or
construction of religion.

5. Fifty years ago people, or at least some people, cared
about their souls; now they hardly know whether they have
souls or not. (1874.)

Strong characters.

Strong characters break up families; either they must
govern and harmonize them, or they must separate from them.
(1874).

The Tyrol.

The forms of the mountains are much finer than in Switzerland (e. g. in the drive from Reichenhall to Berchtesgaden),
also the woods are much finer and more varied. What is it
that makes beauty in nature? The union of what is striking
and abrupt with what is minute and various. The Tyrol is
more cultivated than Switzerland, the hills are sharper and
nearer together, the forms are more 'architectural,' more like
'divine inventions'; and altogether no place in Switzerland
is of so picturesque a character as Berchtesgaden.

Men and the age they live in.

Poets are to some extent dependent on the externals of their
time, but not mathematicians—as we may see from Newton,
Kepler, and La Place; or philosophers—such as Des Cartes,
Spinoza, and Kant; or physicists—like Davy and Faraday;
or historians—like Thucydides, Tacitus, and Gibbon.

We are thus reduced to the small class of great artists and

poets; and these are essentially the same with other great men, only they are more impressible. The whole theory about the influence of an age really comes to this:—

1. That poets and literary men are weaker and more impressible by their own circumstances;

2. That politicians are necessarily more dependent on their age.

What is regarded as the fatalist tendency in art is really the imitative tendency of artists, and for this reason the fatalist doctrine is true of second-rate great men more than of first-rate; for the first are more dependent on imitation and bring less of their own genius to their work. (1876.)

Meditation among the tombs.

Nowhere probably is there more true feeling, and nowhere worse taste, than in a churchyard—both as regards the monuments and the inscriptions. Scarcely a word of true poetry anywhere. The strangest forms of monuments, (1) either purely conventional—the old foursquare stone and brick tomb, the upright tombstone—or (2) ponderous and extravagant, or (3) fantastic and affected. The truth is that neither sorrow nor any other affection finds an eloquent or poetical expression of itself except in those who are poetical and eloquent. (1877.)

Political Economy of the future.

I should like to see a political economy beginning with the idea, not how to gain the greatest wealth, but how to make the noblest race of men. A Greek rather than a modern idea. I would show how the laws of political economy came in to check or to realize this ideal—the form of society best adapted to it.

The first business of mankind is not to make money, but to elevate the greatest number of human souls physically and morally. How the best workman is to be obtained: (1) education; (2) the after education of the professions. (1877.)

Truth.

Can it be said that we ought to preach truth everywhere and at all times, when we think of the effects on character?

In giving the love of truth we take away much more than we give, if we deprive others of the love of goodness, if we isolate them in the world.

On the one hand, the love of truth is so rare a virtue that we cherish it to the utmost; on the other hand, the pretended love of truth = nihilism, vanity, egotism, barrenness. (1877.)

The future life.

The difficulty is how to describe this as indefinite but as real.

At sixty years of age how do I feel about it, not only with respect to myself, but with respect to the uneducated, my old servant—the other good old man who waits on me here at Malvern?

I want to finish three works besides those which I have in hand :—

1. Introductory volume on Greek Philosophy.
2. Commentary on three first Gospels and Epistles.
3. Treatise on Moral Philosophy.

But I would not like to think that this, even if I accomplish it all, is my whole work in life. Yet I can imagine nothing beyond. Still I believe (1) that here my work will be carried on by others; (2) that there I shall myself carry on another work.

A future life has hitherto been a sham or a convention, shocking to doubt, but having no real basis. Who can wonder that such a sham cannot maintain itself against the influence of the nineteenth century?

Two things have been unfavourable to a belief in a future life :—

1. The want of inductive evidence for it, which there neither is nor ever will be.
2. The want of modes in which it may be conceived; these there neither are nor ever will be.

The belief in a future life arises out of our belief in ideas, especially in moral ideas. It can only have its roots in morality, and must therefore be chiefly asserted by character. Without the belief in a future life moral ideas vanish and disappear.

It is one thing never to have had the belief in a future life, or to have had only an indistinct aspiration, and to have renounced or lost a distinct or positive belief in it.

Suppose children trained after secular and utilitarian motives, could education ever succeed in making a fine character ? (1878.)

Moral Philosophy.

A treatise on moral philosophy should arrange the truths relating to human nature in the form of a system, because in this way alone can it gain a hold on the logical faculties;

Should have a poetical beauty and feeling appealing to the imagination;

Should breathe the highest moral spirit, that men may catch from it an inspiration of goodness;

Should enter into and disengage itself from the metaphysical puzzles with which human nature has surrounded itself;

Should have something of an ancient form;

Should express the better part of what everybody is thinking and feeling;

Should embody in an abstract form the lives of individuals. This is the only way in which the abstract can be made interesting. Then every one reads it by the light of his own experience, and says, 'How true that remark is of such an one.' (1878.)

Sermons.

Subjects which ought to be, but never are treated in sermons :—

Love.

The Passions—not generally, but particularly.

Good manners.

Differences of rank.

The right use of money.

The influence of art.

Self-dedication.

The limits of self-denial.

Failure in life.   (1878.)

Hope and Faith.

There is an immense place for faith in human life, but only for a faith which does not fight against experience: there is a faith in goodness, a faith in progress, in a Supreme Being, in the infinite longings and hopes which rise up in the human breast, which still remain and will remain as long as man exists upon the earth. (1886.)

Death.

Hardly any one, when the time comes, is really afraid of death. My sister said: 'I have a great fear, but also a great hope.' This is uncommon. My mother said: 'I wonder whether I shall ever sit in the garden any more.'

I am glad to be nearer death for one reason—because I can see the problems of theology in a truer manner, and can get rid of illusions. (1886.)

Religion.

I. The common view of scientific and educated men. They speak of:—

(a) The reign of law.

(b) The uncertainty of past history.

(c) The unmeaningness and relativeness of doctrines.

(d) The inconceivability of miracles.

(e) The influence of physical causes on moral action.

In none of these tendencies is there reason to expect retrogression; they will go further and further; they are not vague suspicions, but real tendencies of thoughtful minds based on an increasing knowledge and judgement of facts.

But scientific and educated men know little and speak little of religion; and spiritual movements, which greatly affect the minds of women and of the better sort of half-educated men, especially of young persons, do not touch them.

II. The religion of the common mind is of two sorts:—

1. Conventional, which thinks it dangerous to speak of these things—political, conservative, hypocritical, sceptical—which at best hopes to improve the world without unmasking the growth of error and falsehood.

2. Real elements of popular religion:—

(*a*) Belief in the Scriptures and constant reading of them, and fanciful applications of them (or (*aa*) in the sacraments).

(*b*) Aspiration after a higher and better state of life.

(*c*) Prayer and belief in the personal interference of God, and experience of miracles and strange coincidences.

(*d*) Recognition, felt with various degrees of strength, that religion must have a moral basis.

(*e*) [Religious emotions] subject, like all feelings, to revival and depression, dead and living times.

(*f*) Philanthropy, always tending to become formal.

(*g*) Instinct of self-defence against criticism, and even against the progress of knowledge. (1886.)

Moral Philosophy.

I am weary of this endless casuistry of morality and psychology—definition of things impalpable and undefinable.

I would banish the ambiguous words which are used about them, especially pleasure, development, consciousness, utility; and try to find the simplest expression of moral truths, 'the virtues, not many, but one,' the commonest conception of them, as justice and truth, capable of being elevated and idealized into a justice and truth more than human, the simplest form of morality becoming the highest and deepest. (1890.)

Conversion.

It cannot be denied that at any minute of a man's life he may have the most exalted inspiration—that he may be willing to give all that he has and is, to sacrifice reputation, love, ambition, prospects of all kinds, to die without repining if it be the will of God, and that in this [frame] of mind he may continue for a considerable time with great satisfaction to himself. This is probably the experience of many, if not of all, good men. The moments in which we thus taste of the heavenly gift are the most precious of our lives, because they may be made permanent, and lead to everlasting consequences, although, like other feelings usually called love, they are apt to subside into commonplace. Yet it may very well be in either case, whether in the love which is spiritual or that which is sentimental, that the feeling is also lasting, and either lives always or is always reviving. (1892.)

SAYINGS.

Sensitiveness.

Sensitiveness is a great hindrance to action. Other men who have their own ends in view, and perceive that you are sensitive, will not shrink from hurting you. It may be partly overcome. It has some compensating advantages. One enters more into the thoughts of other people.

The beginning of Genesis.

I am afraid mankind must contrive to do without a first parent.

Memory.

A man should make a compact with his memory, not to remember everything. Great memories, like that of Sir William Hamilton, are apt to disable judgement.

Extensive reading.

There is enough time to read all the books worth reading, if you can only get the *mind* for it.

The limit of scepticism.

There must come a reaction towards religion again : the *void* will be too great.

English Composition.

If I were a Professor of English I would teach my men that prose writing is a kind of poetry.

Depression.

Sometimes one feels fit for anything, and then again as if any one could knock you down—(as the Irishman says) with a poker[1].

[1] Cp. the fine saying of Sir Walter Scott in his Diary: 'I feel now as strong as Ailsa Craig : now as feeble as the wave that breaks on it.'

E e

Church extension.

If a few persons would busy themselves in the neighbourhood of Bethnal Green, without looking for preferment—that, and not more churches, is what we want.

Luxury and plain living.

You ought not to say, 'What waste!' when you see a gorgeous dinner. You should rather say, 'How much better this is than what I get at home!'

The dignity of labour.

You cannot say that the man who plasters your hair with yolk of egg has a dignified occupation.

Criticism and popularity.

Criticism cannot be popular, but no good is to be done without it. One ought to show consideration for received opinions only so far as to secure a hearing.

Rank.

I do not doubt that one day such distinctions will vanish. While they remain, I wonder at any one not taking advantage of them.

Youth and age.

I hope our young men will not grow into such *dodgers* as these old men are. I believe everything a *young* man says to me.

The power of kindness.

I have known persons who have made mistakes out of pure kindness; but not often, and kindness is a great power.

Interpretation.

One should be content with presenting *certain uncertainties* in preference to vague guess-work.

Christian evidences.

The man who asks for *demonstration* must be either very ignorant or an utter sceptic.

How to learn to write.

His answer always was 'by writing.' 'I never think I have
done anything unless I have written something: *nulla dies
sine linea.* I used to dream away the time ; I would sit for
hours with the blank page before me.'

Reading.

* ¹ 'Read great and serious books,' he once advised me, 'and
do not spend time upon ephemeral things. Wipe out all
trivial fond records.'

Difference between men.

* Educated men have a common stock of ideas, and so far
are very much on a level ; the difference between one man and
another lies chiefly in their power of expression.

Work.

* He told me that he did a good deal of work, but did not
work very hard. He had never tried to master a subject the
first time he took it up. He contented himself with going
over it superficially, and then returned to it again and again,
deepening gradually as he went on. (1889.)

R. Lowe.

* In 1869 or 1870 he repeated with gusto a story which
Robert Lowe had told him. Lowe had made a friend and
playmate of a bright little girl. They were engaged in a game
of croquet one day, when she stopped suddenly and said: 'They
say you are a great statesman, Mr. Lowe, but I don't think you
can be by the way you play. You make very good strokes
sometimes, but you never can keep your balls together.'

The Whigs.

* I always wonder at the part the great Whig houses have
played in politics ; they have gone on from generation to
generation sapping the foundations of their own order. (1871.)

¹ For the sayings marked thus * I am indebted to Mr. E. Harrison.

Love.

* Young men make great mistakes in life; for one thing, they idealize love too much. (1873.)

Truth.

* I was amusing a little boy with some fantastical and extravagant story, when Jowett checked me: 'You should never tamper,' he said, 'with a child's sense of truth.' (1873.)

Enthusiasm.

Jowett was sometimes thought to have little sympathy with enthusiasm. Yet when he was told the story of Geronimo, the Genoese missionary, who having heard that the aborigines of Australia were the lowest type of savages, went out voluntarily and laboured among them for twenty years 'without making a convert or an approach to one,' he said, 'I should like to have been that man[1].'

[1] The Diary of Geronimo was found among the papers of Commander Owen Stanley (1850).

INDEX

———+——

A

THE END

Lightning Source UK Ltd.
Milton Keynes UK
UKHW011435070720
366156UK00001B/261